Preparing
to Teach the
Disadvantaged

Approaches to Teacher Education____edited by

Bruce W. Tuckman and John L. O'Brian

Rutgers University

Preparing
to Teach the
Disadvantaged

The Free Press, New York
COLLIER-MACMILLAN LIMITED, LONDON

Collier-Macmillan Canada, Ltd., Toronto, Ontario

Library of Congress Catalog Card Number: 69–10280

First Printing

Foreword

W E LIVE in a socially irresponsible society that too often exhibits little concern for its members.

We live in an affluent society that is tragically able to mask our "invisible poor."

We live in a society that says, "Anyone can make it if he just tries," thus displaying its ignorance of the impact of urbanization and of technology and an adherence to outmoded work ethics.

We live in a society where millions of Americans have been systematically deprived of equal educational opportunities and equal economic opportunities by discrimination, prejudice, and exploitation.

We live in a society whose institutions are so complex, so organized, so tradition bound, that they are often unable to serve those who most need their help.

Such a society most severely punishes those youth who have had the misfortune to be born into poor families, minority families, or families with a minimum of education and skills. These are our disadvantaged children and youth. These children—the Negroes and Puerto Ricans of the ghettos of our cities, the rural poor, the children of migrant workers on our farms—will be growing up with the so-called advantaged children in a world that is shrinking in size but increasing in complexity. This society *must* demonstrate the same concern for these children as it does for other children, for it cannot afford any longer this waste of human talent and potential.

The staggering costs of corrective and rehabilitation institutions, the riots in our cities, the "social dynamite" of our unemployed and unemployable youth attest to the magnitude of our past neglect.

We also live in a society where hundreds of thousands of people are dedicated to the principle of service to others. These are people who believe that other people are basically good, who believe that adults want a better life for their youth, who believe that others often need a hand along the way. Many of these people are our teachers. That is what this book is about: our teachers and how we can do a better job of selecting, recruiting, and training them for the demanding and difficult task of teaching disadvantaged youth.

The teacher is the key person upon whom the educational system depends. His behavior and his attitudes, once he closes the classroom door, determine whether his students will learn, become indifferent, or reject learning. The degree to which the critical process of socialization is accomplished is dependent upon his assumptions about teaching, about himself as a teacher, and about children and youth. These perceptions become even more critical when he deals with disadvantaged youth, who often bring to the classroom a very different value system.

The problem is, "How do we train and nurture in a teacher the energy, enthusiasm, intellectual competence, and concern necessary to educate disadvantaged youth?"

This book makes an important contribution in response to that question by first recognizing that educators cannot do the job alone. It is indeed an interdisciplinary task.

A second major emphasis of this book is the link established between the theoretician and the practitioner. Seldom is the gap between them recognized, and even more rarely is it bridged as it is here.

The most important contribution of this book, however, is the translation of the interdisciplinary approach and the experiences of the practitioner into a unique curriculum by means of which students' attitudes as well as skills can be developed.

As Dr. O'Brian states in his chapter, "The curriculum, as it finally emerged, is appropriate for training all teachers who will work with disadvantaged youth." Hopefully this book will encourage other institutions to vigorously examine their programs for training teachers of the disadvantaged.

CARL L. MARBURGER
Commissioner of Education
State of New Jersey

Preface

THIS BOOK represents an attempt to describe some of the characteristics of disadvantaged persons that affect their performance in an educational environment, potential causes of these characteristics, and the qualities of teachers and programs that are required to deal with these characteristics. We have described in detail an educational program for teachers of disadvantaged students that will arm them with the attitudes, perceptiveness, and skills required for even minimal success with culturally disadvantaged youth and adults. We have also brought together some alternative teacher education programs.

There are many books dealing with education of the disadvantaged. Most of these are of quite recent vintage. Many are collections of articles from a variety of sources and dealing with a variety of problems subsumed under the rubric "education for the disadvantaged." This book is different in some important ways. First, all the articles are original and have never appeared elsewhere. Second, the articles were written within the frame of reference of preparing teachers to teach the disadvantaged. The scope of the problem was limited to teacher education, and the contributed papers were focused on this problem area. Third, authors were selected who could approach the problem area from specific vantage points. These writers represent a variety of the social sciences, educators presently running educational programs for the disadvantaged, and educators presently preparing teachers of the disadvantaged. Finally, the educational program for teachers that is offered as a major chapter of the book was essentially the product of the writers of the other chapters, who participated in a group activity that eventuated in the chapter that John O'Brian has written. Thus, the book has a built-in integration as a result of its inception and generation.

To whom might a book such as this appeal? As a *reference* or *source book* it would be of value to both teachers and administrators who are involved in the education of either disadvantaged persons or teachers of disadvantaged persons. This includes professionals at the elementary, secondary, vocational, and higher education levels as well as those involved in Manpower programs, Youth Corps or Job Corps programs, Vista programs, and other "war on poverty" programs. This book can help these professionals understand their students, themselves, and the educational process.

As a *textbook,* this book would rightly fit in a School of Education. Any course dealing specifically with either teacher education or current issues in education would be served by it. As faculties of urban education become a reality, this book will hopefully find its way into courses concerned with urban educational problems and urban teacher education.

The U.S. Office of Education has been placing increasing emphasis on the dissemination of information about youth with special needs in conjunction with in-service education programs. A recent directive requires that all in-service summer workshops in vocational education give consideration to problems associated with youth having special needs. Perhaps the handwriting is on the wall. Perhaps the program that we have brainstormed as a dream will soon become a reality at many institutions of higher learning. Perhaps this book may contribute to that eventuality.

New Brunswick, N.J.   B.W.T.
                                                                         J.L.O.

Contributors

Bruce W. Tuckman is Associate Professor of Education at Rutgers University. He has a B.S. in psychology from Rensselaer Polytechnic Institute and an M.A. and Ph.D. in psychology from Princeton University. He has been a National Institute of Mental Health Fellow, a post-doctoral research associate at Princeton, and a research psychologist at the Naval Medical Research Institute. He is a consultant to the U.S. Office of Education, Westchester County Special Needs Study, and Urban Coalition of Plainfield, N.J.

Leonard Zeitz is a research specialist at the Georgetown University Institute of Criminal Law and Procedure. His undergraduate work was in sociology at Brooklyn College and his graduate work at Columbia University in anthropology. He has been a research associate of the Hospital Review and Planning Council of Southern New York, a research associate at the Cornell Medical College, a consultant for the Newark Housing Authority, instructor to counselors for U.S.E.S. Youth Centers and for counselors of the Kilmer Job Corps, and has had a joint appointment with the Rutgers Urban Studies Center and the Rutgers University School of Law studying attitudes of Negroes to civil rights law.

William M. Phillips, Jr., is an associate research specialist in the Urban Studies Center and lecturer in sociology, Douglass College of Rutgers University. He earned his B.A. and M.A. in sociology at Fisk University and his Ph.D. in sociology at the University of Chicago. He has been a professor of sociology and Chairman of the Department of Sociology at Arkansas A.M. and N. College, a visiting professor of sociology at the University of Alberta, and a Fulbright Scholar at the University of the Punjab, Lahore, Pakistan.

Arnold Buchheimer is Professor of Education at Hunter College of the City University of New York and supervisor of the Guidance Laboratory. He received his basic education in Germany and his Ph.D. from The Ohio State University and has done post-doctoral work in psychotherapy. He is also a practicing psychotherapist with adolescents and has been a social worker, high school teacher, and school psychologist.

William R. Carriker is Professor and Head of the Department of Special Education at The Pennsylvania State University. He earned his B.A. at Nebraska Wesleyan University and his M.A. and Ed.D. in educational psychology and measurements at the University of Nebraska. He has been a teacher of special education, a consultant in special education at the state department of education level, a research coordinator for the Cooperative Research Program, and a teacher trainer. He has also been Director of the Research and Demonstration Branch, Division of Handicapped Children and Youth for the U.S. Office of Education.

Donald Maley is Professor and Head of the Industrial Education Department of the University of Maryland. He earned his B.S. at the State Teachers College, California, Pennsylvania, and his M.A. and Ph.D. in industrial education from the University of Maryland.

Marcus A. Foster is Principal of Gratz Senior High School, Philadelphia, Pennsylvania. He pursued his undergraduate work at the Pennsylvania State Teachers College at Cheyney. He earned his M.A. in education at the University of Pennsylvania, where he is currently working on his doctorate. He has been Principal of the O. V. Catto School in Philadelphia and has been cited by the Pennsylvania Department of Public Instruction for developing an experimental class for preschool children with limited backgrounds.

Sidney N. Chernak received his B.S. from Johns Hopkins University and his M.A. from Columbia University. He is Assistant Superintendent for secondary, vocational, and adult education in the Baltimore City Public Schools. He has served as Principal of four schools in Baltimore including the Carrollton School and Samuel Gompers General Vocational School. He serves as a visiting lecturer on the faculties of Loyola College and Johns Hopkins University.

Paul K. W. Springer is Director of the Manpower Development and Training Center in Rochester, New York. He is a graduate of Cornell University and has done graduate work there and at SUC Geneseo and the University of Rochester. With six years of experience as a teacher of vocational agriculture in Hammondsport, Chateaugay, and Marion, New York, he became Vocational Librarian to the Edison Technical and Industrial High School of Rochester. He then became a guidance counselor, Vice Principal, Evening School Principal and Director of Adult Education of the City School District.

John L. O'Brian is Associate Professor of Education at Rutgers University. He has earned his B.S. and M.Ed. in vocational trade and industrial education at The Pennsylvania State University and an Ed.D. in educational administration from the same university. He has been a director of vocational education, a teacher trainer, and a principal director of the research study entitled "The Development of a Master Teacher Training Curriculum for Teachers of Occupational Level Training Programs."

Harry L. Miller is Associate Professor of Education at Hunter College, and previously held the posts of Chief of Behavioral Science Department for a longitudinal study of child development and Assistant Director of the Center for the Study of Liberal Education for Adults. He directed one NDEA Institute for elementary teachers of the disadvantaged and has taught in several others; he recently completed two research projects on education students' attitudes toward the slum school and is working on the development of a prediction scale for teacher adjustment to these schools. His latest publications in the field are *Education in the Metropolis* (The Free Press, 1966), *Education for the Disadvantaged* (The Free Press, 1967), and *Policy Issues in Urban Education* (The Free Press, 1968).

Julian Roberts is Professor of Education at the Ferkauf Graduate School of Education, Yeshiva University. He received his B.A. and M.A. at Columbia University and his Ed.D. from Harvard University. He taught English at the secondary level and English and philosophy of education at the university level. He is adviser for teacher certification programs at the Ferkauf Graduate School of Education and directed an NDEA Institute for Teachers of Disadvantaged Youth: Reading and Language Arts, Grades 7–9.

Doxey A. Wilkerson is Associate Professor of Education and Director of Project Beacon at Yeshiva University. He earned his A.B. and A.M. at the University of Kansas and his Ph.D. at New York State

University. He was a member of President Roosevelt's Advisory Committee on Education, a member of the Carnegie-Myrdal Study of the Negro in America, Research Director of the Commission on School Integration of the National Association of Intergroup Relations Officials, and Associate Director of the Information Retrieval and Information Center on the Disadvantaged at Yeshiva University. He is a co-editor of *Compensatory Education for the Disadvantaged* (College Entrance Examination Board, 1967).

Maurie Hillson is Professor of Education at Rutgers University and Director of Project DUE (Design for Urban Education), a joint project of the Newark Board of Education and Rutgers University. He has his B.A. from Syracuse University, Ed.M. from Boston University, and Ed.D. from Harvard University in elementary education and administration. He has wide teaching and consulting experience at all levels of education and has served on the U.S. Commissioner of Education's Panel on Educational Research and Development. He has published frequently, including *Elementary Education: Current Issues and Research* (The Free Press, 1967).

Francis P. Purcell is the Director of Social Work Education at San Francisco State College. He has a B.Ph. from the University of North Dakota and an M.S.W. from the University of Denver. He has been Professor of Social Work at Rutgers University and Project Coordinator of Project DUE (Design for Urban Education). He has had considerable experience in community social welfare activities.

Contents

Part Two
The Problem as Viewed by Educational Practitioners

Part Three
Approaches to Teacher Education

Introduction

ALL MEMBERS of society are not afforded the same advantages. All members of society cannot (or do not) take equal advantage of the opportunities that are available. Children who grow up in impoverished homes, reared by parents with limited education, limited occupational skills, limited aspirations, and limited prospects clearly begin life at a considerable disadvantage. These children can be found in the urban ghettos and in the rural communities alike. They are the Negro, the Appalachian white, the American Indian, the Cuban, the Puerto Rican, the southern Negro, and the migrant. We tend to limit our concept of the disadvantaged to the urban Negro and Puerto Rican because of the publicity given to this segment of our disadvantaged population by the mass media. Literature concerning the disadvantaged will show that considerably more has been written about the disadvantaged Negro than about other disadvantaged people. The problems, the unpleasantness, the hardships, and the frustrations are just as real to all so affected.

We tend to refer to those who grow up in the "without" culture as the *culturally disadvantaged*. These people will receive less than their fair share of the necessities and luxuries that the majority of the culture provides for its members.

A prime factor in the limited development of the children of the disadvantaged is the lack of early stimulation in the home. This limits the perceptual, cognitive, and verbal development of the child during the critical formative years. Head Start programs represent an attempt to augment this development but the limiting factor in this program is the limited time available for development and enrichment of the child's background. The parents must be given the incentive and background to provide through home life the stimulation and the enrichment so necessary to the development of their children and so influential on their entire remaining life. The early years have been shown to be the critical formative years.

Children reporting to school with what has been termed a *culture deficit*—and it has been shown that this deficit is cumulative, that is, it increases at an increasing rate throughout the lifespan of the individual—are at a distinct disadvantage in the verbally loaded school setting. And yet, in education lies the greatest hope to break this seemingly unbreakable chain.

There are many reasons for the existence of culturally disadvantaged persons in our society. There are many reasons why the size of this group may continue to grow in terms of total numbers and percentage of the total population. There are many factors that mitigate against the participation of these persons in the fruits of our affluent society and against the elimination of this major social problem. The most favorable change element for the disadvantaged, although by no means a panacea, is *education*. Through education, language and skill deficits can be overcome. (Educators involved in Manpower programs, for example, quickly realized that persons to be helped must possess basic minimum skills in the "tool" subjects.) Through education, aspirations can be encouraged. Programs such as the Great Cities Program encourage the development of aspirations that are so vital to the success of any educational program. We can safely say that through education an individual who begins life at a cultural disadvantage can take major steps to improve his own lot and eventually that of his children. It is conceivable that through education properly presented to enough members of the disadvantaged groups, within a few generations, the majority of the disadvantaged can be brought into the mainstream of American life. To fail in this endeavor will lead to social problems of great magnitude, perhaps too great to describe adequately.

If education is to be the vehicle, or at least one vehicle, by which major social problems are to be ameliorated, then teachers might well be the key to success in carrying out this intent. Satisfactory results are unlikely to be achieved by an educational system built by able and informed administrators and housed in a modern and complete facility, but having a cadre of teachers who lack an understanding of the culture of disadvantaged groups, who lack an understanding of the frame of reference upon which the disadvantaged base and project their value system (and these are different for different disadvantaged groups), and who lack expertise in pedagogical skills that are effective with the disadvantaged. The teachers are an essential ingredient in the tripartition of facilities, administration, and teachers; perhaps the most important ingredient in the admixture of successful education programs. Good administration is necessary; adequate facilities aid the administrative and the teaching-learning processes; but neither alone or both combined are sufficient to guarantee that the objectives of the educational program will achieve fruition. We have a need and a responsibility to provide ways and means as well as motivation for insuring that disadvantaged persons obtain the services of teachers who have a reasonable chance of aiding them to overcome their problems.

Teacher education programs, however, are not noted for their sensitivity to cultural needs; they are slow to change in response to changes in the structure and demands of society. The term *traditional* is typically applied to teacher education in this country. Patterns of change, in the overall picture, seem to stem from the practitioner side of the ledger, and these have not been bountiful. The last decade has witnessed great activity in this area; however, much of this activity is hardware-oriented and parallels recent advancement in industrial technology. A good case can be made relating the sudden and recent flurry in the technology of education to the stimulus provided by federal legislation, beginning with the National Defense Education Act of 1958.

The problem of teaching culturally disadvantaged youth, when these youth come from a culture different from that of the teacher, is one that should receive considerable attention from those who purport to prepare teachers to provide equal educational opportunity for all segments of our society. Teachers who are assigned or who volunteer to teach the disadvantaged and who have not been prepared to cope with the problems of their students are a liability rather than an asset to the student and the system. Teachers working with these students need specific preparation, even if they might have come from a similar background. Many of those few who have broken the chain have lost their empathy for the culture that has been thrown off, and belonging does not assure complete understanding.

Specific teacher training will need to be broader than simple textbook and theory training, though this is an important ingredient. It will need to incorporate first-hand experiences that enable the prospective teacher to apply theory in practical situations. It is doubtful that such experiences can be simulated; this implies, then, that a liberal inclusion of practicums is a realistic consideration for any curriculum designed to train teachers of the disadvantaged. It may well be that new programs of teacher education will have to be revolutionary rather than traditional. It is not expected that revolutionary programs will be accepted without hesitation. However, this point in time finds education and educators more responsive to change than ever before. To be innovative is to be with the "in" group. Here we feel the impact and influence of funds for experimentation that have become available from federal and foundation sources. This receptivity to innovation may be the greatest contribution made by the availability of these funds and may stimulate some meaningful changes in education theory.

As mentioned previously, these teacher training programs will have to teach teachers more about the culture and the society in which the child lives. In addition, teachers will have to become more cognizant of (1) the effects of prior and present experiences on the behaviors and expectations of children, and (2) the wide variety of techniques that can be used to help children build their own self-confidence and explore in a more creative fashion the world around them. Part Three of this book, dealing with teacher preparation programs and institutes, gives concrete examples and recommendations that can be used to achieve these lofty goals.

This book attempts to underscore a need for developing teacher training programs to prepare teachers to teach disadvantaged youths and adults. Several models for teacher education programs are presented. Three approaches are discernible. First, the nature of the problem will be identified, and with this there will be presented some reasonable premises upon which some solutions to the problem can be built. An interdisciplinary point of view that is heavily weighted in a theoretical direction is a feature of this approach. Second, the nature of the problem will be identified and with this there will again be presented reasonable and realistic premises upon which some solutions to the problem can be built. This approach will be from the practitioners' point of view, that is, from the point of view of individuals who are on the "firing line" and who are presently trying to cope with the problem. And finally, there will be presented some comprehensive attempts by educators and educational institutions to develop programs (of which some have been tried) that will provide teachers with knowledge, skills, and background experiences deemed necessary to successfully teach the disadvantaged. Each of these approaches is introduced below.

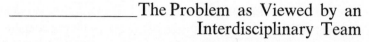The Problem as Viewed by an Interdisciplinary Team

THE TEACHER training curriculum entitled "A Master's Degree Program for the Preparation of Teachers of Disadvantaged Youth" came about through the efforts of a group of individuals representing several different disciplines. The various social science disciplines as well as various aspects of the discipline of education were included. Each of these individuals was invited to come to Rutgers University to present a paper directed to the question, "What can your discipline contribute toward the development of a teacher training program for teachers of the disadvantaged?" The team, which included psychologists, an anthropologist, sociologist, counselor, special education educator, and vocational educators, addressed themselves and the concepts of their disciplines to this problem.

The chapters that appear in Part One of this book are based on the papers that were originally prepared for that conference. There are many common elements running through all of these papers, even though each was written independently and from the perspective of a different discipline. Among these common elements the following requirements for the teacher of the disadvantaged stand out:

1. He must be exposed to a broad range of social sciences, and their contribution and relation to his problems must be made manifest.

2. He must learn new techniques that are appropriate for the student he will face.

3. He must be liberal-minded and willing to work in the face of adversity to help students who need his help but often will not show their "thanks."

4. He must be an innovator rather than a follower.

5. He must be exposed to a range of new environments, both social and educational.

6. He must be willing to accept only minimal success and continue in the face of apparent failure.

7. He must become a student of the subculture he will be working in.

8. He must empathize with his students.

While the above should be goals for preparing all teachers who must confront the subculture of youth, they are particularly critical for the teacher of the disadvantaged and stand out among the statements of the contributing authors.

Second, each of the writers identifies the population in question (for purposes of this chapter called the *culturally disadvantaged*) by a different term, yet in each instance, the term employed is quite specific and meaningful for the discipline represented. Psychologically, this population is identified as the *culturally deprived* and is further specified in terms of specific early experiences and opportunities of which the members of this group have been deprived. The concepts of specific stimulus deprivation have been well documented in many studies in which specific changes in the environment are made in order to restrict opportunities of the individual for stimulation. Although cultural deprivation is not deprivation by choice, it is nonetheless deprivation of specific stimulating experiences, by virtue of the home situation.

To the anthropologist this group is the *alien culture,* alien because it is different. In some cases this group employs different language; in most cases they have a different set of values, norms, and expectations. They are often reacted to in a stereotypic fashion, which tends to overgeneralize their differences and underemphasize their similarities to other subcultural groups.

To the sociologist these are *stigmatized youth,* labeled by their society as being different and inevitably wearing their label as a badge.

The counseling psychologist sees these youth as the *underclass,* considered as below the middle class in many cases by elements of the society associated with employment and employment opportunities. These youth have come to perceive themselves as the underclass.

To the special educator they are *exceptional children,* their area of exceptionality being cognitive, perceptual, and verbal deficits, which it is the role of the educator to overcome. The disadvantaged youngster is exceptional as the genius is exceptional; the mentally retarded is exceptional; the student with social-emotional problems is exceptional; and the physically handicapped are exceptional. Their exceptionality makes it necessary for them to be dealt with in specific ways, ways that are geared to the degree and area of their exceptionality.

To the educator these are *youth with special needs* (as they have been termed by recent educational legislation). It is the role of the educator to identify these needs and hopefully to deal with them in a positive manner that enables learning and attitude change to take place.

It is interesting to note that the perspectives of the various disciplines on this problem are reflected not only in their papers, but in the labels that they use to basically identify the problem and the population with whom they deal.

The Problem as Viewed by Educational Practitioners

TEACHERS of the disadvantaged will teach in a wide variety of programs. These include tutoring, community action, and Manpower Development Training programs; preschool, elementary, and high school remedial programs such as Head Start, Upward Bound, REAP, and Great Cities; disciplinary programs; and programs for the slow learner or underachiever. Administrators of a sampling of such programs were invited to prepare papers addressed to the following five points:

1. A brief description of their programs and objectives.
2. Characteristics of the disadvantaged youth that constitute their student body.
3. The needs of the disadvantaged student that must be met by the school.
4. Personal characteristics needed by teachers of disadvantaged youth.
5. Skills, knowledge, and understanding needed by teachers in teaching disadvantaged youth.

These practitioners—educational administrators—who out of necessity took concrete steps to solve existing problems, developed their papers for a second conference held at Rutgers. These papers formed the basis for the chapters included in Part Two of this book. Education, as other public services, must come to grips with realities of life. At some point, the theorist must consort with the practitioner to evaluate his insights. Likewise, the practitioner must also seek evaluation and try new paths, or modify existing paths, so as to achieve the full potential of theoretical concepts available. This interchange between the practitioner and the scientist is a necessary ingredient to progress. This was the rationale for steps which later led to the development of a curriculum to prepare teachers to work with the disadvantaged.

The chapters presented in Part Two of this volume represent the attempts of practitioners to report their insights and understanding of these students and of the teacher who has proved to be successful with them. Clearly it is necessary to know what kinds of talents, understanding, skills, and personal qualities are needed by the teacher before one can build a program that is designed to inculcate these attributes through controlled instruction and experiences.

_____Approaches to Teacher Education

THE interdisciplinary team that contributed the chapters in **Part One** of this book generated a tentative model Master's Degree program for the preparation of teachers of disadvantaged youth. This project was undertaken under the direction of Dr. John L. O'Brian. The model is the outcome of disciplinary cross-fertilization, under the watchful eye of educational practitioners—individuals experienced with the problem area. It is not a tried and tested program, though its procreators hopefully wish for an opportunity to implement it. It is offered not as the final answer but rather as a medium that will stimulate the exchange of ideas and considerations and the development of innovations that will make it possible for more teachers to become qualified to teach the disadvantaged. The content that has been "tacked" on the model leans heavily on meeting the needs of the disadvantaged Negro. This alternative was chosen because the Negro represents the largest single segment of the disadvantaged and because of the background experiences of those whose joint efforts are responsible for the model. Also, because of the availability of materials, desired examples could be offered that would best illustrate the intent of the committee. The model is just as appropriate for other disadvantaged populations, providing the content, references, practicums, and so on, that are used are germane to that particular population.

Included in Part Three are other models developed by individuals and institutions. These are included to provide the reader with a broad perspective of the thinking of other eminently qualified students of this complex problem. Inherent in these programs are commonalities and differences, some of which are philosophical and others practical, illustrating different interpretations or approaches to the question. These other approaches can provide a broader base for discussion, ideas, and innovations which should be an asset when considering the disadvantaged. An inspection of these other programs will show that some are designed as a Master's program, others are summer programs, and some have been tried whereas others are simply suggested.

It should be pointed out that this volume has specific value not only to the educator who desires to develop a teacher training program, but to all educators and students of education who desire to expand their insights, knowledge, and understanding of the disadvantaged.

The educational institution within our society and the administrators and teachers who make up its personnel are confronted with the responsibility for providing all youth with the skills necessary to lead a useful, productive, and fulfilling life. Such awesome responsibility calls for an open mind and willingness to try new approaches to the task of education. The flow of words is no substitute for the implementation of programs. But history has shown that words can stimulate action. It is to this end that we strive.

Part One

The Problem as Viewed by an Interdisciplinary Team

1 The Teacher and the Psychology of the Culturally Deprived

Bruce W. Tuckman

OUR FIRST question is: "What does it mean psychologically to be culturally deprived or culturally disadvantaged?" An attempt will be made to answer this question keeping in mind that we are dealing with probabilities. A child or adolescent who is culturally deprived is more likely to be characterized by the things that are discussed than is a child or adolescent who is not culturally deprived. What is said may not always apply equally to all individuals who are culturally deprived, but it will be more likely true than false.

First of all, being culturally deprived very often means being biologically deprived; that is, being hungry, underclothed, and in need of medical and dental treatment. Medical and dental treatment are often needed for the individual both because of his general level of poverty—being unable to afford these services—and also because of the fact that the parents of the culturally deprived child or adolescent are very often unaware of the importance of medical and dental treatment.

Being hungry can have many ramifications. Breckenridge and Vincent (1962) have reviewed studies demonstrating that insufficient nutrition affects growth, behavior, and mental performance. From these findings, we can expect the hungry individual to pay less attention in the classroom than would be desired, and to have a reduced mental effectiveness. The work of Schorr (1964) also indicates that malnutrition has an effect on attitudes and behavior. He finds that food deprivation leads to the neurasthenic syndrome: excess fatigue, disturbances in sleep, inability to concentrate, queer bodily sensations, depression, apathy, loss of ambition, and tendency to transfer blame from oneself to others. Poor housing leads to pessimism, stress, poor general health, loneliness when alone, and a high degree of sexual stimulation.

Because of this biological deprivation, the culturally disadvantaged child or adolescent will be anxious to obtain the wherewithal to satisfy his needs, and will not be willing to expend energy for the promise of things to come if he has the alternative possibility of expending energy to obtain immediate gratification of his basic needs. Thus, the culturally disadvantaged youngster is unwilling to delay gratification. This orientation toward immediate gratification or immediate reinforcement is generally coincident with a high state of biological need. The work of Hull (1952) and his associates in the animal laboratory has shown that as the drive state of the animal increases, that is, as the hours since the animal has last been fed increase, the tendency for the animal to perform the desired behavior if reward is delayed is greatly reduced. The same phenomenon appears to hold for human beings when they are biologically deprived or have a history of biological deprivation, as is often the case with the culturally deprived individual. His behavior will be oriented toward satisfying immediate biological needs and he will not be willing to perform educational tasks with a promise of reward forthcoming. Leshan (1952) has shown that lower-class training features immediate rewards based on motor activity and physical gratification, punishments leading to an orientation toward quick sequences of tension and relief, and a strong orientation toward the present rather than the future. Mischel (1961) has shown that delinquents have a preference for immediate reinforcement. *Thus, the first general statement about what it means to be culturally deprived is that it means very often to be biologically deprived and, as a result of this and other training factors, unwilling to delay gratification.*

4
Bruce W. Tuckman

Secondly, individuals who are culturally deprived usually score lower on intelligence tests (Klineberg, 1963, for Negroes). This does not necessarily indicate that a culturally deprived individual has a reduced intelligence. The evidence justifies the inference that culturally deprived individuals have less of their intelligence potential developed than do individuals who have not suffered cultural deprivation; thus, such tests are not valid measures of intelligence for this group. The low score is not native but experiential (Pettigrew, 1964).

The excellent work of Hunt (1961) in bringing together all available relevant literature dealing with the issue of predetermined development and fixed intelligence points out that cultural deprivation almost always produces less developed intelligence but that remedial treatment or improvement undertaken in the years of childhood, even in early adolescence, can modify the situation substantially. Dramatic modifications have been evidenced in the studies of Skeels and Dye (1939) and Wellman (1940). In the Skeels and Dye study, orphans were taken to an institution for the feeble-minded and raised by the patients. Gains as high as forty IQ points were evidenced. Dennis (1960) has shown that many children in an orphanage in Teheran do not walk by four years of age.

Why should all this be so? There is less stimulation in the culturally deprived home in the direction of developing cognitive, perceptual, and verbal skills. Our intelligence tests and the situations that they have been developed to predict for are situations that involve verbal, cognitive, and perceptual skills. This is obviously true of the classroom. In the classroom we call upon the students to manifest these three kinds of skills and all standardized intelligence and aptitude tests are weighted heavily in these three areas (as well as a fourth, numerical).

In the culturally deprived home, as mentioned before, the major orientation is toward the immediate gratification of biological needs. Much energy and emotional involvement by the parents must be spent on this task. Consequently little energy and emotional involvement remain for the development of "intelligence" in the children. The work of Hunt (1961, 1964), Ausubel (1963), and Wolf (1964), among others, points up the fact that a major factor contributing to intellectual development is stimulation in the home by the parents. Moreover, this factor is of peak importance in the early years of life, according to Bloom (1964). The parents themselves in most culturally deprived homes have had little education and are themselves in the situation where their cognitive, perceptual, and verbal skills may be reduced.

They are not aware of many instruments of education that are available for use in the home and they do not have the time and the skill to carry on conversations with their children which are necessary to develop verbal skills. Deutsch (1963) in his examination of homes in depressed areas finds few educational objects and a general absence of parental stimulation appropriate for cognitive, perceptual, or verbal development. The findings of John (1963) lead her to conclude that the "acquisition of more abstract and integrative language seems to be hampered by the living conditions in the homes of lower-class children." This is supported by Bernstein (1962) who finds less language facility among the lower class. Siller (1957) finds less conceptual ability among low status children, status defined on the basis of the Warner Index of Social Characteristics. *Thus, the second general statement about cultural deprivation is that it produces reduced intelligence as a function of lesser cognitive, perceptual, and verbal skills.* However, it must again be stressed that this situation is not permanent, nor fixed, nor unchangeable. It is a situation that can be rectified as a function of the educational situation, as evidenced by the work of Boger (1952) and others mentioned before. This will be discussed in the second half of this chapter.

A third characteristic that is generally produced in conditions of cultural deprivation is an *absence of achievement motivation.* Achievement motivation, which has been widely described, discussed, and researched (McClelland et al., 1953; Atkinson, 1958) refers to the desire on the part of the individual to achieve either for the intrinsic satisfaction associated with achievement or for the rewards society metes out as a function of achievement behavior. This is very strongly associated with the middle class, as McClelland has shown in his book *The Achieving Society* (1961). The American society and particularly the middle class of American society, as shown also by the work of Rosen (1956), is extremely high in achievement motivation.

Where does achievement motivation come from? According to McClelland, achievement motivation is a result of rewards being offered for achievement behavior (that is, approval) and punishments offered for failure. Consequently, the individual who is motivated or oriented to maximize rewards will perform achievement behavior. According to Winterbottom (1958) and to Rosen and D'Andrade (1959), achievement is further enhanced by identification and independence training. The parent puts much emphasis on achievement behavior in the middle class. As a result of success on the part of the potential achiever and

Bruce W. Tuckman

consequent rewards, achievement motivation may well be developed. If the parents are themselves achievers, the development of this motivation in the child will be furthered. Excessive failure and punishment can produce in the individual a motive other than achievement motivation, namely, fear of failure. In the culturally deprived home there is little evidence either that achievement is rewarded or lack of achievement punished. There is little emphasis placed on academic achievement or cultural achievement on the part of the child, and the parent is not himself an achiever by virtue of his own upbringing and lack of present opportunities. The work of Bronfenbrenner (1961) suggests that academic competitiveness is a function of middle-class upbringing but not of lower-class upbringing. Again, the reason for this is insufficient time and a minimum orientation in that direction on the part of the parents themselves. Kahl (1953) has shown that parents interested in getting ahead send their sons to college while those interested merely in getting by do not. *Consequently, as a third generalization it is stated that cultural deprivation usually means having little achievement motivation.*

The fourth and last general area in which cultural deprivation has implications is that of attitudes toward self, toward others, and toward the world. As a result of having to live in general hardship conditions, very often having reduced opportunities, being discriminated against, and, while living in a society that has the highest standard of living ever achieved, not being able to partake of this abundance, the individual may often develop a negative, cynical, fatalistic, and simple view of the world. He may often associate himself with undesirable or criminal elements, move in the direction of juvenile delinquency, and fall into the general clinical category known as psychopathic or sociopathic personality. The underprivileged person feels as a result of the situation that society is doing little for him, giving him little opportunity, and so he is quite right in taking matters into his own hands, and in an asocial fashion, attempting to mold his own situation. If he does not behave asocially, he may simply adopt a set of attitudes that are very negatively related to society. These will be expected to appear in the classroom, since a classroom is a miniaturization of society and the teacher is a representative authority. Hieronymus (1951) has shown a substantial correlation between socioeconomic status and attitudes toward education.

The attitude of the culturally deprived person toward others will be very similar to his attitude toward the world, to the extent that he sees others as being representative of, or exemplary of society in general. That is, he will be negatively oriented toward authority figures and feel that manipulation is a reasonable way to gain his ends. With regard to the attitude that he has toward himself, we can expect that he will have a low level of aspiration, and realistically so, since he sees his contemporaries and his elders having little success in life and having little opportunity to improve their situation. He may come to expect this with regard to himself (Hieronymus, 1951) and consequently may manifest a low level of aspiration and low self-expectations. He may, on the other hand, feel that this inability to improve is a function of his own inability and consequently may develop low self-esteem. Ausubel and Ausubel (1963) and Goff (1954) have shown that social rejection among Negro children leads to low self-esteem and a low level of aspiration.

In reaction to his own unsuccessful situation in society and the unsuccessful situation of his friends and his parents, the culturally deprived person may either become extrapunitive or intrapunitive, using the Rosenzweig concept. That is, he may feel that the fault lies in himself and consequently have low self-esteem, or else he may react extrapunitively toward the source of his frustration via delinquent acts. In either case, low self-expectations and a low level of aspiration can be expected.

Thus, the fourth generalization is that cultural deprivation yields unfavorable attitudes toward self, others, and society, which in turn may result in delinquent behaviors.

It may be said in conclusion that the implication of cultural deprivation for education is to produce individuals with an absence of "learning to learn capability," to borrow a phrase from Bloom, Davis, and Hess (1965). This learning to learn capability is similar to what Harry Harlow (1949) called a "learning set." In Harlow's research with monkeys, the animals learned to solve discrimination problems and oddity problems by learning the general principle, as opposed to reacting to the specifics on a trial-and-error basis in each case. When given three stimuli, one of which was different from the other two, some monkeys were able, after about one thousand trials, to immediately select the odd member of the three and thus achieve a solution without groping. Harlow was not able to produce a learning set in all monkeys, and when he was successful, many trials were necessary. That is, only after much practice with the stimuli and much feedback were some monkeys able to develop a learning set.

Learning to learn encompasses the four principles discussed above.

Bruce W. Tuckman

A person who has learned to learn must be able to delay gratification or reinforcement, for the fruits of education are considerably delayed after the beginning of the effort. Learning to learn means having the appropriate skills on which education is based, namely cognitive, perceptual, and verbal skills. Learning to learn means having the appropriate values, namely values toward achievement. And finally, learning to learn means having the appropriate attitudes toward oneself and one's environment. Having these qualities means being set to learn. Having these qualities means having the strategy for obtaining knowledge. Having these qualities means being able to uncover general solutions and general truths rather than always being restricted to the specific.

Being culturally deprived means not having learned to learn in many cases. What can the teacher do for such a person? It is to this question that the remainder of this chapter is addressed.

When the culturally deprived child goes through school his situation only worsens. His deficit relative to his middle-class counterparts becomes cumulatively greater. Evidence for the accumulation and worsening of the deficit has been provided by Deutsch (1964) and Krugman (1961). Thus, schooling tends not to improve the situation by providing the necessary skills, attitudes, and values upon which learning is based; rather, the deficit becomes greater and greater as the years of education proceed. By the time adolescence is reached the culturally deprived student, according to data collected by Osborne (1960), shows reduced reading skills, reduced arithmetic skills, and a lower mental age relative to a nondeprived group.

Thus, the education system tends to selectively reinforce the good students and to pay little attention, or provide less than the necessary remedial help, for the deprived or disadvantaged students. Major responsibility for improving the situation remains with the administrators and program developers. Enrichment programs at the preschool level are necessary so that deprived youngsters do not enter school with a deficit. Enrichment and remedial programs are necessary all through elementary school and high school, and better counseling, especially in the guidance area, is necessary in the junior high school. However, the major objective of this chapter is to examine what the teacher can and must do when teaching culturally deprived students.

First, it is useful to review some factors that have shown up in various programs that have been carried out. Boger (1952) was able to improve visual perception necessary for perceptual discrimination, in the case of culturally deprived students. Improved perceptual discrimination often led to increases in intelligence test scores because perceptual discrimination in many cases is a prerequisite for problem solving, reading, spelling, and arithmetic. To achieve this end Boger had his students work with jigsaw puzzles and other puzzles requiring visual perception.

Brazziel and Terrell (1962) produced an improvement in pupil readiness as a function of educational television and other experiences. Krugman (1961), in a review of New York City projects, suggested that remedial services, guidance and counseling, opportunities for cultural experiences such as field trips and museum visits, and an increase of care on the part of the school and the teacher all lead to an improved level of skill as well as an improved self-concept among lower-class children. The Manhattanville Project, or Higher Horizons Program, as reported by Schreiber (1958), was able to produce dramatic gains for lower-class students. Remedial programs, tutoring, concentrated training, and systematic attempts at attitude change were perhaps the reason for the success. The project tried to improve the self-images of the students and to help them to develop pride in their cultural background. The project also utilized parent education and vocational guidance.

Shaw (1963), reporting on the Detroit Project and the Manhattanville Project, concluded that the utilization of professional workers, smaller classes, systematic attempts to change the attitudes of parents, and community involvement played a major role in the success of these programs.

And, finally, the experiences from Project Head Start suggest that mere contact between the deprived student and the objects and opportunities of learning can have an effect on performance level and attitudes.

The concept of reinforcement will appear and reappear many times in the statements below. One may ask whether this concept is undergoing a resurgence of interest in the field of education. To be sure, it is increasing in popularity, but caution must be encouraged in its use. The first half of this chapter has attempted to identify the characteristics of the culturally deprived learner, primarily in reward terms, using concepts developed in the learning laboratory. An attempt will be made below to provide some guidelines for working with culturally deprived youth, again with an emphasis on the use of rewards. These guidelines will be modeled around the four major areas of deprivation as described above.

Bruce W. Tuckman

One can take the very hedonistic position that people do things, all things, for a reason—to obtain some gain for themselves. This gain may be universally appreciated and clearly and obviously connected to the behavior that leads to its achievement, such as going to work in order to eat. The gain, however, may be somewhat less than universal, and only very indirectly connected to the behaviors that surround it. This is often the case in our culture. Many people teach because they seek to aid youth in their learning and development, and the "large" sums of money received for it represent secondary gain. The source of this service motive is a complicated one; it appears to be based on rewards and, consequently, learned. However, it is difficult to trace its origin in terms of specific behaviors and rewards. The indirect nature of reward and its delay is not uncommon among the middle class. This is based, in part, on the ready and immediate access of primary rewards, freeing the individual to pursue long-range, moralistic goals. The culturally deprived youngster, as mentioned above, does not often have the luxury of the automatic receipt of primary rewards. Consequently, his behavior is aimed at obtaining satisfaction of his basic needs at the expense of those which his teachers often hold dear. He is often unwilling to perform for the promise of things to come. A history of this leads to a general tendency for such youngsters to develop an orientation to the present and an unwillingness to perform in the present for the promise of any sort of reward in the future, be it basic or otherwise.

For this reason, *the teacher should attempt to reduce the delay in reinforcement as much as possible.* In a very practical sense, this can be done by quick scoring of examinations, by providing the student with continual and immediate feedback as regards his performance, and, primarily by *constantly attempting to relate the school experience to real life experiences.* Much effort is spent on education before the results of this effort can be obtained. Many students who drop out of school are not willing to tolerate this delay; among these often are the culturally deprived.

In order to moderate this delay, the practical significance of education must constantly be pointed out to the culturally deprived student. In addition, materials must be chosen that have an intrinsic interest to the child or adolescent, regardless of their moral value. In teaching the student to read, he should be exposed to the kinds of materials that he would read in his everyday experiences and that have meaning to him, i.e., stories about his heroes, many of whom come from the field of sports. He should have the opportunity to read stories set in the slums, so that he can identify with the characters and be familiar with the situations. The stories chosen should be realistic rather than moralistic. "Kids don't like to be preached at." Students could read destination labels from busses, signs from store windows, descriptions of automobiles and advertisements. Materials should be selected that mean something to the child by relating to his environment. Developing skills to deal with his present environment represents immediate reinforcement for the child. What interests the teacher may not interest the student, and vice versa.

Too often our school situations represent an ivory tower. It is necessary that this distance between school and reality be bridged. While it is not entirely possible for the teacher to do it by himself, he can always keep in mind the fact that the culturally deprived student may not be able to delay reinforcement. He must always think of what he is teaching in the sense of what practical significance does this have for the student.

In the area of skill training, what can the teacher do with respect to the culturally deprived student? The teacher should be aware of the fact that perceptual skills underlie reading, and verbal skills, which in turn underlie cognitive skills. When a student is unable to perform satisfactorily in a cognitive task, it may be because he is in need of remedial help on verbal or perceptual levels. While the teacher may not always be the most skilled person in providing this remedial help, it is necessary that he be able to diagnose where such help is needed and recommend the students to remedial programs, where they exist.

One useful point would be for the teacher to attempt to *teach at the perceptual level as much as possible at all grade levels*. The teacher should teach by showing, by doing, using gestures, pictures, diagrams, schematics, and the chalkboard. The perceptual level should be aimed for and an attempt should be made to avoid the verbal level as much as possible. The students should be given puzzles, like jigsaw puzzles, Chinese puzzles, and other kinds of puzzles that require some degree of perceptual discrimination, in order to improve their skill at the perceptual level. Reading should be included and emphasized as much as possible, even in courses where reading is not directly the subject matter to be taught. Students should read instructions and sketches. An attempt should be made to talk to the students as much as possible.[1]

1. I have suggested above that you teach by showing rather than talking. Now I may appear to be contradicting myself. I am not! By talking, here, I mean conversing, as one converses to pass the time of day, not teaching via extended and complex verbiage. To improve the students' verbal skills they must hear words, but this must occur primarily outside of the pressures of the formal learning process.

Bruce W. Tuckman

Through conversation verbal skills are developed. When a teacher must deal with many students at once this is very difficult, but insofar as it is possible the teacher must talk to the students to provide them with the conversation and the verbal stimulation that is absent in the home. This is especially true with younger students.

In the area of values and achievement motivation, the magic word is REWARD. *The child or adolescent should be rewarded frequently and punished rarely.* He should be rewarded for performances that are less than perfect but have some merit to them. The work of Skinner (1938) in the animal laboratory has shown that behavior can be shaped through a technique called successive approximations. Using this technique, behaviors which bear only slight resemblance to the desired end behavior are reinforced, and gradually this approximate behavior is shaped in the direction of the desired behavior by reinforcing behaviors that are more and more similar to the desired end behavior. The same can be done with children in the area of achievement motivation. By reinforcing only minimally successful behavior to start with, the likelihood of successful behavior will increase and it will be possible to reward more successful behavior in the future and hopefully to shape achievement-oriented behavior.

Punishment, on the other hand, will lead to fear of failure, as the work of Atkinson and collaborators (1958) has shown. Estes (1944) has shown that punishment does not cause behavior to disappear; it simply inhibits its occurrence in the presence of the punishing agent. If failure is punished by the teacher, then the behaviors that lead to the failure may not appear within eye range of the teacher, but they will not cease to exist in the repertoire of the child or the adolescent. Reward, on the other hand, creates a behavior pattern within the individual. Therefore, when dealing with culturally deprived students, for whom achievement motivation is minimal, failure should not be punished. The teacher should wait for some glimmer of successful behavior or achievement-oriented behavior and then reward it. He should attempt through the generous use of reward to develop an achievement pattern in the student. This may be facilitated by posing simple tasks or simple problems for the student and then rewarding successful performance. The difficulty of the tasks can be gradually increased as the generous use of reward has made the possibility or probability of success more likely. Moreover, the rewards should be as tangible as possible. The research of Zigler and DeLabry (1962) has shown that tangible rewards are more successful than intangible rewards with lower-class students, while the reverse holds true with middle-class students. Attempting to make the rewards as tangible as possible is of course limited by the opportunities available to the teacher. One cannot give away money, for instance, or candy, for every good performance. In many cases, the only rewards available to the teacher are such intangible ones as praise, or recognition, or approval. These are important too, and should be made as obvious as possible.

This point is worth stressing in a more concrete manner. It is important for students to succeed because of the intrinsic reward value of success. Success makes the student strive for more success and helps him develop a positive self-image and a sense of worth and competence. A successful student will usually seek a situation which is a little bit harder than what he has encountered before, wherein the probability of success in his judgment is about 50 per cent. He will avoid the very easy and the very hard. The optimal level of difficulty for a middle-class youngster may represent an unattainable level for the disadvantaged youngster, causing him not to try because of anticipated certain failure. This youngster must experience an environment which has been "programmed" for a success pattern, much as the learning program used in a teaching machine is programmed for response success. The teacher should ask the youngster a question or give him a problem that he is sure to answer correctly, and then praise him for his performance—being sure to inform him that he is correct. The next time around, the difficulty of the question or problem should be increased. On each successive instance, the problem should be made successively more difficult, up to about a 50 per cent probability of success level (in the student's eyes—not the teacher's). After each success, the student should be informed of his success and praised for it. In this way fear of failure is replaced by positive achievement motivation.

When it is necessary to use criticism, this criticism should be objective. The work should be criticized rather than the person performing the work. The Lewin, Lippitt, and White studies (1939) gave clear evidence for the fact that group leaders using personal criticism were much less popular than were leaders whose criticism was clearly objective.

Finally, in the all-important area of attitudes, a teacher can make a major impression and inroads into the problems of the culturally deprived. The teacher is a representative of society. He is, moreover, an authority figure second only to the parents as a major source of identification. A teacher can take advantage of this, especially when the parent is not a good identification figure. Using the parent as an identi-

14
Bruce W. Tuckman

fication figure simply perpetuates the ethic of the deprived. To change attitudes of the deprived student toward himself, others, and society, the teacher must be warm, understanding, and sympathetic. In short, he must take a personal interest in the student. If he is likeable yet firm, and takes an interest in the student, the student will attempt to emulate him and use him as an identification figure (Witty, 1947). To the extent that the teacher incorporates prevalent social values, these will be transmitted to the culturally deprived student through identification. If the teacher is fair, then the students' attitudes toward society may well be changed.

Being fair means not playing favorites (especially favoring the brighter students), not punishing when it's not justified, dealing with nonconforming behavior without using damaging physical or psychological punitive measures, supporting students in spite of failures and obstacles, having a warm, stable personality, and practicing what he preaches. Youngsters know when a teacher doesn't like them. Negative attitudes toward one's students are hard to conceal.

As many of the successful remedial projects, such as the Manhattanville Project, have shown, a key to success is working with parents. *The teacher should attempt to involve the parent and work with the parent as much as possible.* If he can change the attitude of the parent, then the possibility of changing the attitudes of the student are doubled, as a result of his own direct influence and the influence of the parent over whom he has exerted some influence. The fact that involvement enhances the probability of attitude change has well been documented. Industrial studies such as those of Coch and French (1948), and studies such as that of Lewin (1952), clearly illustrate that individuals who feel that they are involved are more likely to have their attitudes changed.

Also, the students should be involved in providing some of their own direction in the classroom. Again, the classic Lewin, Lippitt, and White (1939) studies demonstrated that attitudes, motivations, and satisfaction were increased as a result of a democratic group situation, where the group exerted some influence over its own direction. This approach, which has often been called the learner-centered or pupil-centered approach, has been shown in some studies to be highly successful. Culturally deprived students must be able to take on the role of authority in order that their attitudes toward authority can be changed.

Outside of a group-centered or pupil-centered approach, which enables the group to have some control over its fate, *the use of role-playing is also a way of changing attitudes.* The study of King and Janis (1956) demonstrates that role-playing can be used effectively to change attitudes. Letting the students play the game of parents and children and act out a home situation gives them the feeling of what it is like to be a parent or any other authority figure in society. Letting them identify with society and defend society through playing the role of an authority may well change their attitude toward the very society which they often find intolerable. Playing a role which is dissonant with one's attitudes has been shown to cause those attitudes to change (Brehm, 1960).

Praise and approval should be used to change students' self-esteem and self-acceptance. This tells a student that his teacher thinks he is a worthwhile person and capable of good performance. *Students should be provided with tasks of graded difficulty leading to success in order to change their level of aspiration.* Jucknat (1938) has shown that aspirations go up as a function of success, while Sears (1940) demonstrated that success leads to the setting of realistic goals. One must be careful of pushing students too hard and too fast toward higher levels of aspiration. Many culturally deprived students have what Dollard and Miller (1950) call an approach-avoidance conflict with regard to success: they both desire it and fear it. As they expend more and more effort and are pushed closer and closer to success, their fear becomes stronger than their desire (Brown, 1948). Dollard and Miller recommend that efforts be made at this point to reduce the fear associated with school.

Some students will need discipline and will have to be handled in a firm authoritative way; others will need warmth, acceptance, and understanding, and will have to be dealt with in a yielding way. The work of Hunt (1965) is applicable here. Hunt has spoken of the differential diagnosis—differential treatment technique. What this means is that people are different and the teacher must become aware of the differences and not attempt to teach or treat people all in the same way. They must be treated in terms of the differences. *A student who is in need of authority must be handled in authoritative fashion; a student who is in need of acceptance by authority and permissiveness must be handled in a permissive fashion.*

Students who need discipline are generally noisy, inattentive, lacking in self-control, impulsive, egocentric, and immature (Hunt, 1965). These students have not had appropriate discipline at home and are poorly

Bruce W. Tuckman

socialized; they often go on to become delinquents. For this group, the appropriate environment is a consistent, highly organized, yet accepting atmosphere in which they can generally begin to clarify their relation to the world by experiencing consistency of discipline and support. Teachers should use visual aids and demonstrations and should keep the children busy. Class discussions don't usually work out too well. Also needed are rote learning procedures and drilling (Hunt, 1965). As Leshan (1952) has pointed out, disadvantaged children live in the present with little regard to the future. Looking to the future is threatening since their lives and upbringing are so inconsistent; consequently, they do not know what to expect. It is important for the teacher to be consistent.

With disadvantaged students who are already compliant, dependent upon authority, and concerned with rules, some encouragement toward independence is valuable. Well-organized discussions may be useful as long as the children are presented with some performance standard based on teacher encouragement and reward (Hunt, 1965). When both types appear in the same class, as is often the case, it will be difficult to deal optimally with both, outside of individual assignments. The impulsive characters should be given more regimented assignments to build self-control and the more dependent ones some original work to build independence and self-reliance.

The teacher must keep some of these points in mind, namely: (1) to attempt to relate the school experience to the real world experience in order that gratification be more immediate; (2) to attempt to do things in a perceptual fashion and provide as many tasks as possible for remedial training in perceptual, verbal, and cognitive areas and to converse with the students as much as possible; (3) to make frequent use of rewards in an attempt through use of successive approximations to produce achievement-oriented behavior and success while making minimal use of punishments; and (4) to utilize praise, approval, and warmth, and such techniques as role-playing and programmed presentation of tasks in increasing order of difficulty, in order to foster identification with society and to increase self-esteem and level of aspirations. If these things are done, the culturally deprived student may well be able to overcome his initial experiential deficit and cumulative deficit and derive a useful education from his school experiences.

ATKINSON, J. W. (ed.). *Motives in Fantasy, Action, and Society*. Princeton, N.J.: Van Nostrand, 1958.

AUSUBEL, D. P. "How Reversible Are the Cognitive and Motivational Effects of Cultural Deprivation? Implications for Teaching the Culturally Deprived Child." Paper read at a conference of the teaching of the culturally deprived child, Buffalo, N.Y., 1963.

———— and PEARL AUSUBEL. "Ego Developed Among Segregated Negro Children," in *Education in Depressed Areas*, ed. A. H. Passow. New York: Teachers College, Columbia University, 1963.

BERNSTEIN, B. "Linguistic Codes, Hesitation Phenomena and Intelligence," *Language and Speech*, 5 (1962), 31–46.

BLOOM, B. S. *Stability and Change in Human Characteristics*. New York: John Wiley & Sons, 1964.

————, A. DAVIS and R. HESS. *Compensatory Education for Cultural Deprivation*. New York: Holt, Rinehart & Winston, 1965.

BOGER, J. H. "An Experimental Study of the Effects of Perceptual Training on Group IQ Scores of Elementary Pupils in Rural Ungraded Schools," *Journal of Educational Research*, 46 (1952), 43–53.

BRAZZIEL, W. F., and MARY TERRELL. "An Experiment in the Development of Readiness in a Culturally Disadvantaged Group of First-Grade Children," *Journal of Negro Education*, 31 (1962), 4–7.

BRECKENRIDGE, MARIAN E., and E. L. VINCENT. "Nutrition and Growth," in *The Adolescent—A Book of Readings*, ed. J. M. Seidman. New York: Holt, Rinehart & Winston, 1962.

BREHM, J. W. "A Dissonance Analysis of Attitude Discrepant Behavior," in *Attitude Organization and Change*, ed. M. J. Rosenberg. New Haven: Yale University Press, 1960.

BRONFENBRENNER, U. "Socialization and Social Class Through Time and Space," in *Readings in Social Psychology* (3d ed.), eds. Eleanor E. Maccoby, T. M. Newcomb and E. L. Hartley. New York: Holt, Rinehart & Winston, 1958.

BROWN, J. S. "Gradients of Approach and Avoidance Responses and Their Relation to Level of Motivation," *Journal of Comparative and Physiological Psychology*, 41 (1948), 450–465.

COCH, L., and J. R. FRENCH. "Overcoming Resistance to Change," *Human Relations*, 1 (1948), 512–532.

DENNIS, W. "Causes of Retardation Among Institutional Children," *Journal of Genetic Psychology*, 96 (1960), 47–59.

DEUTSCH, M. "The Disadvantaged Child and the Learning Process," in *Education in Depressed Areas*, ed. A. H. Passow. New York: Teachers College, Columbia University, 1963, 163–180.

————. "The Role of Social Class in Language Development and Cognition." New York: Institute for Developmental Studies, 1964. (Mimeographed.)

18
Bruce W. Tuckman

DOLLARD, J., and N. E. MILLER. *Personality and Psychotherapy.* New York: McGraw-Hill Book Co., 1950.

ESTES, W. K. "An Experimental Study of Punishment," *Psychological Monographs,* 57 (1944), No. 263.

GOFF, R. M. "Some Educational Implications of the Influence of Rejection on Aspiration Levels of Minority Group Children," *Journal of Experimental Education,* 23 (1954), 179–183.

HARLOW, H. F. "The Formation of Learning Sets," *Psychological Review,* 56 (1949), 51–65.

HIERONYMUS, A. N. "Study of Social Class Motivation: Relationships Between Anxiety for Education and Certain Socio-economic and Intellectual Variables," *Journal of Educational Psychology,* 42 (1951), 193–205.

HULL, C. L. *A Behavior System: An Introduction to Behavior Theory Concerning the Individual Organism.* New Haven: Yale University Press, 1952.

HUNT, D. E. "Conceptual Systems Assessment in Planning Differential Educational Treatment and in Measuring Developmental Change." Paper presented at the meetings of the American Psychological Association, Chicago, Ill., 1965.

HUNT, J. McV. *Intelligence and Experience.* New York: Ronald Press, 1961.

———. "The Psychological Basis for Using Pre-School Enrichment as an Antidote for Cultural Deprivation," *Merrill-Palmer Quarterly,* 10 (1964), 209–248.

JOHN, VERA P. "The Intellectual Development of Slum Children: Some Preliminary Findings," *American Journal of Orthopsychiatry,* 33 (1963), 813–822.

JUCKNAT, MARGARETE. "Leistung, Anspruchsniveau, und Selbstbewusstein," *Psychologische Forschung,* 22 (1938), 89–179.

KAHL, J. A. "Educational and Occupational Aspirations of 'Common Man' Boys," *Harvard Educational Review,* 23 (1953), 186–203.

KING, B. T., and I. L. JANIS. "Comparison of the Effectiveness of Improvised versus Non-Improvised Role-Playing in Producing Opinion Changes," *Human Relations,* 9 (1956), 177–186.

KLINGBERG, O. "Negro-White Difference in Intelligence Test Performance: A New Look at an Old Problem," *American Psychologist,* 18 (1963), 198–203.

KRUGMAN, M. "The Culturally Deprived Child in School," *National Education Association Journal,* 50 (1961), 22–23.

LESHAN, L. L. "Time Orientation and Social Class," *Journal of Abnormal and Social Psychology,* 47 (1952), 589–592.

LEWIN, K. "Group Decision and Social Change," in *Readings in Social Psychology,* eds. G. E. Swanson, T. M. Newcomb and E. L. Hartley. 2d ed. New York: Holt, Rinehart & Winston, 1952.

———, R. LIPPITT, and R. K. WHITE. "Patterns of Aggressive Behavior in Experimentally Created 'Social Climates'," *Journal of Social Psychology,* 10 (1939), 271–299.

McCLELLAND, D. C. *The Achieving Society*. Princeton: Van Nostrand, 1961.
—— et al. *The Achievement Motive*. New York: Appleton-Century-Crofts, 1953.

MISCHEL, W. "Preference for Delayed Reinforcement and Social Responsibility," *Journal of Abnormal and Social Psychology*, 62 (1961), 1–7.

OSBORNE, R. T. "Racial Differences in Mental Growth and School Achievement; a Longitudinal Study," *Psychological Reports*, 7 (1960), 233–239.

PETTIGREW, T. "Negro American Intelligence: A New Look at an Old Controversy," *Journal of Negro Education*, 33 (1964), 6–25.

ROSEN, B. C. "The Achievement Syndrome: A Psychocultural Dimension of Social Stratification," *American Sociological Review*, 21 (1956), 203–211.

—— and R. D'ANDRADE. "The Psycho-Social Origins of Achievement Motivation," *Sociometry*, 22 (1959), 185–218.

SCHORR, A. L. "The Non-culture of Poverty," *American Journal of Orthopsychiatry*, 34 (1964), 907–912.

SCHREIBER, D. "Identifying and Developing Able Students from Less Privileged Groups," *High Points*, 40 (1958), 5–23.

SEARS, PAULINE S. "Levels of Aspiration in Academically Successful and Unsuccessful Children," *Journal of Abnormal and Social Psychology*, 35 (1940), 498–536.

SHAW, F. "Educating Culturally Deprived Youth in Urban Centers," *Phi Delta Kappan*, 45 (1963), 91–97.

SILLER, J. "Socio-economic Status and Conceptual Thinking," *Journal of Abnormal and Social Psychology*, 55 (1957), 365–371.

SKEELS, H. M., and H. B. DYE. "A Study of the Effects of Differential Stimulation on Mentally Retarded Children," *Proceedings of the American Association for Mental Deficiency*, 44 (1939), 114–136.

SKINNER, B. F. *The Behavior of Organisms: An Experimental Analysis*. New York: Appleton-Century-Crofts, 1938.

WELLMAN, BETH L. "Iowa Studies on the Effects of Schooling," *Yearbook of the National Society for the Study of Education*, 39 (1940), 377–399.

WINTERBOTTOM, MARIAN R. "The Relation of Need for Achievement to Learning Experiences in Independence and Mastery." In J. W. Atkinson (ed.), *Motives in Fantasy, Action, and Society*. Princeton: Van Nostrand, 1958, 453–478.

WITTY, P. A. "The Teacher Who Has Helped Me Most," *Elementary English*, 34 (1947), 345–354.

WOLF, R. M. "The Identification and Measurement of Environmental Process Variables Related to Intelligence." Unpublished doctoral dissertation, University of Chicago, 1964.

ZIGLER, E., and J. DeLABRY. "Concept Switching in Middle-Class, Lower-Class, and Retarded Children," *Journal of Abnormal and Social Psychology*, 65 (1962), 267–273.

20
Bruce W. Tuckman

2 An Anthropological View of Poverty

Leonard Zeitz

GEORGETOWN UNIVERSITY INSTITUTE OF
CRIMINAL LAW AND PROCEDURE

FROM AN ANTHROPOLOGICAL point of view, any program designed to aid the "culturally deprived" may be seen as a problem in the inducement of culture change. Such terms as diffusion, acculturation, ethnocentrism, and culture contact loom large in any anthropological discussion of culture change. These terms will be touched upon in the course of this chapter.

As a starting point, certain premises about the nature of society and the nature of culture must be stated. Society, roughly defined, is an aggregate of individuals who, having worked together and lived together over a period of time, develop an *esprit de corps* based on cooperation, predictability, and commonly held sets of ideas, values, and ways of doing things (Linton, 1936). Culture, more difficult to define, may at least be described as the totality of these commonly

21

held sets of ideas, values, and ways of doing things of a particular society (Kroeber and Kluckhohn, 1963).

All cultures are subject to change, and indeed do change. Westerners, used to the dramatic shifts and upheavals produced in our own societies, are prone to look at "primitive" societies as static; our popular literature teems with references to "people still living in the Stone Age." While it is true that many human groups have not developed their technology beyond the use of stone artifacts, it is equally true that their culture has not stood still. Shifts take place, perhaps in the art forms used to decorate stone tools, or perhaps in religious or other social structures. These changes may take place in any of three ways: (1) through independent invention and discovery; (2) through acculturation; or (3) through "scientific" acculturation (Foster, 1962).

In the first way of changing a culture, individuals or groups within a particular society hit upon a new technique which may facilitate accomplishment, or ease or enrich life in some fashion, and find that the new technique is accepted by a large portion or all of the society. While this form of change does occur, it is far less likely to occur than change through borrowing. This second form of change introduces the concept of acculturation, which may be defined as the process of altering culture via the borrowing of traits, techniques, ideas, and the like from another culture, when two societies having different cultures are in contact over a period of time (Redfield, Linton, and Herskovits, 1936). When these culture borrowings occur over a large area incorporating many societies, the process of passing the trait is referred to as diffusion. Change through acculturation has, in the past, been accidental, in the sense that whether introduced forcibly as in a conquest situation, or introduced simply through contact and recognition of value, the process has been haphazard and subject to chance. Thus, the third form of change takes place when one society deliberately seeks to alter the forms and structures of another society via its use of sociological, psychological, and anthropological knowledge.

It is obvious, then, that the anthropologist disputes any argument implying that attempts to change cultural situations are doomed to fail by virtue of man's immutable nature. The anthropologist argues not for change in "human nature," but for change in "human culture," i.e., the way men do things, the beliefs and values they hold. He bases this belief on his certain knowledge that societies do change their cultural forms and content, and that these changes may be induced from outside sources through contact and experimentation. The question posed,

Leonard Zeitz

therefore, is not: "Should change be attempted?" The questions are rather: "When is change necessary?" "When is change appropriate?" "When is change feasible?" After these have been answered, the next questions follow: "What should be changed?" "How shall we make the desired changes?"

The anthropologist, generally working with small units of mankind, has, in the past, failed to understand the intricacies of modern industrial society. His outlook was a simplistic one, viewing culture as homogeneous throughout a society. It was not until Redfield's studies (1941) in Mexico, which emphasized urban-rural differences, and Warner's studies (1941), which demonstrated that there were different classes in the United States and that values and behavior could be directly related to class status, that American anthropologists recognized and accepted the possibility of subcultures, related to, but different from, the parent culture. Whether the poor in our society may indeed be called a subculture is debatable. Using this term hypothetically, however, we can see that a significant proportion of the population of the United States, by virtue of historic accident (or other causes) has developed a way of life sufficiently removed from the main cultural developments as to be significantly different. This "subculture," then, may also be seen as having developed patterns and values, many of which are detrimental to the society as a whole.

_____The Subculture of the Disadvantaged

IT IS hardly likely that anyone will dispute the statement that it is *now* necessary, appropriate, and feasible that the subculture of the disadvantaged be changed. What remains to be decided is what specifically is to be changed and how this change is to be effected.

From the anthropologist's perspective, it is perhaps best to view the people of this subculture as he would the people of any alien culture: similar to him by virtue of universal manhood, different in respect to behavioral patterns. Seen in this light, comparisons, analogues, parallels with other situations known to anthropologists may yield clues to what should be changed and how change may be effected. Some general observations of the subculture of the disadvantaged are as follows: They tend to suffer from a wide variety of mental and physical illnesses and social pathologies (Crocetti, 1959); They lack political control over their own destinies (L. Zeitz, 1965); Their nuclear families are often fragmented and disorganized (Reissman, 1962); They are prone to legal problems, both criminal and civil (Wald, 1965); They do not readily accept aid proffered by middle-class institutions (L. Zeitz, 1964); They attempt, as often as is practicable, to give help to one another rather than to seek institutional aid (Koos, 1946); They often accept the parent culture's estimation of their "innate" inferiority (K. Clark and M. Clark, 1950); At the same time, they may also react against this evaluation of the parent culture, by a *bouleversement* of the parent culture's values (Cohen, 1955).

All of the above tendencies are paralleled to some degree in the behavioral patterns of the peoples of the world who have been dominated by Western powers. To suggest that the position of the subculture of the disadvantaged in relation to the parent culture in the United States is analogous to colonially dominated cultures vis-à-vis the conquering cultures is to offer a harsh indictment of our behavior. The analogy is offered, however, not in the harsh spirit of judgment, but rather as an effort in understanding why we have failed to help the poor in the past, and why our present efforts may fail.

"Colonial Domination" of the Disadvantaged

LET us examine the parallels. Riessman (1962) has argued that the "culturally deprived child" understands the advantages of our education in our society but fails to make full use of his schooling because of the condescension and lack of cultural understanding of his middle-class teacher. The teacher (and the social worker) have traditionally been the "missionaries" of the middle-class culture, and in their zeal to convert, have ruthlessly sought to exterminate all aspects of the lower-class subculture. Bascom (1953) has pointed out the same phenomenon in missionaries working among indigenous populations in Africa. Where destruction of indigenous values has taken place, there has been little effort at compensation by incorporation into the dominant culture. The reasons for this are many and complex, but looming large are the following: (1) persistent belief in the innate inferiority of those whose cultures are being destroyed; (2) political and economic exploitation of the members of the subordinate culture. As to the former factor, both native and "culturally deprived" populations are quickly sensitized to recognize the validity of the Orwellian proposition that while all men

Leonard Zeitz

are equal, some are more equal than others. Missionaries spread the new gospel and then withdraw when equality of peoples may result. South and Central African religious separatism is partially the result of educated native religionists being placed in positions of marked inferiority to their white coreligionists (Sundkler, 1948; Vilakazi, 1960). In the United States, Warner (1941) has shown that specific religious denominations are components of class determination, and a recent study (E. Zeitz, 1966) in Washington, D.C., reveals that integration of previously white Protestant churches is considered successful by the ministers when the percentage of Negro parishioners reaches two.

As to the political and economic exploitation which prevents entrance into the dominant culture, we need merely point to a Rhodesian government whose white minority has declared its independence of Great Britain in order to prevent political domination by a native majority. And in some southern states of the United States, Negroes attempting to register in order to vote have often been met with threats, subterfuges, physical violence, and economic reprisals. On a much more subtle level, the colonial peoples and the disadvantaged suffer immediate consequences when there are international fluctuations in politics and economics. The world-wide depression of the 1930s hurt many peasants economically and left them bewildered as to the reasons, and the financial burden of the Vietnamese war has seriously threatened the antipoverty war in the United States.

How do the colonized and the disadvantaged react to their situations? They react as described above, but also with specific actions and with marked similarities. Compare, for example, Hollowell's (1940) portrait of the apathy and dissoluteness of the Saulteaux Ojibwa of Lake Winnipeg, with similar descriptions of the people of Toby Town (Douglas, 1966) or the people of Appalachia (Caudill, 1963). Apathy, however, is but one possible response to pressure. Behavior predicated upon fantasy components is a frequent form of response. Again, compare the aggressive, militant fantasy of the Black Muslims, who demand a separate black nation within the United States, and the adherents of Kitawala (a Central African Bantu form of "Watchtower"), who have announced that they will drive the whites into the sea when Christ returns (Cunnison, 1951). Or compare the nostalgic Ghost Dance of the Plains Indians seeking a return to a time when only red men roamed after the buffalo (Mooney, 1896) and the number of religious movements in the United States that perpetuate a traditional system and ameliorate discomfort through manipulation of expressive symbols

(Fernandez, 1964). Or compare the absurdity of Enoch Mgjima's statement in South Africa, in 1921, that the bullets of the whites would turn to water in the face of the faithful (Lea, 1926) and Colonel Jeru Ahmed Hassan's statement in Washington, D.C., in 1966, that his Blackman's Volunteer Army of Liberation intends to free Central and South Africa (Ridgeway, 1966).

Note that whether absurd, militant, or regressive, all of these movements are movements precisely because they recruit enough followers to attract attention, that their recruits are the products of subordination in either the colonial or the subcultural situation, that they are manifestations of protest against subordination, and that in spite of historical and cultural differences, there are marked similarities in the movements of both the colonized and the disadvantaged.

It is the argument of this chapter, therefore, that up to the present moment in our history, all efforts at changing the condition of the poor have been in the nature of missionary efforts, destined to fail because they have implied superiority and manifested condescension; and that these efforts have been subordinated to the wills of economic and political exploiters. Further, our present effort is likely to fail if we are unable to shake off our middle-class ethnocentrism that says we are offering the most precious gift (our way of life), and to reject it (or any part of it) is the sign of innate inferiority. One must also add that to accept the gift is a sure sign that one's original culture must have been inferior. In the theoretical acculturative process, it is *both* cultures which undergo change; the dominant culture does not simply impose its will on the subordinate.

Preparing to Teach

WE MUST not assume that the allocation of funds for a war on poverty (an inadequate allocation in the eyes of many) is the proof that we have come of age, that we have shed our missionary mentality. Past efforts, having been in the nature of attempts to denude completely the culture of the disadvantaged, have always failed. Today one may well argue that assimilation into the middle class is not necessarily a bargain, considering the tensions, the anxieties, the over-emphasis on material status that the present middle class suffers. There are values in the subculture of the disadvantaged that deserve preservation, among them the generalized nonconforming tendencies, the effort at self-help,

Leonard Zeitz

and the general resourcefulness in the face of hardships. As an example of these traits, there is the tale going the rounds that is probably apocryphal but deserves repetition. In one antipoverty program, young boys being paid minimum wages would pool their money at the end of the week, buy wholesale quantities of marijuana, and sell the smokes retail, with handsome profits! We are not commenting here upon the morality but upon the ability of the disadvantaged to seize opportunities resourcefully, to cooperate, and finally, to become entrepreneurs in a business repugnant to the middle class but acceptable to the disadvantaged.

In a program of preparing teachers of the disadvantaged, the first function of the anthropologist, therefore, is to force the neophyte instructor to re-examine his premises about the nature of society and of culture. These premises, learned early and reinforced over time, are deeply embedded in the sociopsychological matrix. They are the ethnocentric biases of a dominant middle class, bent upon self-perpetuation and determined not to yield. The anthropologist must make the instructor aware of these cultural biases so that the instructor may analyze himself in this light. Given such a cultural reappraisal, the teacher of the disadvantaged should become aware of the virtues and flaws of his sociocultural system and the virtues and flaws in other such systems. Prepared early in his training, the neophyte teacher should be able to cast aside the behavioral accouterments of the crusader, the missionary, and the benevolent paternalistic colonizer and to become instead the expert instructor in a particular field, sensitive to his own and to his students' cultural needs.

In addition to sensitizing the instructor to cultural phenomena, the anthropologist should be prepared to teach about culture from theoretical points of view: its nature; its functions; its incredible variety as seen in the various groups of mankind; its relationship to the natural environment and to historical developments; its manifestations under the large institutional rubrics, such as social, political, religious, and economic organization.

In the field of social organization, the anthropologist may make a unique contribution to the teacher, since anthropology has long theorized about and studied the origins and development of the family, and has amassed vast quantities of cross-cultural data on family organization and its functions.

Because of his emphasis on cross-cultural data, the anthropologist can make contributions to the teacher in the fields of comparative religion and political organization. In the area of political organization, anthropology can help the teacher of the disadvantaged to recognize indigenous leaders often overlooked by the middle class. Knowledge of comparative religion may make the teacher more aware of the function of forms and structures alien to him, but not to his students.

Concerning economic organization, the unique contribution of the anthropologist has been his understanding of its integrated relationship to other aspects of a culture, which often transforms economic behavior into noneconomic sets of values. That is to say, economic activity may be pursued for other than material profit, and failure to understand how this comes about and why often leads the observer to condemn the economic actor as irrational or childlike (and hence, inferior).

While other disciplines have made great contributions to our understanding of race and racial problems, the anthropologist takes pride in the work of his peers in this field. More than any other social science, all branches of his discipline—physical anthropology, linguistics, archaeology, and cultural (or social) anthropology—have done exhaustive studies vis-à-vis race. The anthropologist has endeavored to comprehend this phenomenon holistically and to present his findings accurately to the public. The outspoken segregationist, Carleton Putnam (1963) condemned thirteen academicians, eight of whom were anthropologists, for their position on race; anthropologists must take pride in being thus singled out. Anthropological teaching concerning race attempts to determine the origins of different races and emphasizes the term "race" as a taxonomic and classificatory device valuable in isolating populations for the purpose of studying their cultural and physical histories. The anthropologist stresses this classificatory aspect because not in his physical, nor in his archaeological, nor in his cultural (or social) studies has he found any evidence to support the contention that race is a determinant of cultural development. It may also be pointed out that there is a recent trend among anthropologists (Titiev, 1959) to drop the term race because of the invidious meanings that now cluster around it, and to substitute instead, stock, with race now referring to the subspecies of a stock.

Specific Guidelines

Since the end of World War II, a new set of beliefs has come into being about the relationships governing the West, Asia, Africa, and Latin America, and also about the responsibilities of industrialized nations to developing nations. A variety of technical aid programs have begun, sponsored by business concerns, voluntary and church agencies, nations, and UN agencies. It has been the good fortune of the anthropologist to be either participant or observer of many of these programs, and he has seen successes, failures, and all other observable points on a success-failure continuum. As a result, he has often attempted to establish criteria for future programs. One such set of guidelines (Foster, 1955) is offered below with appropriate modifications for the specific thrust, that is, for teachers of the disadvantaged:

1. *Know the specific culture in which the work is to be done.* This point is obvious and yet requires constant repetition. While Oscar Lewis (1959) may assert with validity that there is a universal culture of poverty, it is also true that the disadvantaged Puerto Ricans in El Barrio in New York City behave quite differently from the disadvantaged Sioux in the Rosebud Reservation of South Dakota.

2. *Know exhaustively the integrating aspects of the various parts of the culture in which the work is being done.* The change in a single item of the culture may create a ripple effect, touching all parts of the culture. Given an understanding of the interrelationships of the parts of a culture, one may reasonably predict the effects and consequences of a newly introduced item. Failure to predict the effect of such an introduction may have catastrophic consequences. As an extreme example, the introduction of the potato into Ireland, Ireland's development as a one-crop nation, and the consequences of the potato crop loss in the Nineteenth Century are still being felt.

3. *Learn to recognize those new beliefs and customs which are compatible with and which can be readily absorbed into a culture.* Foster (1962) gives the example of the physician who was unable to convince a group of Mexican Indians that the boiling of milk might prevent dysentery in children. Instead, he urged them to feed an herb tea to babies. The tea had been in use for other ailments and was readily acceptable. In spite of the fact that the Indians believe that the ingredients of the tea are therapeutic for sick babies (rather than the boiled water), a valuable item based upon compatibility has been added to their cultural inventory.

4. *The teacher must know his own culture.* This point has been stressed above, and requires no further discussion.

5. *Take advantage of the pragmatic nature of people.* Years of frustration and disillusionment have left their marks on the disadvantaged in the form of cynicism toward ameliorative efforts. This cynicism

can only be removed by demonstrable (and, hopefully, cumulative) success. Thus, it is not enough to simply encourage or praise the talented writer in the English class; perhaps a better tactic would be to submit the talented pupil's work to a school magazine or a national scholastic contest. In this context, note the success of the writer Budd Schulberg in seeking out literary talent among the disadvantaged of the Watts section of Los Angeles.

6. *Do not ask people to threaten what may be an already very narrow margin of material security.* The teacher may feel that through the use of extracurricular activities he has found an important means of developing rapport and understanding with his students and of developing feelings of belonging and/or pride. In spite of these positive advantages, demands upon the free time of a boy who must work after school to help support his family, may, in the long run, be more detrimental than beneficial.

7. *Use existing community leadership wherever feasible.* Active participation by leaders of a community is essential if the community is to become involved. The success of the Cornell University Medical Project on the Navajo reservation (McDermott et al., 1960) is at least partially due to the enlistment of Navajo medicine men as respected peers. In this case, the Cornell workers convinced the medicine men of their good intentions by referring to the medicine men Navajos suffering from ill-defined maladies curable through Navajo psychotherapeutic techniques. As time passed, the medicine men began referring to the Cornell Clinic Navajos whose diseases (for example, tuberculosis) defied the traditional medical techniques.

8. *Learn to detect who the community leaders are.* As a result of our middle-class biases, we are prone to seek out lawyers, physicians, "respectable" ministers, police officials, and politicians as the leadership element. The choice of these personnel may be at total variance with the views of the community. In a Puerto Rican neighborhood the leader may be the local *herbalista* who runs a tiny, almost insignificant *botanica* where she dispenses good-luck charms, love potions, and advice. In a Negro community, it may be the poolroom proprietor, a tavern owner, the beauty salon or barbershop proprietor. In all poor communities, the itinerant preacher, the store-front minister, the fortune-teller, or the spiritualist may be of vast but undetermined importance in creating and maintaining the value of these communities. Even such antipathetic (to the middleclass) characters as the hoodlum may be of pivotal significance in the direction which a community takes. Note the transforma-

Leonard Zeitz

tion in the character of the Chicago Blackstones (Washington Post, 1966) from gangfighters to predators to community organizers.

9. *Think in terms of both the economic and social potentials in the local community and in the wide area.* It almost goes without saying that the training of men for computer programming in a barely literate community is a cruelty, as is also training for any job which is soon to disappear as a result of either obsolescence or automation. Such efforts, which presumably are meant to be stopgaps and palliative, become further sources of exacerbation.

10. *Select the more "progressive" student for intensive teaching, rather than the more "conservative" student who may need the teaching to a greater degree.* This point is, of course, subject to sharp debate. The argument against it is that basically it weasels out of a difficult assignment by concentrating on those whose success seems most guaranteed. Those who advocate this point stress that it is practical in view of the limitations of time, money, and manpower. There is a second argument for this point that lays aside short-term "practicality," namely the argument that those who successfully bridge the gap between two cultures (or subcultures) are most qualified to translate the new cultural items to the conservatives, and can also be held up as models for the conservatives to emulate. As an example of this approach, the Cornell University Medical Project (McDermott et al., 1960) found that its first concrete successes in attracting Navajo patients came when the project-trained Navajos who had been in the Armed Forces, that is, somewhat acculturated Navajos, were chosen to act as medical liaisons between the Cornell physicians and the Navajo community. The Navajo workers' ability to interpret to their community some or all of the complexities of Western medical technique helped to alleviate fear and insecurity. Further, the acceptance of the Navajo medical aide by the whites as an invaluable addition to their medical team approach impressed the Navajo with the sincerity and goodwill of the Cornell physicians. This approach is now being used in Newark where a Legal Services to the Poor Project (Newark, 1965) is under way. A number of "progressives" from the disadvantaged areas of Newark will be trained by lawyers in their legal rights. They will then be encouraged to spread their new knowledge in their communities. Additionally, these law trainees will act as liaisons between the disadvantaged and the legal profession, in an effort to induce the disadvantaged to freely utilize the professional legal services when necessary and advisable.

11. *Require payment for services, where such payment is appli-*

cable. This is not meant to be a cruel or greedy act. Rather, it has definite practical advantages. In field situations, anthropologists have discovered that free dispensation of even such cheap patent medicines as aspirin has often been met with rebuffs and evasions. There seem to be two disparate reasons for refusal to accept, or grudging acceptance of, these free items: (1) The offer of free aid places the recipient in a position of indebtedness from which he is hardly likely to escape, since he has so little to offer the Westerner. This indebtedness now compounds his feelings of inadequacy and inferiority in relationship to the person of the donor culture, who has made what on the surface, appears to be a magnanimous gesture; (2) An offer of something for nothing is often suggestive of an inferior product. It is almost universally recognized that the best things in life are not free; rather, you get what you pay for. Thus, the teacher or the community worker cannot expect to be accepted in an alien culture by professions of the work to be done as a labor of love. This may indeed be the case, but it is hardly likely to attract the disadvantaged. A much wiser tactic is to stress the fact that the teacher is being paid to do the job he does and that he has been chosen on the basis of his expertise and qualifications.

12. *One's expertise should give one authority, and this authority should be presented as a fact to the class.* There is no suggestion here of undisciplined exercise of power, but a simple emphasis put on acknowledgment of authority in a particular field. It is likely that groups will respond with respect and attention to those whose strength of authority is felt. Fragmentary evidence at the moment suggests that an approach of this type is probably most felicitous among Puerto Ricans and other Latin American groups. Latin Americans have derived from the Mediterranean *compadrazgo* religious system of god-parenthood their own form which stresses *padron* ("boss") relationships. In such a system, a man does what a *padron* wishes in exchange for future requests for aid that he may make of the *padron*. As an example, at Cornell Medical College, New York Hospital Center, a project which was designed to measure the health levels of welfare patients was failing in its efforts to induce Puerto Rican welfare recipients to enter the clinic. Dr. Elena Padilla, an anthropologist and specialist in Puerto Rico, was called in as consultant. After studying our interview schedules and procedures, Dr. Padilla pointed out our errors. We offered the putative patients a wide choice of dates and hours for clinic attendance and always included the phrase "please come." This was interpreted by many of the Puerto Ricans as a sign of weakness and a lack of authority, something no

Leonard Zeitz

padron would show. She suggested that we limit the choice of dates and hours, and that we substitute the phrase, "You will come. . . ." When we instituted Dr. Padilla's suggestions, Puerto Rican clinic attendance doubled.

13. *Do not anticipate being loved.* Anticipate, rather, anger, hostility, and resentment. It is hardly likely that after the years of distress, pain, frustration, and disappointment, the culturally disadvantaged will accept overnight the "new" teacher as humane, sincere, and dedicated to his vocation and to the unique needs of his pupils. It is much more likely that you will be greeted cynically and perhaps contemptuously. Even initial successes may not win your group over, since they may feel that these successes were long overdue (and certainly they are justified on this score). Some students may exploit you unmercifully, developing better hustler's techniques as they go along (recall the story of the marijuana salesmen). Still others may remain apathetic no matter what individual effort is forthcoming. If, for whatever personal reasons, your need to be loved overrides other sources of gratification such as monetary reward or internal satisfaction for successful teaching, then it is incumbent upon you to leave the field.

References

BASCOM, WILLIAM. "African Culture and the Missionaries," *Civilisations,* 3 (1953), 491–504.

CAUDILL, HARRY. *Night Comes to the Cumberland.* Boston: Little, Brown Company, 1963.

CLARK, K. B., and M. P. CLARK. "Emotional Factors in Racial Identification and Preference in Negro Children," *Journal of Negro Education,* 19 (1950), 341–350.

COHEN, ALBERT K. *Delinquent Boys: The Subculture of the Gang.* New York: The Free Press, 1955.

CROCETTI, GUIDO. "Suicide and Public Health," *American Journal of Public Health,* 49 (1959), 881–887.

CUNNISON, IAN. "A Watch Tower Assembly in Central Africa," *International Review of Missions,* 40 (1951), 456–468.

DOUGLAS, WALTER B. "Apathetic Toby Town to Greet Yule in Same Muddy, Delapidated Setting," *The Washington Post,* December 24, 1966.

FERNANDEZ, JAMES. "African Religious Movements," *Journal of Modern African Studies,* 12 (1964), 531–549.

FOSTER, GEORGE M. "Guidelines to Community Development Programs," *Public Health Reports,* 70 (1955), 19–24.

———. *Traditional Cultures, and the Impact of Technological Change.* New York: Harper & Row, 1962.

HOLLOWELL, A. IRVING. "Aggression in Saulteaux Society," *Psychiatry,* 3 (1940), 395–407.

KOOS, EARL. *Families in Trouble.* New York: King's Crown Press, 1946.

KROEBER, A. L., and CLYDE KLUCKHOHN. *Culture: A Critical Review of Concepts and Definitions.* New York: Vintage, 1963.

LEA, ALLEN. *The Native Separatist Church Movement in South Africa.* Johannesburg: Juta & Company, 1926.

LEWIS, OSCAR. *Five Families.* New York: Basic Books, 1959.

LINTON, RALPH. *The Study of Man.* New York: Appleton-Century-Crofts, 1936.

MCDERMOTT, WALSH, et al. "Introducing Modern Medicine in a Navajo Community," *Science,* 131 (1960), 197–205, 280–287.

MOONEY, JAMES. "The Ghost Dance Religion and the Sioux Outbreak of 1890," *Fourteenth Annual Report, Bureau of American Ethnology,* 2 (1896).

PUTNAM, CARLETON. "These Are the Guilty," *Washington Putnam Letters Committee,* February 1963.

REDFIELD, R., R. LINTON, and M. HERSKOVITS. "Memorandum on the Study of Acculturation," *American Anthropologist,* 28 (1936), 149–152.

RIDGEWAY, JAMES. "Black Mischief," *The New Republic* (December 24, 1966), 14–16.

RIESSMAN, FRANK. *The Culturally Deprived Child.* New York: Harper & Row, 1962.

SUNDKLER, BENGT G. M. *Bantu Prophets in South Africa.* London: Lutterworth Press, 1948.

TITIEV, MISCHA. *The Science of Man.* New York: Holt, Rinehart & Winston, 1959.

UNITED COMMUNITY COUNCIL. "A Proposal for a Legal Services to the Poor Project in Newark as Part of the Antipoverty War," February 1965. (Mimeographed.)

VILAKAZI, ABSALOM. "African Religious Concepts and the Separatist Movements," *AMSAC Newsletter,* 2 (March 31, 1960).

WALD, PATRICIA M. "Law and Poverty; 1965," Report to the National Conference on Law and Poverty, Washington, D.C., June 23–25, 1965.

WARNER, W. LLOYD, and PAUL LUNT. *The Social Life of a Modern Community.* New Haven: Yale University Press, 1941.

WASHINGTON POST. "The Blackstones Are Coming," December 10, 1966.

ZEITZ, EILEEN. "Integration in Washington's Churches, George Washington University," 1966. (Unpublished Paper.)

ZEITZ, LEONARD. "Survey of Negro Attitudes Toward Law," *Rutgers Law Review,* 19 (1965), 258–316.

34
Leonard Zeitz

3 Inventing an Education for Teachers: A Sociological Perspective

William M. Phillips, Jr.

RUTGERS UNIVERSITY

THIS CHAPTER will describe some contributions sociology can make to a program designed to train teachers of stigmatized youth: (1) A presentation will be made of a conception of education today, including "higher" and "lower" education. (2) Something will be said about the general problem of the teaching process. (3) An attempt will be made to meaningfully connect education, teaching, sociology, and stigmatized youth as they fit into the contemporary urban world.

The Process of Education

IT CAN be argued reasonably that all education today in the United States must be concerned with the constant ferment of every facet of contemporary society. If so, the concern bluntly and pointedly must center on problem solving. Problem solving, moreover, cannot be compartmentalized away from the crucial humanistic, intellectual, and social issues and forces of today. None of the future generations can be allowed to escape a sense of obligation and responsibility for involvement in the dynamics of our entire societal and communal life. Youth, stigmatized or not, must not be educated technically or vocationally without securing as well the problem-solving key and the moral imperative to participate fully in contemporary society.

The paternalistic ideology that permits educators to indulge in the immorality of devising pseudoeducational or training programs aimed at preparing teachers to train any youth merely for low-level, marketable, but semiskilled jobs requiring minimal mechanical aptitudes can no longer be tolerated. The plain fact is that the world now, and as far as the shape of things can be imagined in the future, is not receptive to youth who have been prepared robot-like for low- or high-level work activity. This fact is accompanied by the companion fact of the miseducation of practically all of youth today for life in an urban, industrial, overdeveloped society. The ultimate test of the validity of these facts may include the clear symptoms of revolt against much of the conventional educational system by some segments of youth today.

This is why the concept of problem solving must be used as the basic theme of any educational scheme designed to be applied to youth today. Problem solving, to be useful, must be viewed in the larger sense; that is, as the freeing of the capacities of each individual—teacher and student—for the attainment of new levels of awareness, intellect, emotion, and involvement. This approach focuses on the idea of education as an instrument to help each individual youth to fully "become," and thus to permit each to be a positive contributor to the continued existence and development of human society. Social as well as "hardware" problems do exist; and the educational process must involve teachers and students in confronting social issues, understanding them, and developing whatever it takes to confidently see, define, and work rationally toward their management and solution.

This conception of the education process, then, is based upon a personal estimation of the needs of youth in the world of human relations today and in the future. All youth need to master the formal disciplines of logic and mathematics, the beauty and utility of communication, and the disciplines of experimentation, natural history, and aesthetics. If these are mastered, one has learned to learn, and commitment to human society is possible. Such a commitment would be a

William M. Phillips, Jr.

clear alternative to a passive acceptance of the status quo. A commitment means taking one's place in the public and impersonal world, knowing the costs of modern life and being willing to pay them. Essentially the thrust is toward a moralizing and a nonmoralizing concept of education—one in which youth are taught how to view, analyze, and accept human society in all its complexity, and then to commit themselves to judge and to act toward the attainment of universal humanistic goals. Youth should be and must be presented with a realistic and thus, quite often, a depressing view of social reality.

A tough-minded analysis of American society is proposed, therefore, as the core of a teacher training program directed toward stigmatized youth. This problem-solving educational approach, in addition, is conceived as being messianic and idealistic. It deliberately must focus on utilizing the entire educational system to counteract adverse influences by peers, parents, neighborhoods, and communities on youth. Moral, or if another word is preferred, character training has to be included too: teachers ought to be encouraged and induced to stress vigorous intellectual as well as physical/athletic activity, and aggressive participant roles by their students in the worldly affairs of man. Such a program should lead students to become preoccupied with major societal and humanistic ideals, values, goals, and problems.

Devising a program to train teachers to teach stigmatized youth demands, then, a curriculum that confronts major societal forces bearing implications for the contemporary and the future educational systems. One such force is the continued urbanization trend in American society. This trend has radical educational implications for youth of the so-called minority or racial groups. Then there is the continued thrust toward affluence of an industrial society; one with a very advanced technology, very high productivity, and great surplus. There is the pattern of the work force's being increasingly used to perform economically defined activity in giant and complex bureaucratic, or even meritocratic, organizations. Evidence is available as well that the entire nonprofessional work force may be seriously threatened by automation. There is the trend in our society for some class lines to become blurred, and yet, in the forming of this pattern, there are many left-behinds or left-outs. These societal forces may imply, as well, the evolution of new kinds of social values and norms: the recognition of a collective and individual responsibility for human welfare, a diminution of emphasis on dysfunctional competition of the old style and its replacement with some kind of transcendental ideology.

THIS leads to the general problem of teaching. The sad truth of the matter is that teachers today (as in times past) appear to lack a revolutionary zeal. In dealing professionally with students, teachers tend not to think so much in terms of change and revolution as of adjustment and accommodation, a characteristic particularly out of tune with the social forces of today. This fact was brutally and pathetically made clear during a recent research study conducted by the Urban Studies Center involving the public schools of a large metropolis. Consistently the attention of the teachers, as they rather innocently stated and demonstrated, was not toward the schoolchildren and the cognitive processes of learning. They were seriously concerned with making no trouble for the school and the principal; with the establishment and maintenance of discipline; with belittling the inherent abilities and capacities of their pupils; with scandalizing the families and neighborhoods of their pupils; and with arranging transfers away from their assigned posts. They were incessantly adjusting and accommodating, not innovating and creating change nor rebelling against the nonlearning patterns of their educational situation. Teachers have developed a massive array of coping devices to prevent confronting youth with the facts of social life. A predictable response from youth is their loss of confidence in them. It is not completely absurd to consider the notion that many youth may intensely dislike teachers and educators. Students recognize, often painfully, that many teachers are mere lackeys, without deep roots of integrity and commitment and that they are not intellectual and cultural leaders and involved citizens.

One conception of the art of teaching is that it is at the center of the whole educational process. If it fails, then education fails. It is just possible, too, that the role of teaching may lie at the heart of all the excitement, agony, and conflict of human relations in society. It is through the teacher that youth are inspired to know their heritage, to produce new knowledge, and learn how to deal with social change. The education of the teachers of youth, then, cannot be separated from the ebb and flow of contemporary life in all its complexity and contradiction.

Teacher training programs must somehow transmit to teachers the arts and commitments that enable the students they teach to learn how to learn. This does not mean courses, credits, subjects, and degrees required to certify a teacher. Rather, it means training teachers to their

38
William M. Phillips, Jr.

calling of using their wits to find the ways of being useful to their students and their communities. A way must be found to enhance the personal and intellectual growth of the person who is learning how to become a teacher. A consideration of the societal forces operative today leads to the inevitable conclusion that responsible educators must somehow instill in teachers of all youth an awareness of their real role in the processes of disenchantment and social commitment. Charles S. Johnson (1943) of Fisk University (a former teacher of mine) put it well: "The teaching role is a painful one. It essentially is a controlled struggle of inducing strain between processes of disintegration and integration. It is a cultural process of transmission and transformation of people who are more or less in conflict."

There are no pat proposals at hand to offer for the radical reform of teacher training and retraining. Moreover, it is impossible to see how youth can be taught how to learn "to be" by their adult models unless they know that such models have integrity and a deep sense of meaningful attachment to the real world, and possess as well the art, craft, and science of their profession. A clear and concrete example of the teacher role being performed in this way is delightfully described by Sylvia Ashton-Warner (1963) in *Teacher*. Thus, the teacher training program to be proposed in this book ought to be defined as a part of a total revitalization movement. Teachers so trained should be involved in a complete personal and professional transformation. The crux of this conversion process should be the shaking and repudiation of the old way. A thrust must be made toward shifting them to the acceptance of a new commitment and purpose to teaching and learning.

_____Youth, Excluded or Otherwise

A WORD about the concept of "disadvantaged youth." Somehow this can be usually read as "Negro" "black youth." Several observations are relevant here. One may strongly suspect that Negro youth intensely dislike the way they have been traditionally handled by teachers and the school system. They do not fall for the old line, "We are color-blind." They know, only too well, that teachers and the schools have never been color-blind, and they see little evidence of their becoming color-blind now. They know the old ploy, too, about their families and homes being responsible for their not learning; these kinds of youth have been "playing the dozens" long before they were exposed to insult and injury by teachers and schools. Teachers of such youth must be made aware of the sharpness and accuracy of their students' perception of them and the educational system, and their feelings about it. Secondly, teachers of such youth must know and appreciate that in all truth Negroes are infamously stigmatized by the American way of life. Most Negro youth have grown up in a predominantly lower-class, poverty-stricken, relatively isolated social world that often has its own distinctive social and cultural organization. Social goals and the means for their attainment may be uniquely defined, established, and accepted in such a social world. And, above all else, they have met always from the white members of American society—as far as isolation and segregation permitted—an immutable denigration of their worth, dignity, and being. The results are easily evident to their teachers; and if such youth are to learn how to learn, these problems and their consequences must be coped with intelligently by their teachers.

Negro youth do not exhaust the membership category included within the "disadvantaged" label. There are collectivities of other so-called racial, color, and ethnic groups to be included; such as Mexican-Americans, Puerto-Rican Americans, Indian- and Eskimo-Americans, Oriental-Americans, "other"-Americans. In addition, there are youth who are treated as outsiders or disadvantaged by teachers and schools because of such factors as their rural, Appalachian, or share-cropping background; their migratory way of life; the poverty or "low-class" community positions of their families; and even those who displease aesthetically by being obese, too tall, too short, too thin, and even too ugly! All such categories may be euphemistically thought of as left-outs, potential dropouts, socially deprived, culturally deprived, disinterested, handicapped, reluctant and/or alienated.

Regardless of how one may label, identify, or stigmatize these youth, teachers and school systems operating within democratic traditions, and especially as prescribed by the imperative of equality of opportunity, must deliberately prepare them by developing their critical facilities, improving their creative and judgmental skills, and building up their capacity to learn. These youth must be prepared, not for satisfactory adjustment to the status quo or for the occupancy of some insignificant vocational and societal niche, but for awareness of what the status quo is and how by learning they can be a part of changing the status quo.

It cannot be stressed too much that American society and the present institution of education can no longer avoid confronting the problem of the existence of an inferior and an unequal system of education af-

William M. Phillips, Jr.

forded such disadvantaged youth. The situation must be made plain as a first step, and even painfully so, to those electing to pursue a career of teaching such students; only then can problem solving in terms of the ruthless destruction of the situation and the urgent recreation of an adequate teaching and learning system be devised and put into effective operation.

Two other points quickly can be made about the roles of teachers and educators with those youth called disadvantaged. It is suggested that, for a moment, stigmatized youth be considered as a type of dissenter. In a democracy not only is dissent to be tolerated, but something worthwhile can be learned from it. Dissenting youth, then, could possibly teach something; and there might be much risk in losing whatever they are trying to teach. It just could be important.

The last observation is about unintended consequences. Educators may run the risk of unintentionally further stigmatizing disadvantaged youth by providing them with special teachers and special educational programs. At the tenth grade, for instance, certain youth are recruited for a special vocational-technical educational program under specially trained teachers. It has to be a special track because, commonly, regular vocational-technical schools reject disadvantaged youth, as do the regular high schools. What do you think such youth will think and feel? What do you imagine they will do? What do you think the cadre of specially trained teachers will think and feel? Is more isolation and segregation one of the goals of the special educational program? The possibility of the intrusion of such unintended consequences compels the educator to deliberately consider the educational process as it pertains to all youth.

There is a more concrete way to minimize this risk of unintentionally further stigmatizing some of our youth with esoteric educational programs. It is based upon the premise that the ideal and the policy of equality, in all its senses, is to be afforded all youth. If this explicit value is granted, then strategically disadvantaged youth, however identified, must be given preferential educational treatment. Such a program of compensatory education for disadvantaged youth must be based upon the proposition that such youth have to catch up with more fortunate youth and, moreover, that the conditions contributing to the old-styled patterns of privilege in our society have to be drastically subverted. Tactics relevant to the particular educational frame of reference of this paper include the highest quality of teacher training and excellence; experimentally derived and oriented curricula; preferential selection for occupational career opportunities and entry into the job market or for more varied and higher educational chances; special tutoring, counselling, and guidance for youth and their teachers; intensive involvement and cooperation between families or homes and the educational system; and by a stern and continuous scheme of total program evaluation.

The suggestion that preferential educational and vocational treatment for disadvantaged youth may minimize the risk of their further stigmatization in no way contradicts the basic view of this paper of abhorrence of special educational regimes for the wretched of our society —especially as they have been devised and carried out in the past. The central feature of this matter hangs on two pegs: the nature of stigma, and justice.

Stigmatized persons, or groups, are bound up in social situations and relationships of nonacceptance or of deep discreditation. A key fact about social action and response with stigmatized persons in such situations is that not only do those who stigmatize hold a set of beliefs and pursue a common set of actions toward the stigmatized, but that those stigmatized somehow tend to accept the beliefs held about them and suffer the actions that flow out of the attributed condition. Goffman (1963) terms this a sociological problem of identity. Thus, if one wished not to stigmatize, or to unstigmatize, the course of action is clear. Invent an educational program that clearly does not and cannot invest its participants with disgrace; that accepts and awards positive credit to all participants.

The matter of justice can be treated with dispatch. Our society, historically and presently, behaves with arrogance toward those who constitute the bulk of disadvantaged youth—nonwhites. The point needs no substantiation. The costs to all members of our society are literally unmeasurable. Our debt to them is clear from almost all canons of ethics and morality. Let us then mobilize our tremendous resources to remove these costs and to pay off these debts, with interest. A preferential educational program could be one phase of this societal purgation.

One final word on this matter. Recognizing and removing stigmas and attaining justice or excellence in modern society, as they pertain to the education of the disadvantaged, presumes a readiness for social change. Social change inevitably involves discarding of the old, the conventional, and the traditional ways of social life. There must, then, be a clear and deep commitment for the goals of a society unlike that in which we presently exist. There must be, in other words, utopian elements in our educational programs.

42
William M. Phillips, Jr.

THE discipline of sociology can make rather specific contributions to the curriculum of a program designed to train teachers of disadvantaged youth. It follows, as well, that the discipline of sociology can profit from becoming involved with educators in training teachers; although this aspect of the issue is not of immediate concern here. Orville G. Brim, Jr. (1958), among others, has dealt comprehensively with this topic.

Sociology, as an academic discipline, has several functions directly relevant to teacher training. It is, above all else, dedicated to the deliberate search for truth about and an attempt to understand the world of human relations. It has the equally important mission to provide clarification of and corrective solutions for the great problems and issues of societal life. These functions can be translated concretely to the topic of teacher preparation.

The following six questions are submitted as inherently sociological. Their relevance to a teacher training program designed for those who will teach stigmatized or nonstigmatized youth will be explored briefly.

1. What are the ways in which the members of American society really behave?

2. What are the ideologies, goals, and values (actual and professed) that members of American society hold?

3. What are the main social structures or entities into which members of American society organize themselves, and what are the connections between such entities and their consequences?

4. What are the principal agents, agencies, and channels of change among members of American society?

5. What are the unsolved, unresolved, persistent, and recurrent problems or failures of the members of American society?

6. What behavior models of deviance and conformity do we observe among the members of American society?

For each of these general sociological inquiries, subsidiary questions naturally follow: What is the actual fact or situation? Who is involved? Why are they so involved, that is, who gets and who gives? In what ways are these parties involved? What are the rational and irrational results of the situation—the ramifications of such actions and interactions?

Teachers of any youth can be affected (one might even say "corrupted") by sociology by following this approach to the world of man. For one thing teachers will gain "disillusioning" insight into the rational and irrational sources of social life. They must have this objective and disenchanting knowledge before they can successfully engage youth in the transforming aspects of the learning processes. Moreover, teachers can be brought to understand and accept the educational utility of divergent thinking. This condition functions efficiently in permitting the identification and avoidance of cant, dogma, and indoctrination. The old aphorism, "Whatever is, is right" may be tested and rejected; and the lesson then transferred to the youth who are attempting to learn how to learn. Pursuing the above questions nullifies the tendency toward phoniness and make-believe explanations or justifications of the social world, which are so quickly recognized by our astute youth of today. Finally, "conning" teachers into dealing with such questions leads them irreverently and inevitably to problem solving. The premise is offered that the discipline of sociology has a mission to help clarify and to point out alternative resolutions of the problems emerging out of an analysis of society in this way. By confronting prospective teachers with the complexities of human life, sociology can contribute to the attainment not only of truth but of integrity, significant attachment to the real world, and commitment to the career of teaching youth about the joys and the agonies of societal life.

Let us look at sociology and teacher training from a more concrete perspective. The major problems of American society today center around the following issues: urban-industrial life; race and racism; complex organizational structures or systems; the world of youth; work and leisure; the educational institution; international relations; the nature of social change. No teacher worth his salt can induce and control the learning process without a competent and confident acquaintance with the character of such basic American problems and processes. Any treatment of the major sociological inquiries previously listed must confront directly these focal issues of our times. Sociology, then, has an indispensable role in training prospective teachers to cope with youth as they learn and acquire the courage to live and face the future.

Prospective teachers, through the intervention of sociology, will acquire the conceptual and theoretical equipment to conceive of human society logically as a dynamic social system. They will view society as a model of social power and conflict; involved with ideology, ethics, and incessant change. The imaginations of such teachers will be stretched by treating the fact and the forms of deviancy and the variety of social worlds that make up society. They will be able to describe and interpret the facts of urban life and bureaucratic or complex organizational structures, leadership phenomena, and collective behavior. They will be able

William M. Phillips, Jr.

to deal intelligently with the inhumanity, the problems, and the consequences of our obsession with race and color, and probably to understand its implications for other structures of American society. The worlds or cultures of youth will be explored, permitting the identification of the special needs—especially with reference to education—of members of such groups. Finally, teachers can acquire an intimacy with the complex organizations of work and the educational system.

There is one final potential contribution that sociology may make to a teacher training program. The breed of man called sociologist tends to be hopelessly, shamelessly, wanting in reverence about or pride in the object of his study—the world of man. He is fascinated by anything that men do. He is not too snobbish to study the lowest social settings, the most despised undertakings, and the most sordid passions. This he does to find answers for his questions. Berger (1963) puts the point well:

> It is not the excitement of coming upon the totally unfamiliar, but rather the excitement of finding the familiar becoming transformed in its meaning. The fascination of sociology lies in the fact that its perspective makes us see in a new light the very World in which we live our lives. This also constitutes a transformation of consciousness.

C. Wright Mills (1961) calls this quality of the intellectual discipline "the sociological imagination." This quality, if successfully transmitted to prospective teachers, guarantees that they face the requirement of their profession: to demonstrate to youth a sense of their understanding and appreciation of the reality of youth and the complexities of social living.

Conclusion

ALTHOUGH all youth should be trained by their adult models in the perplexities and utilizations of problem solving, those youth identified as stigmatized or disadvantaged especially and urgently need this knowledge. These youth have qualitatively and quantitatively more problems than other youth. Finally, it is possible to discern a common approach by agents of American society, including teachers, toward stigmatized youth. This approach amounts to locating the onus of their problems in the youth themselves. Thus, the strategies used tend to come under what is termed discipline, regimentation, group and individual therapy often of a psychoanalytic nature, physical and social isolation or segregation, and often threats, coercion, force, and violence. This approach is greatly disturbing. It assumes implicitly, at least, that those who have a problem condition caused it, that this internal cause must be exorcised, and that such a unidimensional strategy alone is the answer to their problems. The approach most commonly boils down to more of man's inhumanity to man.

The premises or the consequences of this approach must not be accepted by educators. Regardless of the criteria used to identify and manage those youth termed stigmatized or disadvantaged, it is suggested that they are primarily symptoms of social conditions, predicaments, encounters, and processes. The strategies used by teachers must deal with these same social conditions and processes. Youth has to be led into an objective perception of the real world and how it works. Their difficulties must be understood as they are within the world as it is. Teachers and youth must deal with the strategies and tactics of mobilization and involvement in changing the world; and youth must be led to know the results to them and all of society if they do or if they do not become alive to the reality of the world of man. The discipline of sociology can be a powerful instrument for preparing teachers to engage in this way with all youth for the purpose of genuine education.

References

ASHTON-WARNER, SYLVIA. *Teacher.* New York: Simon and Schuster, 1963.

BERGER, PETER L. *Invitation to Sociology.* Garden City, N. Y.: Anchor, 1963.

BRIM, ORVILLA G., JR. *Sociology and the Field of Education.* New York: Russell Sage Foundation, 1958.

CLIFF, VIRGIL A. "Educating the American Negro," in John P. Davis (ed.), *The American Negro Reference Book.* Englewood Cliffs, N.J.: Prentice-Hall, 1966, Chap. 7.

DAVIDSON, HELEN H., et al. "Characteristics of Successful School Achievers from a Severely Deprived Environment." School of Education: The City University of New York, October 1962. (Mimeographed.)

GOFFMAN, ERVING. *Stigma.* Englewood Cliffs, N.J.: Prentice-Hall, 1963.

GOSLIN, DAVID A. *The Search for Ability: Standardized Testing in Social Perspective.* New York: Russell Sage Foundation, 1963.

HERNDON, JAMES. "The Way It Spozed To Be," *Harper's Magazine,* September 1965.

JOHNSON, CHARLES S. *Educational and the Cultural Process.* Nashville, Tenn.: Fisk University, 1943.

William M. Phillips, Jr.

KAUFMAN, BEL. *Up the Down Staircase.* Englewood Cliffs, N.J.: Prentice-Hall, 1964.

KORNBERG, LEONARD. "Meaningful Teachers for Alienated Children," in *Education in Depressed Areas,* ed. A. H. Passow. New York: Columbia University Press, 1963.

LANGBERG, GEORGE, and PHILIP I. FREEDMAN. "Self-Selection of Student Teachers," *Integrated Education,* Issue 16–17, August/November 1965.

LITEAK, EUGENE. "Notes on the Relationship Between Neighborhood, Educational Achievement, and Good Citizenship." "Notes on the Relationship Between Internal Administrative Structure and Goals of Educational Achievement and Good Citizenship." (Unpublished.) August 1961 and October 1961, respectively. School of Social Work, The University of Michigan.

MACKLER, BERNARD, et al. "The Successful Urban Slum Child: A Psychological Study of Personality and Academic Success in Deprived Children." Institute of Urban Studies, Teachers College, Columbia University, March 1965.

MCCREARY, EUGENE. "Teaching the Culturally Different," *Integrated Education,* Issue 13, February/March 1965.

MILLS, C. WRIGHT. *The Sociological Imagination.* New York: Grove Press, 1961.

SKINNER, B. F. "Why Teachers Fail," *Saturday Review,* October 1965.

TURNER, RICHARD H., and NICHOLAS A. FATTU. *Skill in Teaching.* School of Education, Indiana University, Vol. 36, No. 3 (1960).

WALLER, WILLARD. *The Sociology of Teaching.* New York: Russell and Russell, 1961.

————. "The Bridge Project: The Preparation of Teachers for Schools in Culturally Deprived Neighborhoods." New York, Queens College, 1965.

4 Explorations in the Role of Guidance for Youth from the "Underclass"

_____Arnold Buchheimer

THE CITY UNIVERSITY OF NEW YORK

WHEN POLITICAL, psychological, economic, and cultural factors are so overwhelmingly arrayed against some pupils, what is the task and role of those who work in a guidance capacity in a vocational school or, for that matter, in any school? How does the following definition of guidance fit students who dwell in the slums, who do not seem to benefit from formal education as it exists at the present time?

> Guidance helps a student to find order in the complexities of decision making, helps him to enrich his experience by examining it, and helps him to become the conscious artist of his own career.
> (Katz, 1963, p. 59)

Gilbert Wrenn's answer to these two questions is a cautious, help-less, plaintive attempt to relate the needs of these youth to the guidance movement that has evolved for the last fifty years (Schreiber, 1964). It is shocking to find one of the sages of the guidance movement so helpless until one examines Alan Haber's unpublished manuscript entitled "The American Underclass" (1965). The array of economic, social, political, and cultural forces against the poor, as cited by Haber, is so overwhelming that one begins to understand Wrenn's qualified view of the guidance function and the economists' open pessimism about the worth and value of an education, as we know it, for those who belong to the underclass.

Yet, so far as vocational education is concerned, we are in a situation where education and economics meet and consort with each other. In the guidance movement there has been a long dialectic between manpower utilization and self-development—manpower utilization being an economic concept whereas self-development is more or less a psychological and educational concept. Today we are involved in a dialectic between those who are concerned with social change and those who are concerned with individual change. Some feel that individual change, however dramatic it may be, is predicated on changes in social conditions.

But as Katz (1963, p.14) has said, "Clearly an individual's vocationally oriented choices are social as well as psychological events—they always involve some transaction with the cultural environment." This basic sense of choice is not as available as it is to the middle class.

Wrenn (in Schreiber, 1964, p.193) defines guidance as a point of view which is, or should be, a part of a working philosophy of every school. He thinks that the school counselor should influence others to provide a more meaningful environment, both school and nonschool; should modify others' perceptions of urban youth in the direction of better identification and understanding; and, should modify self-perception of urban youth so that they may be able to relate better to others and also to know how to make more adequate use of whatever environmental resources are available to them. Wrenn conceives the environment of the counselor, as well as the youth with whom he works, as three concentric circles: the innermost is the social environment we all live in; the second circle is the educational environment; the third circle is the psychological environment. These circles are in constant dynamic interaction with each other. This chapter will be addressed to the guidance task in each of these environments within a school—any school—vocational, academic, general, elementary, secondary, trade, or technical.

50
Arnold Buchheimer

_____Modification of the Social Environment

So FAR as the underclass, Negro or white, is concerned, opportunities have become more and more limited. These limits are because of obsolescence due to automation, because of limited occupational mobility due to substandard education and substandard living conditions, and because of our caste and ghetto structure. Guidance and school personnel can be effective in three distinct ways: first, by modifying their own attitudes toward the poor; second, by becoming involved in the many community action programs that now are being created and developed under local, state, and federal sponsorship; and third, by modifying the opportunity structure.

Modification of Personal Attitudes

In our Protestant ethic, the poor are considered a public nuisance, socially disruptive and morally incorrigible (Haber, 1965, p. 12). We value work, thrift, and the survival of the fittest. The poor are obviously unfit. These feelings may be strongest among those who themselves have been recently uplifted from this state of "sinfulness." It seldom occurs to us that people are poor today because of forces over which they have had little control, for which we of the middle class are directly responsible, and from which we benefit directly.

We need to look at our own values, prejudices, and social attitudes and question their validity. This may be a difficult task, and an uncomfortable one. But it is no more uncomfortable or difficult than it is for a slum youth to give up being a junky, become socially responsible, and report to school or work punctually. Indifference to social plight and the enjoyment of caste privileges may be equally irresponsible, sinful, and morally reprehensible to those whom we deride as being socially misfit. I am neither a moralist nor a sentimentalist when I speak as I do, but a hard-headed realist. The old song, "She's more to be pitied than censured" in no way pertains. The poor need neither pity nor censure; they resent both. They do need responsibility and public advocacy; they need allies with unlimited commitment. The guidance person in a school should be such an ally, deeply committed against the exploitation of the poor, deeply committed to the eradication of the caste and color line, wary of viewing poverty and the underclass in terms of a puritanical ethic.

Personal Involvement in Community Action Programs

In acting on such a commitment, consideration should be given to psychological moonlighting. For his own edification on the conditions of poverty, as well as an insight into the aspirations and frustrations of the poor, every person should devote some time to working in community action programs. It is recommended that the principle of the tithe be applied to our social involvement, that we give a certain proportion of our time and our professional know-how to these programs. Not because there may be an extra buck made—this may be voluntary time—but because as professionals we owe it to ourselves to become involved at the blood, sweat, and tears level in a great American social enterprise. If we are indeed at war with poverty, then, as in any other war, we must tighten our psychological belts. In this war the sacrifice is not our lives but the abandonment of white middle-class smugness and privilege and the attitudes that foster these states of mind. In the poverty programs around the country, especially those geared to the ghetto areas, there is an alarming tendency to involve only those who are themselves of the ghetto culture in the community action programs.[1] This is alarming, not because this practice often has overtones of nepotism and political patronage, but rather because it maintains the caste structure. The principle that "a house divided against itself cannot stand" was eloquently pronounced over a hundred years ago. It would be truly ironic if now, on a different level, under different circumstances, government policy, federal support, and the established institutions aided and abetted the maintenance of the caste structure. The moral imperative of all our civil rights and manpower legislation is to eradicate the underclass and the "other America." Yet it is understandable that the spokesmen for the poor and the "out-caste" would be wary of involving the uncommitted or the outright enemy in their struggle for freedom. It is up to us to show our commitment, especially since our professionalism is needed. Our involvement in community action is essential if we are to be modifiers of the environment; our skills are necessary to bring us closer to the democratic ideal of the Great Society. Our indifference is tanta-

1. This comment is not meant to diminish the value of efforts to create work programs and community action programs involving indigenous persons. This paper was written before the advent of the "Black Power" slogan. The concept of Black Power cannot be supported in its racist connotations; but insofar as it offers glamour to its workers in community action programs, it has value for its motivational effect.

Arnold Buchheimer

mount to resistance to change, and open resistance to change is akin to sabotage in wartime. We have no choice but to become involved. But if we are involved, it must be an involvement of humility and equality rather than one of benevolence and paternalism.

Modifying the Opportunity Structures

"Opportunities are mediated by gate keepers . . . the gate keeper makes ability judgments about an applicant's risk . . ." (Haber, 1965, p. 14). "A gate keeper is one who has direct control of access" (Haber, *ibid.*). As guidance workers, we control the route out of the underclass. Every time we make a judgment about a youngster, a judgment which is "reality oriented"; every time we do not send an able boy to explore a job opportunity because he may not be hired because of his race; every time we counsel a child out of a chosen field because his opportunities are limited by discriminatory practice; every time we counsel a child in terms of our stereotypic notions of the work force; every time we participate in discussions that restrict the opportunities of training or induction into the labor force for any reason whatsoever, we commit an act of sabotage in the war on poverty. We have only one role and one single purpose: to counsel in terms of *potential* regardless of what the present reality may be. Any action short of counseling, developing, and training for potential is an action against the national and personal interest. Employment restrictions of today may be—will be—the real opportunities of tomorrow.

The only honest, moral, and decent attitude we can take as professionals is to say to each individual youth, "This is what we think you can do; we will train and educate you to do it; and we will use all of the influence and endeavor at our disposal to see to it that you have the opportunity to do what you can do and what you are trained and educated to do."

_____Modifying the Educational Environment

DURING the last five years, a rather acrimonious dialogue has developed among those who are exploring the reasons why children do not stay in school; indeed why they do not succeed in school. Approximately 50 per cent of the noncollege-bound population does not finish high school,

Explorations in the Role of Guidance for Youth from the "Underclass"

and another 50 per cent of the college-bound population does not finish college.

The immediate reaction to such figures is that something is wrong. Either there is something unnatural, in developmental terms, in asking children to stay in school for twelve to sixteen years of their lives; or, the institutions are not offering what is needed. Levine (1965) speaks of customizing and tailoring education to the needs of individual youths. Where is this concept in relation to the above figures? The acrimony of the dialogue is intensified by the contention that the slum schools are different from schools in middle-class areas. There is a third force, represented by Goodman (1964) and Friedenberg (1959), which contends that all schools and most colleges are generally outmoded and that they are meeting the needs of our youth and our society in a most limited and limiting way.

There are those who feel strongly that systems of special secondary schools that usually exist in large cities—academic schools, vocational schools, and general schools—and practices of grouping children homogeneously, either by reading achievement or by IQ, contribute to educational and social pathology.

The Dimensions of the Problems

The frustration with the dialogue between these contending forces, those who seek modification in education practices and those who feel that the schools are doing the best they can do, is best characterized by Martin Mayer's reaction to the proceedings of a conference on the school dropout sponsored by the N.E.A. (in Schreiber, 1964, p. 209).

> For this participant, the most distressing moment at the conference was a superintendent's retreat to administrative rigidity when a partial solution to a piece of the problem was offered at the table. . . . Nobody doubts that the schools must work harder with slum children than with suburban children to achieve even remotely comparable results. But, as the handicapper of a race track once said to a starter who tried to keep a horse out of a race on the grounds that he was troublesome to start, "If it was no trouble to start horses, we'd hire the milkman at five dollars a day."

Let us, therefore, look at the controversy with the assumption that providing a meaningful education for all children is an extremely taxing but socially significant task. The controversy has three distinct aspects

Arnold Buchheimer

to it: home versus school, compensatory versus integrated education, vocational versus general education.

Home vs. School

The University of the State of New York (1965) reports that children from the underclass in high school possess the following characteristics and are therefore not educable:

1. Overage.
2. Retardation in grade level.
3. IQ below 90.
4. Lack of interest in school.
5. Low school marks.
6. Reading retardation of two grade levels.
7. Uncooperative parental attitudes.
8. Poor or fair general personal and social adjustment.
9. Nonparticipation in out-of-school activities.
10. Absenteeism and truancy.
11. Underlying racial tensions.
12. Rejection by in-school peers.
13. Members of large families (five or more children).
14. Resentment of controls.
15. Parental achievement of Grade 7 or below.
16. Poor personal health.
17. Short attention span.

Those who blame the schools, as such, say the problem is attributable to the teacher rather than the child. Harlem Youth Opportunities Unlimited (1964) claims the following:

1. The school in itself is responsible for the decline in verbal skills.

2. Social characteristics, such as family income, overcrowded housing and broken homes, do not contribute to education deficiency.

3. The slum schools should have their fair share of experienced teachers.

4. There is a necessity for multiracial content in the texts and the course of study.

5. School personnel have distorted perceptions of the educability of the poor.

6. The poor attitudes of school personnel are due to lack of direct contact with the poor.

7. Poor attitudes are due to an overemphasis on competition.

8. Poor attitudes are due to stereotyping and patronizing attitudes.

9. Poor attitudes are due to lack of identification with the poor and, conversely, with lack of opportunity for the children of the poor to identify with people like themselves. (This is especially true of Negro children in the cities.)

10. Authority figures are too different and distant from the children.

11. The slum children themselves have a low self-image.

12. The status system in the school overemphasizes intellectual achievement.

13. The self-fulfilling prophecy is expressed in this way: "When teachers and principals have a low opinion of the children's learning ability, the children seldom exceed those expectations."

These allegations about the schools are echoed by sociologists like Edgar Friedenberg and Frank Riessman, social critics like Paul Goodman, and economists like S. M. Miller. Paul Goodman (1964) contends that the function of compulsory education is based on the economic motive to keep children out of the labor market. He likens it to conscription. He suggests that it may well be a violation of our civil rights! He characterizes schooling—elementary, secondary, and college —as mis-education, an oppressively boring experience which barely engages any aspect of the person, physical, psychological, or intellectual.

Miller (in Schreiber, 1964, p. 13) classifies students who are unsuccessful in school into four categories:

1. School-inadequate.
2. School-rejecting.
3. School-perplexed.
4. School-irrelevant.

He estimates that the truly school-inadequate number is small. My own experiences as a school psychologist tend to confirm this impression and to say that the truly school-inadequate—the intellectually retarded or emotionally ill child—is well identified, if not provided for. Miller estimates that most school dropouts are either school-rejecting or school-irrelevant.

The foregoing is an impressive list of allegations and counterallegations. It clearly indicates that schools have much self-examination to do without ever being concerned about remedying directly the factors of social pathology affecting growth and development. Both factions are right in describing the condition that exists.

We as school people are told that we are uncomprehending, distant, prejudiced, discriminatory, and distorted in our value system. This is something to deal with in undefensive ways, requiring genuine self-examination and revision of our basic value systems within the school, regardless of what goes on in the society at large. If our school curricula are irrelevant and perplexing, then it is up to us to create less puzzlement and more relevancy.

I disagree with Goodman's point on separating educational purposes from economic purposes, it seems somewhat unreasonable since education is economics. However, his observation that schooling, as practiced, administered, and experienced by all concerned—teacher, administrator, and pupil—is an oppressive bore is supportable. If anyone doubts it, he need only listen to children, administrators, or teachers in the counseling room or in graduate courses, respectively.

Some of the street academy programs developed by the New York Urban League come close to what Goodman advocates and they illustrate his point very well. The street academies are store-front schools populated by high school dropouts, who are recruited by street workers. The facilities are poor. They would not meet minimum standards of the most liberal school-building code. The teaching is done by college students who have little formal training in education. The street academy students take formal academic courses part of the day and participate in a work program the rest of the day. It is very much the way Paul Goodman describes what a school ought to be and very much unlike what schools in an urban school system are like. Children who have dropped out of school, or who have been kicked out of school, are engaged in the study of algebra, civics, journalism—they write their own newspaper—and dramatics.

The school authorities notwithstanding, the participants in the street academy program are not uncommunicative. The restless school attenders, the hard-core kids, are actively engaged in an academic program. They respond positively to authority. They attend classes and are engaged in highly verbal pursuits. They can concentrate. They do not have a low attention span.

What differentiates these schools from a public school other than the already noted poor physical facility? The charisma and commitment of its staff! Much, much emphasis is placed in the street academy on the fact that the counselor, the teacher, and the street worker really care. There is constant evidence of the commitment to the child even to the extent that his teacher or street worker will go to his home to get him out of bed in order for him to come to school. Boredom and irrelevance have been replaced by the feeling that someone really wants him in school, that someone cares about his educational development, and that there is a way of upgrading himself through education. The street worker will speak disparagingly of the professional guidance worker. It is as though he assumes that the professional training and status have taken away the charisma.

A part of the home *vs.* school issue that touches on an issue raised at both the federal and the local level is that of compensatory *vs.* integrated education.

Two government reports were recently published in Washington. One is the U.S. Office of Education survey, "Equality of Educational Opportunity" (Coleman et al., 1966), and the other is "Racial Isolation in the Public Schools," published by the United States Commission on Civil Rights (1967). Both reports emphasize the importance of integrated education. Both reports point to the limited value of compensatory education. Yet both reports are generally unacceptable to the educators. There seems to be a striving within the field of education to maintain segregated education and increase compensatory education, even though the evidence in most public documents points to the limited value of compensatory education.

What, then, is a counselor to do in the stand that he takes, assuming that he has a commitment, especially since one of the most important features in most compensatory education programs is the increase of special services, including guidance? It is recommended that he take a moral stand, as well as a professional stand; and morally he can take the position only on the side of integrated education. His commitment, therefore, to compensatory education can only be a limited commitment in the sense that the remediation of insufferable conditions is an interim step toward the desired goal of integrated schooling. Even while he may be engaged in a compensatory educational effort, he must not lose sight of the fact that the only real educational attainment is integrated schooling. This is the sense of the Office of Education survey.

There are some people who are now talking of "quality segregated" education, boosted and beefed up through compensatory programs. It is almost as though these people are bent on reversing whatever small achievement has been attained as a result of the Supreme Court decision

Arnold Buchheimer

of 1954, and would revert again to a segregated school system, North and South.

A Suggested Resolution

Schools have always been the primary force of social mobility and social progress in our society. In the past they reflected the philosophy of free enterprise and personal achievement and improvement. We are embarking on an age of automation, which necessitates social planning on all levels of our economy. An automated society cannot be an unplanned society nor a free enterprise society. Thus, the social emphasis in our schools has to shift from a free enterprise philosophy to a social welfare philosophy. Such a shift leads of necessity to a reevaluation of our entire competitive emphasis. We need to reevaluate our status and reward systems in our schools, both for the teacher as well as for the children. *First, so far as elementary school children are concerned, it is recommended that we totally abandon special classes and special grouping practices for all those children who do not fall into the "school-inadequate" category.* In other words, elementary schools should practice heterogeneous grouping for all children whose potential is not hampered by a high degree of emotional disturbance or clear intellectual retardation.

On the other end of the scale, for children who are so clearly superior that their potential and full development augurs social contributions of the magnitude of a Freud, Mozart, Weiner, Einstein, Beethoven, Menuhin, Mendel, DaVinci, Mills, or Shakespeare, I advocate a completely personalized tutorial educational program with whatever group and social experiences the individual situation requires. All other children should be grouped without regard to intellectual assessment or intellectual achievement. Status systems in schools are obsolete and have a deleterious effect on the achievement of children.

The most ardent objectors to these suggestions are school personnel themselves. They are thoroughly entrapped in their own mystique. They will refer to "good classes" and "bad classes" and "good schools" and "bad schools" without ever knowing what they are saying. Recently a principal of a vocational school showed me his class rosters and his attendance records. The "good classes," those who were achieving up to grade level, were regular in attendance. Those who were in "bad classes" were chronically truant. Consider for yourself how long you would willingly continue in an environment if you were continually told that you were undervalued.

It would undoubtedly take considerable retraining of administrative and teaching personnel and the general public to abandon the investment in homogeneous grouping. Every classroom in a school should represent the entire range of differences of the educable children within a school—sex differences, class differences, race differences, and intellectual differences.

A constructive step toward equalizing educational accessibility would be to take another look at the way we group children and at the way school tracks become fixed. Those who are impressed with the mystique of grouping should be reminded that "it does not necessarily follow that organizations designed to simplify the act of teaching through reduced ranges will enhance children's learning" (Buchheimer, 1965, p. 40).

In defense of those who resist the inauguration of heterogeneous grouping, it must be said that class size needs to be reduced so that individual attention can be given. On the other hand, it must be emphasized that reduction of class size does not guarantee individual attention or differentiation of educational approach.

Secondly, a policy of saturation for all children, especially those who are deficient in some way, is recommended. When children are deficient in reading they should have more reading rather than less, with new and different approaches. If five periods of English don't seem to do the trick, seven periods might. If seven periods don't eliminate the deficiency, nine might. When a person shows a dietary deficiency, we don't water down the diet further; rather, we supplement and enrich. Educational programs need enrichment rather than watering down. This is not to say that we do not need to start where children are, or that all children should end up the same way. Rather, all children need the same commitment and their differences are an educational challenge rather than an educational handicap. Our curricula and courses of study need to be differentiated, but our educational setting needs to be equally accessible and available to all.

The third recommendation is the adoption of a policy of inclusion rather than exclusion. This would include eliminating the possibility of school exclusion as a punishment. Contrary to Paul Goodman, such a policy would be seen as a commitment, an act of faith, rather than as mandatory conscription. It is interesting to speculate about the effect on the dropout rate or the truancy rate in our schools if pupils were told

Arnold Buchheimer

that, as an endorsement of their educability, suspension from school would no longer be used as a disciplinary measure. When this policy was adopted by the Greenburgh #8 School System in New York, their dropout problem was nonexistent.

A fourth recommendation is to adopt a deliberate policy of color sensitivity, rather than color-blindness. In fact, the problem of teaching the disadvantaged is intimately bound up with the problem of racial discrimination. The Negro believes and knows this.

> "The color of your skin does make a difference, believe me."
> "It makes no difference to me," she said.
> "In my country it makes all the difference in the world."
> "I know how you feel," she said tonelessly. "I don't blame you."
> "No," he replied, "you don't know how I feel. You can't know how I feel."
>
> (Killens, 1964)

Color sensitivity means letting the Negro know that we can and will understand how he feels and that we will do all in our power to take these feelings into consideration.

The above recommendations are sweeping and largely psychological and cultural in consequence. They are difficult to enact and their effects are difficult to evaluate objectively. We are dealing with deeply felt emotions and attitudes. Each generation has a "rendezvous with destiny." Our rendezvous is with ourselves and with the beliefs and attitudes we hold. Our destiny is to change the socially damaging practices that result from these attitudes with more than "deliberate speed."

Vocational Education vs. General Education

A part of the larger issue of segregation that has developed recently is the issue of vocational *vs.* general education. Where does the counselor take his stand? The vocational school has become a *de facto* segregated school. This is true not only in New York City, but also true in Detroit, St. Louis, Philadelphia, and any other urban center with a large ghetto population. The trade concept on which most vocational schools were built is now obsolete. Therefore, it would seem almost inevitable that the present-day counselor would have to take his stand on the side of a general, comprehensive school.

It may appear that in advocating the creation of a comprehensive high school, in the dissolution of the vocational school, vocational education is being abandoned. Not at all! It is being extended. If one of the functions of vocational education is to provide a balanced secondary education, there is no reason why it cannot be received in a regular comprehensive high school. This still leaves open the question of the two other purposes of vocational education: preparation for earning a livelihood and for vocational competence.

Today we are told by labor and industry that a criterion for employability is a high school diploma; that vocational training and vocational competence are a function of industry and management or post-high school training in technical schools, community colleges, private trade schools, or special institutes. The Public Education Association of New York declares (1963, p. 15):

> The ultimate goal, however, is to have all high schools operating under a single system and attaining such excellence that the specialized schools of today may no longer be a necessary or a desirable part of public education in New York City.

They advocate the postponement of vocational-skill training until after high school and recognize that workers with a single skill may have increasing difficulty in adapting to the labor market (*ibid.*, p. 15). On the other hand, one can examine the program of what is called a Unit Trade High School in New York City. This is a school which prepares students for employment in the trades of a single industry, such as food trades, printing, or aviation.

In some unit trade schools, in addition to mathematics, science, English, and history, a student is required to take courses in basic electricity, woodwork, hydraulics, weights and balance, and engines, before he takes the courses specifically related to the industry. (This is also true of the diversified trade vocational schools.) The courses for the specific trades are given primarily in the twelfth grade and require special shops and equipment.

One can certainly make a good case for the fact that no one's education is complete if he does not have a working knowledge of motors, electricity, and principles of hydraulics and weights. Within a few years, as we become more and more automated and there are fewer semiskilled occupations, we may be forced to do our own repair work rather than rely on handymen to do it for us. Mechanical illiteracy may be as much a problem in a few years as reading deficiency is today.

The vocational training within a comprehensive school may be more

Arnold Buchheimer

akin to what is called industrial arts. It is, however, absolutely essential that such a program should involve the entire student body, not merely a special group. Programs requiring special equipment could be housed in special centers. Students could travel to these centers.

The new Vocational Education Act (U.S. Department of Health, Education, and Welfare, 1965) mentions certain occupations, specifically taking cognizance of the need for new types of service occupations, such as the following:

1. Repairmen for new types of appliances.
2. Heating and ventilating occupations.
3. Health subprofessions, such as dental aides, nurses' aides, and hospital aides.

Pearl and Riessman's recent book, *New Careers for the Poor* (1965), suggests such job descriptions and titles as Family Counselor, Neighborhood Coordinator, Home Economist, Group Work Aide, Neighborhood Health Aide, and Home Visitor. These careers are based on the assumption that community action programs demand widely extended social services and that jobs such as Health Aide are entry jobs to more professional levels of training. Even more forceful is the argument that the poor be hired to serve the poor and that community action programs are for the poor, with the poor, and by the poor. As has been indicated above, the exclusiveness of this approach is objectionable, although perhaps socially necessary. Certainly any training basic to entry into the expanding social service professions involves the skills and competencies acquired in a comprehensive high school program.

Do schools educate only those who are basically like the school staff itself? If the answer to this question is affirmative, then the poor have no choice but to go off on their own with federal aid to establish competing institutions and training centers.

The comprehensive high school is a school that will need to provide much flexibility, diversification, and tailoring of programs to fit individual needs. Fixed tracks, particularly, are a practice of the past in the socially viable school.

Many who question the ideas of comprehensive schools in a large city are concerned about bigness and depersonalization. They feel that segregation is as likely to occur within a school as within separate schools. This is true! Present educational practices of homogeneous grouping, fixed tracking, and the highly competitive academic emphasis all contribute to *de facto* segregation by color, caste, and class lines within a school. Individualized programming would help. For example, a boy who is really gifted in mathematics should have the opportunity to take math courses leading to advanced placement in college without being obliged to be equally high in his history performance, or in biology.

A standard high school diploma would be useful—a diploma without the specification of what kind of program it represented. Anyone who needs to know can ask for the school transcript to get more specific information. Another practice is also suggested: the school within a school, provided it is organized to include a balanced representation of the various differences that exist within the school population.

We already have such schools within schools. The career guidance program in the junior high school of New York City is one example. Another is the college discovery program, funded by O.E.O. and co-operatively developed by the board of education of New York City and the City University of New York. But both these schools within schools emphasize remediation and are basically crash programs. The same principle could easily be applied to typical school groups. The house plan in the Newton, Massachusetts, school system approaches the school-within-a-school concept. There are answers to the problem of depersonalization without segregating young people, creating a fixed status structure within a school, or jeopardizing intellectual stimulation.

Dealing with Skill Deficiencies

Much has been said here about a balanced education, but little about education either for a livelihood or for vocational competence. Nor has the potent problem of skill deficiencies in high school been discussed as yet. Consider the latter first.

A counselor in a vocational school, a diversified one offering twenty-eight different vocational and technical trade subjects, recently said that the biggest problem she encountered was the substantial educational deficiencies with which the children came to school. Because of these deficiencies, the boys could go only so far in their shop work. The roster was similar to ones seen in other schools. The truants were the same as the skill-deficient. Picture the frustration and despair. The children unable to cope with the task at hand, the teacher unable to communicate, and the administration on the spot for being unable to hold the pupils. This particular twenty-eight track school does attempt to offer remedial help outside the classroom to those with skill deficiencies. But one wonders about the tenacity of the teacher in the classroom who persists in ignoring the basic educational dictum of starting children where they are, rather than starting them where the course of study says they ought to be. One cannot help wondering how much the practice of homogeneous grouping in itself has contributed to the lack of learning. How long were those boys at the bottom of the ladder before they ever came to this school?

Skill deficiency is an important problem in all our schools. Neither remediation nor modification have had much impact against the problem. Saturation, not modification, may be the answer. The richer the diet, the more palatable the program.

New York City vocational schools with entrance requirements, and thus with greater status, also have a greater holding power. A counselor in a unit trade vocational high school with such an entrance examination gleefully revealed: "They used to think that we were the dumping ground; now they are." "They" referred to the general track in the academic high school. This same school closes its doors for a period every spring for the sole purpose of interviewing and testing every applicant. The interview is crucial to the selection. When a boy does not meet paper qualifications, he may nevertheless be admitted, depending on the judgment of the interviewer. If he is admitted with a deficiency —below the cut-off point on the test—an enrichment program is arranged for him. The dropout rate for this school is low and their achievement level is consonant with the rest of the city's academic schools. Every boy admitted feels that the school made a commitment to him.

If secondary schools are unable to deal with skill deficiencies that have accumulated throughout elementary and junior high school years, then other institutions have to be found to do the job. One such institution may be a skills center where people of all ages may go to overcome deficiencies. Such a center is an educational "cafeteria" whose primary purpose is to offer educational services on an individualized basis for those who need to make up deficiencies in training. Such a center could be staffed by educational consultants who could assess needs and then work out an individualized program of training. The object of the skills center would be to direct the person either toward a formal school program or toward employment. A proposal of this kind was made by the Public Education Association of New York City for the purpose of helping dropouts and men and women needing retraining for new jobs.

The issue of compensatory education and the remediation of skill deficiencies are closely linked. It is the counselor's job to diagnose and make the prognoses about skill deficiencies. It is the counselor's job equally to help develop curricula where skill deficiencies are not created by the school.

There are those who say that the school itself creates the deficiencies and impedes learning. The counselor, together with the rest of the faculty, should develop curricula that are as relevant as possible. The issue of skill deficiencies that are created by the home involves the notion of compensatory education; it is the counselor's responsibility to develop programs of compensatory education that begin as early in the history of the child as possible. The earlier the beginning, the narrower the gap.

From what we learn through the Head Start programs and through various research, it is possible and relatively easy to bridge the experiential and cultural gap between the child entering school from the middle class or the lower class, when this is done early in the child's development. It is, therefore, the counselor's obligation to participate in general education programs wherein the experiences are designed to compensate for learning deficiencies created by the culture of poverty.

Education for a Livelihood

Whatever educational approach is used, certain youth need to earn their livelihood at the same time as they attend school. With many it is a matter of economic need. With others it is a matter of self-respect. In some cases it is a part of the cultural pattern. A fifteen-year-old Puerto Rican boy recently reported to his counselor that his family treated him differently. They listened to him now. When the counselor asked why this was so, he told her that he now had a part-time job. Manhood is an important value. Manhood may mean girlfriends, a car, status, often in place of school success. All of these things cost money, and a job is the way to attain them.

Any high school program planning for the needs of youth, especially the needs of poor youth, must take into consideration that the need to attain manhood or womanhood cannot be postponed until after graduation. In the streets one becomes a man or a woman long before being recognized as one in school. It is for these youth that work-study programs are essential. The results of the STEP program—another school-within-a-school—indicate that more students were held in school when the following was done:

1. Students either earned money while going to school or were given a stipend.
2. There was an effective program of skill development and enrichment.
3. Basic educational requirements remained flexible.
4. Work and study were combined.

(University of the State of New York, 1965)

A Mt. Diable, California, school principal sums up his experience with a work-study program:

> Work experience helps in the adjustment of youngsters in an important developmental stage. They learn to adjust to real life situations. They achieve some degree of independence in which they must live with themselves and at the same time get along with other people.

(Burchill, 1962, p. 41)

If this is the value of a work-study experience, why not make the experience available to all students who wish to participate in such programs, not merely to those who are problems to the school? The work-study approach to education is not a new one. It goes back to the continuation centers which are the forerunners of our vocational schools, predating the Smith Hughes Act.

Work-Study Programs

The work-study programs may be of two types. Type 1 consists of work experiences that are essentially exploratory in nature. The purpose of such a program would be for a young person to understand what the work situation is like and to understand the different types of work involved in the occupational structure of a community. Exploratory work experiences, if they could be arranged, might be appropriate for any child, especially at the junior high school level. Such exploratory work experience would logically follow Super's findings. These are the years for which exploratory experiences are particularly appropriate.

It is possible to develop a program in the junior high school years whereby industry and the schools would cooperate directly in orienting children to the world of work through exploratory work experiences. If

Explorations in the Role of Guidance for Youth from the "Underclass"

such exploratory work experiences were truly open to all children and conducted on a completely nonsegregated basis, they would certainly be instrumental in expanding the horizons of children whose experiences are otherwise limited because of their ethnic background and because of their life in the slums.

The second type of work-study program, which would be consistent with the principle of general education, is the typical work-study program which has already been mentioned, such as STEP, cooperative education, and the programs described above by Burchill (1962). These programs should not be open only to youngsters who would otherwise not remain in school, although as Burchill states, involvement in work has been a factor in the holding power of the school. They should be available and relevant to any interested child.

The counselor is often the placement person in such programs. If such programs were truly nondiscriminatory, and if counselors insisted through the school placements that the law of the land be enforced, then again the work-study program, considerably expanded, would perform a valuable role and function in the modification of the opportunity structure.

I am not sure whether it is really necessary to require so much schooling for many jobs, even highly verbal jobs, especially when industry does the training and when many tasks performed by the work force are not self-fulfilling or particularly gratifying. Are we not perhaps overemphasizing the value of a high school education for work? The following is an illustration. A top executive of a major insurance company recently returned from a conference on high school dropouts. He was perplexed and frustrated by what were offered as solutions to the problems of dropouts. Being of an experimental mind, he told his employment people to go out and hire seventy-five "hard-core kids." The boys were put through the training program and assigned to foremen who were thought to be sympathetic. The foremen were told that the hiring of the boys was in excess of their quota and budget and that their work would have no bearing on the quality-control procedures. A third of the boys did not last; they were let go. Another third was incorporated into the company and they have made a good adjustment to the work force, availing themselves of training opportunities within the firm. Another third either went back to school when they realized that a limited education means limited work opportunities, or they went to other jobs. In the case of these boys, the company cooperated with JOIN to find appropriate job opportunities for those who did not fit

68

Arnold Buchheimer

into their work force. This company is continuing to hire high school dropouts, and is even recruiting them. It is generally pleased with the results of a two-thirds success. This experience certainly casts some doubt on the assumption made by most employers: that persistence in school is an indication of persistence on the job and a basic criterion of employability.

Earning a livelihood while in school will always be a factor affecting school attendance. There will always be a group of students who need, for economic, social, or psychological reasons, to work while attending school.

The matter of technical and vocational competence is less clear in the light of our rapidly changing economy. There seems to be general agreement by those who predict labor trends and by those who advocate specific vocational training in schools (as opposed to industrial arts training) that this specific training be postponed to the last year of high school and two years of post-high school.

_____Modifying the Psychological Environment

THIS brings us to the outermost aspect of Wrenn's three concentric circles, the counseling task itself. What must the counselor know about the psychological environment of the youth of the underclass? Perhaps the best answer to a question like this is that he must "meet him on his own turf." What distinguishes a street worker in the slums from any other individual who may do group work or youth work? Here again the term *charisma,* however elusive it may be, comes to mind. Someone who cares, someone who can show commitment, someone who is willing to extend himself personally and psychologically and to enter the world of the slum dweller. To the youth of the underclass the schools have no charisma.

In order for the counselor to understand the psychological environment of the youth of the underclass, he must develop in some way the charisma that is so difficult to define. He must be able to understand and to communicate with the slum dweller. The tools that he needs are those he would ordinarily receive in his professional training and they are related to the whole problem of whether the counselor is an activist, or whether he intervenes, or whether he remains available only to those who seek him out.

The Rankian concept of counseling and of social work is essentially a middle-class concept, whereas the activist concept is more applicable to working with a lower class. The Hull House concept of social work needs to be revived and adapted to present-day needs. The school in the slums is as much a social agency as it is an educational institution, and the counselor in an urban school is at once a social worker and an educational counselor.

How can the counselor develop the techniques to counsel youth from the underclass? They are best developed through active involvement and direct contact with residents of the inner city, sometimes referred to as indigenous persons. The school is not an island set apart from the community, but rather it is an active agent creating change within the community. It is incumbent, therefore, on the counselor to become a community worker, to be directly involved in community action programs, and indeed in the ferment that may occur within the community.

Through such involvement and through the charisma that he may be able to develop within his community, he may actually be able to learn about the psychological environment of "slum children," and develop the essential tools that he needs to communicate with these children and their parents. It is necessary to communicate directly with the people of the inner city. In educating the counselor to develop these understandings, our approach may well need to be anthropological. We may have to recognize that within our society an "alien" culture exists. With this recognition we may need to borrow the tools of the anthropologist, especially his field-study methods. Field study is as important as articulation and orientation.

Let us take a close look at one of the necessary guidance functions, articulation and orientation, as it evolves from junior high school to vocational school.

In New York City there are now more than 130 junior high schools that feed children into some thirty vocational schools. Some of these high schools have special entrance requirements; others do not. The process of exploration begins in the eighth grade where children consider various high school alternatives. Plans for school and vocation are discussed in a general way during group guidance classes. Depending on how enterprising the counselor or grade adviser is, the schools may be thoroughly researched and detailed information may be made available.

At the beginning of the ninth grade, youngsters who wish to take the various entrance examinations required by selective schools are rounded up, again depending on the enterprise of the counselors and

Arnold Buchheimer

grade advisers, and are prepared for the examinations. (The exams are usually tests of spatial visualization or mechanical aptitude, which emphasize an understanding of basic physical principles of mechanics.) Applications are filled out. Films are shown of prospective schools; wherever possible, speakers from schools are heard. Applications are then processed. From November to March the counselor is so involved in the bureaucratic web of processing applications, he has little time to do anything else. The children, for the most part, are an adjunct to the procedure, bringing in their papers on time, appearing in the right place at the right time. There is little actual exploration of the schools and their curricula themselves, nor is there opportunity for the children to explore their own interests and goals. Yet this decision certainly has vocational implications, even though the implications are minimized by recent findings. It seems that many graduates are not employed in the trade for which they are trained.

The entire orientation and articulation process is meant to orient the receiving school about the child to be received, rather than to orient the child about the school to which he is to go. Most counselors find this an arduous and frustrating task. Their quandary is aided and abetted by the operation of several biases:

1. Underachievement in school may be remedied through work with one's hands.

2. It is good to know a trade whether one has use for it or not.

3. It is good to go to school in a masculine environment.

4. A general diploma from an academic high school is better than a vocational diploma, or vice versa.

The able counselor believes none of these, but he does have to deal with them. In addition, particular schools have particular images. There has been a general decline in the vocational school enrollment over the past twenty years because of image, or lack of charisma.

The able counselor, furthermore, knows that he is acting contrary to the best knowledge in his field. From everything we know from our studies in vocational development, the end of junior high school is the time for vocational exploration rather than for decision-making. Yet, on the flimsiest of information, without any real exploration, a boy choosing a unit-trade high school is making a vocational decision.

Articulation and orientation in a typical urban school system is, by and large, a meaningless process to the children involved and a bureaucratic exercise to counselors. It is an exercise designed to accommodate to institutional rather than to children's needs.

Let us now examine the vocational counseling process. Understanding general vocational trends, personal abilities, interests and accomplishments, and local industrial conditions, and effecting a good synthesis of these three disparate forces, is a concept deeply ingrained in the guidance movement. But, on the other hand, the economist tells us this (Miller, in Schreiber, 1964, p. 18):

1. An anarchical, unorganized, inefficient labor market prevails.
2. Technological change is occurring at a rapid clip.
3. Economic growth is limited (an unusual event during technological innovation).
4. The push from rural and agricultural areas is leading the new migrants to large cities.

Another economist, Levine (1965), describes the economic picture as follows:

One school of thought attributes the unemployment situation to the failure of the economy to expand sufficiently. . . . Another school explains unemployment in terms of imbalances between the characteristics and qualifications of . . . job seekers and the hiring specifications and requirements of existing job openings.

In the face of these basic economic problems, how can the counselor take into account the "realities" of labor trends and labor conditions? The only course he has open to him is to counsel for potential, for the maximum utilization of personal abilities. This is especially true for the poor because the affluent or semiaffluent are employable by virtue of their status, though this may not be true much longer of white-collar workers. If a girl wishes to be an architect and has the gifts and interests for it, she should be encouraged to pursue her goal, regardless of the fact that this profession is now practically closed to women. If a Negro boy wants a trade that is presently closed to Negroes—the trades seem to be more closed than the professions—and he has the potential for the trade, he should be encouraged by the counselor to pursue his goal. Conditions of the labor force are simply not reliable enough to make valid predictions. We have a good idea of what jobs will not be, but we do not know what jobs will be.

In the case of the "occupational level" student, the recommended emphasis in training would be for the personal service professions such as restaurant, home maintenance, and the entry fields into the social

Arnold Buchheimer

service professions alluded to earlier. But one should be guarded about the present criteria of the occupational level child and the limits of educability these criteria employ. In the words of Samler (in Burchill, 1964, p. 71):

> [W]e are the people who hold the keys to unlock the doors. . . . None of our educational and counseling practices should be beyond questioning. . . . Aptitudes and capacities are trainable to a point. . . . Whatever it is, intelligence may or may not be genetic, but its development is strictly a product of culture as are the instruments that measure its functioning. Even modest increases in aptitudes and capacities would greatly ease the training problem.

So one of our tasks is not only to emphasize potential but to "increase" it as well.

Certainly our whole theory of intelligence testing has been called into question. We have to look again to see what these tests mean, how we interpret them, and what their relationship to achievement is. What can be done, honestly and with integrity, to improve scores? As guidance counselors and specialists in assessment, we have an important role to play. Intelligence testing is a valid and important practice. If the tests are no good or no longer appropriate, they need to be revised and made more representative.

_____Guidance Personnel and Training

WHAT kinds of people should staff the schools with which we are concerned? There is no point in reciting the standard requirements of vocational-education training or guidance training. The reader already knows them. They are, first, competence in a particular vocational area, and second, competence in the academic areas. In addition, guidance must have a pervasive point of view and a developmental point of view.

A teacher should be a person who can be a positive model to children, a person with whom they can identify, a person who can be direct without being authoritarian. Most of the recent studies about discipline confirm that discipline is not taught and behavior is not changed by a reward-and-punishment approach to learning. These studies indicate that acceptable behavior is learned from the models

Explorations in the Role of Guidance for Youth from the "Underclass"

that children have and by the identification with adults that they are able to make. It is especially important that children who have had poor models outside the school have good models within the school.

As has already been indicated, it is important that teachers who teach the disadvantaged can identify with them as persons, and with their problems and their conditions. This is probably a crucial dimension about which we still have a great deal to learn—an area in which we are most lacking.

A more specific characteristic is the capacity to deal with hostility without responding defensively or retaliating in a hostile manner. Finally, an important trait is flexibility, the capacity to meet a child where he is and to start there to help him grow at his own rate.

These characteristics of teachers have been listed so often that they sound like educational cliches. However, the last five are more often honored in the breach than in the observance.

A short time ago, some of the Job Corps personnel involved in urban centers revealed that they do not find vocational education or school guidance people very helpful in teaching their vocational education programs or in conducting their guidance activities. It took a long time to ferret out the basis for their dissatisfaction. Aside from the middle-class orientation, so often talked about, there are some more specific factors that need to be considered.

With regard to the classroom teacher, three factors seemed to be particularly crucial. They were (1) preoccupation with abstraction, (2) rigidity, and (3) language of condescension. Preoccupation with abstraction means that there is too much time spent on cerebral activity and not enough time on the physical, the actual concrete involvement with the job (the taking apart of the motor, the handling of the tools, and so on). The people in the Job Corps feel that their most successful experiences involve situations where the physical has preceded the cerebral. This is certainly not a new concept in education; but it is often violated.

Flexibility means something similar to what the programmed instruction people are talking about—the possibility of moving through a sequence of learning tasks without a prescribed time period. If, for example, a boy can build his own transistor radio in two weeks, and completes it by September 15th, he should not have to wait until October 15th, when the next unit is scheduled to begin. This is "customized" instruction in its most concrete form.

Arnold Buchheimer

The language of condescension is a phrase not unique to this chapter, though it seems very descriptive and appropriate here. It was alluded to in speaking of color sensitivity. The man who coined the phrase is, at the present time, developing a glossary of the language of condescension. Such phrases as "you people" and "boy" might be in this glossary.

So far as guidance personnel are concerned, the two crucial characteristics necessary for working with disadvantaged youth seem to be (1) a de-emphasis on verbal communication skills and (2) an understanding of primary and secondary relationships. Counselors are apt to demand highly verbal behavior from counselees. The disadvantaged youth is apt not to be very conventionally expressive in an interview. Thus the formal interview, as we know it, will not be particularly helpful. What is likely to be more helpful is the frequent, short, informal contact. This would require the counselor to be highly mobile, to be present in many places, and to be highly sensitive to situations and incidents as they arise. These incidents could then be dealt with on the spot, in the context in which they arose.

The problem of primary and secondary relationships is related to this point. The counselor and guidance person dealing with children from the underclass has to be much more like the parent than the counselor of a middle-class child. This is a broad distinction, but the counselor of the middle-class child is probably in the position where his role is one of counteracting parental influence where such influence has been too dominant; while the counselor of the child of the underclass is apt to be more like the parent. What the middle-class child will discuss with his parents and never bring to his counselor, the child from the underclass may well bring to his counselor if he learns to trust him.

When we talk of teaching and counseling children of the underclass, the basic competencies and basic training are similar for any school, and the basic preparation is the same. Sensitivity, however, is a very special factor; we know very little about how to train for it.

There has been much discussion about training teachers and counselors of the disadvantaged by exposing them to the children and the conditions under which these children live and go to school. Exposure is necessary, but exposure must be accompanied by identification. It does not help very much to expose a person to conditions and situations with which he cannot identify.

Explorations in the Role of Guidance for Youth from the "Underclass"

Summary

GUIDANCE is a point of view which fosters creative self-discovery and the personal artistry of coping with life's responsibilities and developmental tasks. It is a point of view which pervades the entire learning atmosphere of an institution.

The traditional guidance concepts of intelligence, aptitude, and achievement need to be thought through again. The current format of techniques of assessing these three basic aspects of behavior is not applicable to children of the underclass.

Motivation is as much a problem to the institution as it is to the persons with whom we are concerned. Much institutional behavior and many institutional demands are irrelevant to the needs of youth from the underclass, and perhaps from the middle class as well.

Effective techniques of dealing with these youths are predicated on the capacity of the worker, be he teacher or counselor, to identify with such youth, and for such youth to be able to identify with the worker and to see him as a model.

References

BUCHHEIMER, ARNOLD. "From Drudgery to Anxiety," *Vocational Guidance Quarterly,* Winter 1965.

———, JESSE GOODMAN, and GERALD SIRCUS. *Videotapes and Kinescopes as Situational Tests in the Training of Counselors.* Hunter College of the City University of New York, 1965.

BUCHHEIMER, NAOMI, and ARNOLD BUCHHEIMER. *Equality Through Integration.* New York: Anti-Defamation League, 1965.

BURCHILL, GEORGE W. *Work Study Program for Alienated Youth.* Chicago: Science Research Associates, 1962.

COLEMAN, JAMES S., et al. *Equality of Educational Opportunity.* Washington, D.C.: U. S. Office of Education, Government Printing Office, OE-38001, 1966.

FRIEDENBERG, EDGAR Z. *The Vanishing Adolescent.* New York: Dell Publishing Co., 1959.

GOODMAN, PAUL. *Compulsory Miseducation.* New York: Horizon Press, 1964.

Arnold Buchheimer

HABER, ALAN. "The American Underclass." Ann Arbor, Michigan: Institute of Labor and Industrial Relations, 1965. (Unpublished manuscript.)

Harlem Youth Opportunities Unlimited. *Youth in the Ghetto.* New York, 1964.

KATZ, MARTIN. *Decisions and Values.* New York: College Entrance Examination Board, 1963.

KILLENS, JOHN OLIVER. *And Then Came the Thunder.* New York: Pocket Books, 1964.

LEVINE, LOUIS. "Implications of the Anti-Poverty Program for Education and Employment," *Vocational Guidance Quarterly,* 14 (1965), 8–15.

PEARL, ARTHUR, and FRANK RIESSMAN. *New Careers for the Poor.* New York: The Free Press, 1965.

Public Education Association. *Reorganizing Secondary Education in New York City.* New York: 1963.

SCHREIBER, DANIEL (ed.). *The School Dropout.* Washington, D.C.: National Education Association, 1964.

U. S. Commission on Civil Rights. *Racial Isolation in the Public Schools,* Vols. I and II. Washington, D.C., 1967.

University of the State of New York. *Developing Work-Study Programs for Potential Dropouts.* New York, 1965.

_____Additional Sources

BRYAN, H. M., and R. D. WENRICH. *Vocational Education and Practical Arts in the Community School.* New York: Macmillan Co., 1956.

California State Board of Education. *Interim California Plan for Vocational Education.* Sacramento: California State Department, 1964.

CONANT, JAMES B. *The American High School Today.* New York: McGraw-Hill Book Co., 1959.

———. *Slums and Suburbs.* New York: McGraw-Hill Book Co., 1961.

DAVIDOFF, LOUIS. "Staffing Difficult Schools," *Strengthening Democracy,* 8, No. 15 (1956).

MAYER, MARTIN. *The Schools.* New York: Harper & Row, 1961.

McKEAN, ROBERT C., and H. H. MILLS. *The Supervisor.* Washington, D.C.: The Center for Applied Research in Education, 1964.

MILLER, C. DEAN, and EDWARD STANSON (eds.). *Automation, the Threat and the Promise.* Washington, D.C.: National Vocational Guidance Association, 1964.

MOORE, G. ALEXANDER, JR. *Realities of the Urban Classroom. Observations in Elementary Schools.* New York: Praeger, 1967.

Publication Education Association. *The Secondary School Program in New York City.* New York, 1964.

RIVLIN, HARRY N. *Teachers for the Schools in Our Big Cities.* New York: The City University of New York, 1962.

SAVITSKY, CHARLES. "Social Theory Advances on the Disadvantaged," *High Points,* 46, No. 2 (1964), 54 ff.

SLAYTON, WILLIAM L. "The Influence of Urban Renewal on Education," *School Life,* June 1962, 9–12.

SMITH, HAROLD T. *Education and Training for the World of Work.* Kalamazoo, Mich.: Upjohn Institute for Employment Research, 1963.

SPELLMAN, OLGA. "Staffing Difficult Schools," *Strengthening Democracy,* 8, No. 5(1956).

U. S. Department of Health, Education, and Welfare. *The Vocational Education Act of 1963.* Washington, D.C.: Government Printing Office, 1965.

————. *Vocational Technical Education for American Industry.* Circular No. 530. Washington, D.C.: Government Printing Office, 1958.

————. *Administration of Vocational Education.* Bulletin No. 1, General Series No. 1. Washington, D.C.: U. S. Government Printing Office, Rev., 1958.

78
Arnold Buchheimer

5 Special Education for Teachers of Disadvantaged Youth

William R. Carriker

THE PENNSYLVANIA STATE UNIVERSITY

THE INHERENT WORTH of each child is not given to him by man; it is his birthright. This right sets the individual above the state, and the purpose of education should be focused on the development of the individual; any benefits that accrue to the state should be secondary to those derived by the individual. Therefore, every child has a right to share in and to expect to benefit from the educational system, which is a common wealth of our nation. Whether or not he can materially contribute to its support should not jeopardize this right.

Problems of exceptional children and disadvantaged youth are somewhat parallel as they relate to this philosophy and to the definition of equal educational opportunities. Both groups have suffered as a result of apathy or lack of understanding.

Probably Dr. Conant's *Social Dynamite* (National Committee for

Children and Youth, 1961) was the stimulus that set off the fuse in awakening the public from its apathy toward the critical need for an appropriate education for deprived youth. The field of special education began to move from its doldrums in the late 'forties and early 'fifties but did not really surge until the early 'sixties, and then especially because of the impact of federal legislation under Public Law 88–164. It was shortly thereafter that the war on poverty began, along with special concern for the education of disadvantaged youth.

The definitions that can be found pertaining to disadvantaged youth are varied (compare, for example, Bloom, Davis, and Hess, 1965; Frost, Hawkes, et al., 1966; Crow, Murray, and Smythe, 1966). However, each has included or implied in his definition such factors as educational retardation, lack of motivation due to years of futility and failure, and disorganized cognitive development due to environmental depressants.

One could almost modify the same elements for the education of the disadvantaged child as are involved in the education of the exceptional child. These modifications of the usual school programs are generally made in regard to specially trained personnel, special methods or materials, and special facilities. Most definitions of special education for exceptional children include these three elements.

Dunn (1963, p. 2) defines exceptional pupils as "those (1) who differ from the average to such a degree in physical or psychological characteristics (2) that school programs designed for the majority of children do not afford them opportunity for all-round adjustment and optimum progress, (3) and who therefore need either special instruction or in some cases special ancillary services, or both, to achieve at a level commensurate with their respective abilities." As is readily seen, this definition could well be applied to the disadvantaged.

In the following discussion, a number of statements will be made in regard to the education of exceptional children. Following each will be a brief discussion pertaining to such special education and how this relates to the education of the disadvantaged.

1. *Wide individual differences exist among children within each area of exceptionality as well as among children within each special class for exceptional children.*

Most of the following discussion will refer to special programs or classes designed for the mentally retarded or the emotionally disturbed. Although separate classes for the retarded have been established on a national basis, they are not alike. Evidence of this can be found in the

William R. Carriker

large numbers of different curriculum guides being used throughout the nation as well as in the many different administrative organizational structures being used in an effort to meet the needs of the retarded children.

Even within each class of retarded children there will be found a wide range of individual differences. They will be alike in only one way in that they will be educationally retarded. Even in this aspect their abilities and educational achievements will vary significantly. In addition to educational retardation there is a wide variance in their ability to do abstract thinking. In many cases one or more other handicapping conditions are in evidence. They certainly, as a group, have more than their share of sensory, speech, neuromuscular, and emotional handicaps.

The educational programs for the disadvantaged must also be designed to meet the wide variances among individual needs. Certainly the *basic* needs of disadvantaged youth in the slums of metropolitan areas are the same as are the *basic* needs of disadvantaged youth in small, run-down coal-mining communities in Appalachia. However, the way of meeting these basic needs must be different, as is evidenced by the various types of curricula being used from one area to another plus different administrative organizational structures.

As in the special classes, there is also a wide range of individual differences among disadvantaged youth. They are alike only in that they are affected by deprivation that has resulted in various degrees of educational retardation. Their remaining handicapping conditions will vary in degree as a result of the severity of the impact of such factors as physical or mental illnesses in the home; family unit disintegration; poverty; inability of the family to cope with the demands of modern urban living; and deep-rooted family history of educational and cultural deprivation.

As can be seen, there are likes and differences between the two groups, that is, the exceptional and the disadvantaged. To assume however that all groups of mentally retarded or any other special group are alike or that all groups of disadvantaged are alike is a false assumption.

2. *There is a need for early screening, identification, and school placement in special programs if exceptional children are to make maximum progress.*

Probably no phase of educational planning should receive as much attention as that which could be done during the first five years of a child's life and in his first year of school. The results of overlooking problems at this level are very costly, not only emotionally but economically as well. Ideally, children who are likely to have school problems should be identified and their needs met before the problems obtain.

Kirk (1958) concluded, from data based on eighty-one children between the ages of three and six with IQ's from 45 to 80, that those retarded children who were from inadequate homes tended to retain their rate of development or dropped in their rate of development as they grew older. He also felt that his data gave evidence that the reversal of this tendency could be accomplished if compensatory environments such as preschool programs were provided. Foster-home placement and preschool experience resulted in an even more marked changed in the developmental rate. These results lend support to the value of early educational treatment as a way of increasing the rate of mental growth of children from psychosocially deprived homes.

Too often educable retarded children are placed in special classrooms after they have learned how to be failures. Early identification and placement is especially important in relation to emotionally disturbed children too. A preventive program should be provided for them rather than to wait until it becomes necessary to provide a therapeutic and corrective program. With a preventive program, the chances for success in relation to the welfare of the child will be much greater.

This particular need for early identification and treatment is as true for disadvantaged youth as for retarded youngsters. Because problem areas can be recognized, certainly there ought to be an effort made to do something about them. This is one of the major purposes of Project Headstart. Even with all of its problems and certain questions that have resulted, this program offers real potential, especially if it can be continued beyond its present typical offering of six to eight weeks in the summer. There will, of course, be a need for a continual upgrading of the personnel involved and many of the facilities being used.

A considerable body of theory and research evidence supports the concept of the value of the first years of life as being a critical period for later learning. This evidence can be found in such animal studies as those by Hess (1959), Scott (1963), and Harlow (1962). Their evidence seems to point to the fact that deprivation of social interaction during early life will probably result in inappropriate behavioral patterns at a later period, and that the behavior may be irreversible. For example, Harlow's monkeys who were reared with artifical mothers were unable to breed and care for their own offspring as well as animals reared by real mothers.

William R. Carriker

3. *Comprehensive case study and planning will involve a team of medical, social, psychological, and educational specialists but educational diagnosis and placement must be the responsibility of the educational agency.*

This particular position is one that states, in essence, that educators cannot stand alone in relation to the total welfare of an exceptional child. In an effort to meet the needs of an exceptional child, the various disciplines must be involved and their positions stated, their findings reported and integrated into a total educational program designed for the needs of the individual child. The educational program becomes the responsibility of the education authority in charge.

It appears that there is an analogy between the program planning for special education and for an educational program planned for disadvantaged youth. In both programs there must be a reliance upon the sociologists, the psychologists, the anthropologists, the political scientists, and the economists as the program relates to an effective educational curriculum for disadvantaged youth. However, the responsibility for coordinating and implementing this educational program rests finally upon the shoulders of the educators.

4. *Successful special education classes for various types of exceptional children are dependent upon meaningful criteria for placement so that children with other types of needs and problems are not inappropriately enrolled.*

As possible teacher training programs for disadvantaged youth are developed, attention should be given to avoid the position in which the discipline of special education has found itself, namely, compartmentalization and possibly inappropriate classification placement and serving of children. The recent past-president of the Council for Exceptional Children, Harry M. Selznick, has suggested that the discipline of special education reconsider the classification and grouping of pupils found in special education programs over the past years. He states (1965, p. 357):

> Although good programs of training provide the special educator with broad aspects of understanding he is essentially an educator. The techniques and skills which he brings to the school situation are intended to enhance the learning opportunities for the children with whom he works. Too often the children are placed in a given class because of a similarity in a medical diagnostic label rather than because of a similarity in learning needs. We, in special education, must recognize our areas of competence and direct our energies and

attention to the types of groupings which will best contribute to the accomplishment of our responsibilities. Although we are educators, we have permitted medical diagnostic labels to bring about type compartmentations which frequently bear little relation to learning needs and abilities.

There should be an avoidance of classifying for educational purposes all disadvantaged into one or more categories based on such criteria as socioeconomically deprived, Negro culture, urban, rural, and so on. From experiences gained from special education, it seems that educational compensatory experiences via special classes for the culturally deprived should be based on the individual needs as identified within the groups that are to be served.

5. *There is a need for specialized curriculum, materials, and equipment.*

This position has been held by the discipline of special education for many years. Obviously, the quantity and type will vary from area to area of exceptionality. For example, the specialized needs in the area of the mentally retarded certainly differ from those in the area of the physically handicapped or of the visually handicapped. The variances in ways of meeting the needs within a special area are not nearly as obvious as the variances between areas and the tangible changes in the improvement of school facilities, special equipment, and so on. For example, if one were to look at the changes in classroom methods that have taken place in the teaching of retarded children over the past few years, one might have some difficulty in seeing any basic differences. This seems to be so, even though there is some factual evidence in regard to special materials and curricula differences.

Many of the materials are designed to meet the needs of the retarded through using concrete approaches, avoiding abstract principles, and use of materials that are within the realm of the retarded child's community. Ideally, the process of teaching should include tangible and immediate reinforcement of appropriate behavior, overlearning, and minimal change.

The analogy to be drawn between the retarded and the deprived is that probably the child's alienation from the school is not so much of a reflection of discriminatory or rejecting attitudes from the teachers and other personnel but rather of a curriculum that is too demanding. As a result there is a cumulative effect of frustration, confusion, resentment, and lowering of self-confidence, which will inevitably result in failure, aggression, and withdrawal, and eventual dropping out.

William R. Carriker

6. *There is a need for individualized teaching of a clinical nature based upon each pupil's abilities and disabilities.*

This position as it relates to individualized teaching procedures is not new. Kirk (1953) stated emphatically that special education should be based on clinical procedures. This type of teaching—that is, clinical teaching—must involve the identification of the specific learning problems manifested by the child and then the remediation according to effective principles of learning. It is probable, however, that too many special education teachers have not been trained in clinical teaching procedures. Many, however, who have had an opportunity to involve themselves with clinical teaching procedures based on differential diagnosis have dropped the procedures by the wayside, not because they do not wish to use this approach but because its use is almost impossible as it relates to the type of grouping that has taken place.

As teacher training programs for disadvantaged youth are developed, consideration might be given to the following direction for grouping of exceptional children, which was suggested by Selznick (1965). He recommended that grouping be on the basis of communication disorders, behavioral disorders, or special learning disorders. He felt that various programs and services could be developed for children who possessed one or a combination of disorders. Each child could receive a special service or a combination of special services, and clinical teaching could be provided in each of the classrooms so that a variety of approaches might be tried with the individual child.

In an effort to further the possibility of effective individualized and clinical teaching procedures for the disadvantaged, grouping could be based on certain major disorders or combinations of disorders found within the disadvantaged groups. These might include communication, behavioral acting out, and special learning disorders.

Riessman (1962) has suggested a number of characteristics that represent the pattern or style of the deprived child which could well be utilized as a baseline for individualized instruction and clinical teaching. He suggests that instruction be oriented toward such factors as: (1) physical and visual activities; (2) content- and problem-centered experiences; (3) inductive thinking activities; (4) external cues; and (5) slow, careful, and patient procedure in areas that are particularly important to them. These characteristics should also be considered very carefully as the baselines from which to develop an individualized and clinical teaching approach with the disadvantaged.

As proposed by Ausubel (1966, pp. 237–238), there are three considerations that must be emphasized in the teaching of the disadvantaged; these are also appropriate in teaching the retarded:

> (a) [T]he selection of initial learning material geared to the learner's existing state of readiness; (b) mastery and consolidation of all ongoing learning tasks before new tasks are introduced, so as to provide the necessary foundation for successful sequential learning and to prevent unreadiness for future learning tasks; and (c) the use of structured learning materials optionally organized to facilitate efficient sequential learning.

7. *There is a need for a continuous re-evaluation of children, school programs, and teacher education programs.*

In reference to evaluation of the effectiveness of special class placement versus regular class placement of retarded individuals, one would have to say the whole field of special education is still in a turmoil. Present research seems to indicate that there are no basic differences between the two in relation to the achievement and probably the social competencies of the retarded child. There have been some basic methodological flaws in research design pertaining to these kinds of research projects. However, in regard to special classes for the retarded, Sparks and Blackman (1965, pp. 245–246) make the following observation:

> [P]roof must be forthcoming that there is more special about special education than the children assigned to these classes. If the null hypothesis relating to the differences between regular and special classes cannot be rejected, then the field of special education represented primarily by teacher trainers and administrators, will be required to do some soul searching.

They go on to discuss the problem as it relates to the special teacher training:

> A survey of the literature to determine whether the special teacher's approach to the special child actually differs from the regular teacher's approach to the normal child did not unearth a single study comparing the two teaching procedures on any dimension. A review of the literature to determine the basis of sequences of courses leading to certification of a teacher of educable mentally retarded children reveals no validation study nor any claims for teaching the mentally retarded. On the basis of existing evidence, it is only possible to conclude that the special education teacher has superior qualifications to teach exceptional children to the degree that the consensus of intelligence and experience of special edu-

William R. Carriker

cators is accepted. Empirical proof of the validity of special preparation does not exist.

This sounds awful and rather damning. However, the area of special education does not seem to stand alone in relation to this criticism.

Cyphert (1964, p. 1) stated in his summary report of a conference on research in teacher education:

Preeminent among the problems which teacher education today is fraught is its apparent inability to provide for its own systematic improvement. Concomitantly the extant research in teacher education is neither extensive nor profound. Existing teacher education research has had only a minimal impact upon teacher preparation and curriculum. Teacher education content and method have been generated almost exclusively on logical ground without explicit empirical reference to a clear definition of criterion behavior and has been neither empirically validated nor refuted.

An additional contention is that research in teacher education has been poorly conceived and defined so as to exclude from study perhaps the most important elements of the education of teachers. Much of the educational research which might have implications for restructuring teacher education is not integrated with the literature of teacher education. Many would contend that teacher education research has been approached in the main in an unimaginative fashion and with no communicable conceptual frame of reference.

The opportunity to evaluate programs for the disadvantaged is here and now. Evaluation should be an integral part of the development of a curriculum to train teachers of disadvantaged youth as well as the curriculum designed for the children. Some of the general questions that need to be answered include: (1) Is there a need for special grouping? (2) What are the realities of the stated goals? (3) Are the characteristics that obtain in the disadvantaged irreversible? (4) Can local schools assume the financial responsibility without Federal support? and (5) Can the school expect significant changes in the disadvantaged without accompanying changes in the family structure and community?

8. *Each student needs placement assistance and should be contacted periodically after he leaves school.*

This particular statement has become of special concern within the past decade. The work-study program for educable mentally retarded, secondary age youngsters is now a blooming and successful program. It has been known for a number of years that retarded individuals could hold various types of jobs, but no concerted and systematic effort was made to bring the mentally retarded to the job nor to introduce the employer to the capabilities manifested by the educable mentally retarded. Placement, assistance, and follow-up are not the sole responsibility of the school, however. Effective follow-up and placement of individuals should be an integral part of the total interdisciplinary program planning for educable retarded individuals and probably can be one of the most important facets of program planning for disadvantaged youth.

They, both the retarded and the disadvantaged, need to have a focal point of help; for example, if problems develop with the employer, they should be able to come back to an individual within the school for counsel, guidance, and assistance. Syden (1962, p. 331) summarizes such a coordinated program as follows:

> During the past decade many school systems have inaugurated programs for the educable mentally retarded of secondary school age. . . . Curriculum content, whether organized under traditional titles or under core units of study, is socio-occupationally oriented. The goals of the program are to develop the individual's capabilities and assist him in discovering his place in the economic society upon completion of his formal schooling. In addition to academics taught by special education teachers and electives in classes for normal students, the special education curriculum (for the educable mentally retarded) provides for work experience as a bridge between school and the world of work coordinated and correlated by special education personnel.

As attempts are made to delve into special programs for teacher training and to determine what methods and competencies are important, it would be well to reconsider what Dewey (1913, p. 202) has to say about methods:

> Strictly speaking, method is thoroughly individual. Each has his own instinctive way of going at a thing; the attitude and the mode of the approach and attack are individual. To ignore this individuality of approach, to try to substitute for it under the name of "general method," a uniform scheme of procedure, is simply to cripple the only effective agencies of operation and to overlay them with the mechanical formalism that produces only a routine conventionality of mental quality.

Consideration might also be given to the experiences gained by the group at the Norfolk Division of Virginia State College. Their research demonstration project concerned with training the hard-core unem-

William R. Carriker

ployed has provided some profitable insights for those concerned with specialized teacher education programs. Brooks (1964, p. 116), emphasizing the aspect of the worthwhileness of the individual and of the dignity of man, makes the following observation:

> Before the project could be considered a success, the ninety men who had been recruited and trained had to be employed on jobs which would allow them and their families to live at a decent standard. To many, this was the proof of the project (the pretraining workshop with industrial and business men was helpful at the time of employment) yet the project team had to overcome patterns of discrimination in some areas [and] skepticism. . . .
>
> The crowning point . . . was the rising sense of dignity and worth in the men. . . . It was a thing that gradually caused hitherto shy and deprived men to talk with pride and confidence when people in high positions from all parts of the Nation came and sat in their classrooms. . . . It is the story of a working commitment to the dignity of man, it is the story of the kind of deep experiences that may become the heart of manpower, poverty and other programs that will help the disadvantaged and defeated climb up on the main road of human dignity.

Summary

AN ATTEMPT has been made to review ways in which a number of the educational problems of the disadvantaged are analogous to those of the exceptional (retarded) child. Likewise, there are many comparable problems in the planning of special programs and the training of teachers. Some of the aspects referred to were the following:

1. Both the disadvantaged and the exceptional child have suffered as a result of apathy and lack of understanding.

2. The area of special education received an additional impetus from and the needs for the disadvantaged were recognized with programs initiated during the early 'sixties.

3. Both the retarded and the disadvantaged are educationally retarded.

4. Both the retarded and the disadvantaged are not achieving at their best levels owing to such factors as lack of motivation as a result of past failure and environmental depressants that result in disorganized cognitive development.

5. Both the groups need specially trained personnel, methods, materials, and in some cases, facilities.

6. There are wide individual differences both within groups of retarded youth and within groups of disadvantaged youth.

7. Evidence from research that reports the debilitating effect of early deprivation on later behavior has special implications for educational programming for both the retarded and the disadvantaged.

8. The need for a team approach of specialists from various disciplines has been pointed to as an effective procedure in meeting the needs of both groups.

9. The importance of an individualized teaching approach of a clinical nature was referred to as a common need.

10. Both groups have the same need for assistance and follow-up in job placement in an effort to maximize their success on the job.

References

AUSUBEL, D. P. "A Teaching Strategy for Culturally Deprived Pupils: Cognitive and Motivational Considerations," in *The Disadvantaged Child Issues and Motivations,* eds. J. L. Frost and G. R. Hawkes. Boston: Houghton Mifflin Co., 1966, 237–238.

BLOOM, B. S., A. DAVIS, and R. HESS. *Compensatory Education for Culture Deprivation.* New York: Holt, Rinehart & Winston, 1965.

BROOKS, L. B. "The Norfolk State College Experiment in Training the Hard-Core Unemployed," *Phi Delta Kappa,* 46 (November 1964).

CROW, L. D., W. I. MURRAY, and H. H. SMYTHE. *Educating the Culturally Disadvantaged Child. Principles and Programs.* New York: David McKay Co., 1966.

CYPHERT, F. R., et al. *An Analysis and Projection of Research in Teacher Education,* Cooperative Research Number F-015, Ohio State University Research Foundation, 1965.

DEWEY, J. "Method," in *A Cyclope of Education,* ed. M. P. Monroe. New York: Macmillan Co., 1913, 202–205.

DUNN, L. M. (ed.). *Exceptional Children in the Schools.* New York: Holt, Rinehart & Winston, 1963.

FROST, J. L., and G. R. HAWKES (eds.). *The Disadvantaged Child: Issues and Innovations.* Boston: Houghton Mifflin Co., 1966.

HARLOW, H. F. "The Heterosexual Affectional System in Monkeys," *American Psychologist,* 17 (1962), 1–9.

HESS, E. H. "The Relationship Between Imprinting and Motivation," in *Nebraska Symposium on Motivation,* ed. Edward E. Jones. Lincoln, Neb.: University of Nebraska Press, 1959, 44–47.

KIRK, S. A. "What Is Special About Special Education?" *Exceptional Child,* 19 (1953), 138–142.

————. *Early Education of the Mentally Retarded.* Urbana, Ill.: University of Illinois Press, 1958.

National Committee for Children and Youth. *Social Dynamite—The Report of the Conference on Unemployed Out-of-School Youth in Urban Areas,* 1961.

RIESSMAN, FRANK. *The Culturally Deprived Child.* New York: Harper & Row, 1962.

SCOTT, J. P. "The Process of Primary Socialization in Canine and Human Infants," *Monograph of the Society for Research in Child Development,* 28 (1963).

SELZNICK, H. M. "Direction for Future Action." *Exceptional Child,* 31 (March 1965), 357.

SPARKS, H. L., and L. S. BLACKMAN. "What is Special About Special Education Revisited: The Mentally Retarded," *Exceptional Child,* 31 (January 1965), 242–247.

SYDEN, M. "Preparation for Work: An Aspect of the Secondary Schools' Curriculum for Mentally Retarded Youth," *Exceptional Child,* 28 (February 1962), 331.

ZEDLER, E. Y. "Public Opinion and Public Education of the Exceptional Child—Court Decisions 1873–1950," *Exceptional Child,* 19 (1953), 187–198.

6 The Teacher in the Education of the Disadvantaged: An Educational Perspective

Donald Maley

UNIVERSITY OF MARYLAND

THIS CHAPTER DEALS with two groups of teachers involved in the education of the disadvantaged individual in the vocational curriculum. The first section will be devoted to the vocational teacher, with emphasis on his special requirements. The second section will attempt to establish the direct relationship between the vocational teachers and the "continuum of teachers" that the individual experiences, extending from the early primary years to those of the vocational levels.

The Vocational Teacher

THIS discussion is based on the assumption that vocational and occupational teacher education programs will be successful to the extent that they can produce the quantity and quality of teachers who have the interest and desire to teach boys and girls, as well as men and women, with wide ranges of social and economic differences, of ability, and background in the technological process and advancements of society.

This does not mean that any one or several teachers would be capable of such versatility. The essence of the requirement is that there be a sufficient quantity of quality teachers at each level of need in order to accomplish the ends of education in a society in which the dignity of man, his maximum development, and his maximum contribution are of primary concern.

This presentation is devoted to a projection of the kind of person the teacher-education curriculum would hope to produce. This is a discussion of the *quality goal* for the proposed curriculum.

The early establishment of statements describing the product of a curriculum would provide the goals or objectives that the curriculum could be designed to achieve. The statements presented here have been developed as a result of a broad study of the vocational and occupational fields and of a number of years of dedicated observation of the trends in occupations and vocations. The following ten points are also a result of prolonged analyses of the requirements of those who teach in these fields. Each of the ten points is followed by a statement or rationale that supports the teacher quality under discussion. It is also important to mention that the writer has no delusions about the absolute inclusiveness of the qualities.

The following ten points are presented as teacher quality goals or objectives towards which the ultimate curriculum growing out of this study may be directed:

1. *The vocational teacher of the future must acquire a sensitivity to the changing role of man in relation to work.*

This sensitivity must be developed to a depth that will permit the teacher not only to generalize on its consequences, but also to design learning experiences that will enable the student to assimilate the concept into his attitudes and behavior.

Venn, in *Man, Education, and Work* (1964, p. 1), wrote about "a new relationship between man, his education, and his work, in which education is placed squarely between man and his work." Essentially, this is an emphasis on the role of education in the affairs of man. It not only presents education as the key to the door that opens into the world of work, but it also implies that education will be imperative to continue to work.

The importance of education and the pressing need for increased education in the future is well known. What is important in this respect is to have teachers who are capable of such attitudinal stimulation of the student. Likewise, it is important that the teacher recognize this same fact in his own development.

2. *The teacher of the future will be required to interpret and make use of research findings and community analyses far beyond the activities of his predecessor in these areas.*

The current multidisciplinary emphasis in vocational education is clear evidence of the trend of thought in this area. It is an obvious outgrowth of inadequacies found in the past education of vocational teachers and administrators.

Vocational education can no longer afford the easy route of selected students or compilations of skills to be taught based upon a narrow interpretation of the trade. Nor can it base the program of studies on a limited local industries' pressure or survey for specific skills. Teachers, administrators, community representatives, and a host of consulting personnel will form the backbone of future curriculum development activities. This will require that the preparation of teachers in this field involve a greater insight into the factors that affect vocational education in the contemporary age. It will require a working knowledge of the tools and findings of research and scholarship by which such insights are developed.

The narrowness of the traditional teacher preparation processes and requirements have definitely set the vocational teacher apart from the other professionals in education. This is especially obvious in the areas of research, scholarship, and cross-discipline utilization.

3. *The vocational teacher of the future will place greater emphasis on people—the development of people rather than the making of things by his students.*

The central issue here is one of putting first business first. The only defensible product of the American vocational school is people. This concern for people is excellently portrayed in a 1961 publication by the President's Commission on National Goals (p. 3):

> The status of the individual must remain our primary concern. All our institutions—political, social, and economic—must further enhance the dignity of the citizen, promote the maximum development of his capabilities, stimulate their responsible exercise, and widen the range and effectiveness of opportunities for individual choice.

The attitude has prevailed among too many vocational educators and administrators that display-case filling, project fairs, as well as state and national project contests are the primary goals of instruction. The professional teacher must develop the thinking that all of the school's equipment, libraries, laboratories, and personnel have but one function —the maximizing of the performance of the individual. Essentially, what this means is that the teacher's attitude and his actions will cause him to diligently pursue the task of making Johnny or Mary the best persons they are capable of becoming. This notion of teaching would cause the vocational teacher to take greater interest in the psychology of human behavior, learning theory, human growth and development, and sociology. The tools of teaching are in essence the principles of psychology that aid the teacher in his efforts to affect a change in the student's behavior or intellectual equipment. The tools, machines, materials, and devices commonly found in the laboratory are merely the assisting implements through which these other behavioral changing tools work.

This effort in behalf of people cannot be accomplished in a splintered process with each teacher or segment of the school acting independently. The human grows as an organism and it is essential that the educational establishment direct its attention accordingly. This would call for a team concept with the total faculty being the team members. This idea alone is worthy of considerable emphasis in the teacher education curriculum.

4. *The vocational teacher of the future will find himself a specialist among other specialists in the professional setting.*

This is not to merely infer a specialization by such categories as agriculture, trade and industries, business, or home economics. The specialization will go beyond the specialities of clothing or foods for home economics, or the specialities of machining, plumbing, carpentry, or electricity for the trades and industries person. What is meant here is the specialist among people—the specialist in dealing *effectively* with the disadvantaged, the specialist for working with the dropout, and the specialist for working with such other groups as the "slow," the accelerated, the highly skilled, or the man on the job who needs new skills because of displacement. It has been clear that these specialities call for different people, and the records of teaching will amply attest to this point. The teacher requirements are considerably different for those who teach the boy or girl from the disadvantaged socioeconomic sectors of the society than they are for the teacher who deals with the highly skilled and advanced technical aspects of vocational education.

Donald Maley

The implications for the teacher education curriculum would stress the need for more specialized courses in sociology, anthropology, communications, and special education for certain teachers. Others may require concentrations of work in the sciences, adult education, economics, and so on.

5. *The teacher of the future will be much more skillful in the design of learning experiences.*

The true artistry in teaching and ultimately the net result of education is dependent upon this very important design facility on the part of the teacher. Ralph Tyler, in *Basic Principles of Curriculum and Instruction* (1955, p. 41), emphasizes this point as follows:

> The term "learning experience" refers to the interaction between the learner and the external conditions in the environment to which he can react. Learning takes place through the active behavior of the student; it is what he does that he learns, not what the teacher does. It is possible for two students to be in the same class and for them to be having two different experiences.

The concept of environment is one of the problems of education in the traditional sense. The isolationism of the school from the great laboratory of life has indeed restricted the potential for learning as well as the teacher's design of learning experiences. The vocational setting in the school with the usual laboratory facilities provides an opportunity for creative and ingenious learning-experience design that many of the academic settings lack. The vocational setting in the school provides the opportunity for planning, constructing, experimenting, testing, evaluating, researching, demonstrating, lecturing, viewing and listening of all forms, as well as many other kinds of student experiences.

6. *The vocational teacher of the future will be required to have an adequate and ever-increasing knowledge about, as well as an increasing facility with, the newer media of instruction.*

The vocational teacher of the future will constantly find himself faced with a need for the tools of teaching. These will be vastly different from the tools of the vocational or occupational area he teaches. These tools with proper use are designed to affect the processes of communication, and in turn to have an influence on the behavior of humans. Such devices as television, radio, teaching machines, pupil-response mechanisms, projectors of all kinds, tape recorders, bulletin boards, chalk boards, models, mockups, collections, specimens, charts, graphs, maps, and many more (new and old) will constitute the tools of the professional teacher.

The effective use of these items is a must in a society experiencing an explosion of knowledge, a society dedicated to the education of all its people, and a society witnessing a population explosion. Furthermore, this need is emphasized by an increasing demand on the intellectual and performance requirements of the individual.

7. *The future teacher of vocational education must be more articulate about his work and his purposes than has been the case with past teachers in this area.*

One of the serious areas of deficiency among vocational and occupational teachers is that of not being capable, and at times willing, to discuss their work, their purposes, and the values of their work. Yet, if these teachers are to be effective in the *broad* range of their responsibilities, and if the support and strengthening of vocational and occupational education is to come from the teaching staffs in these areas, it is apparent that verbal articulation is essential. The decisions in faculty meetings, Parent-Teacher Association meetings, and board of education meetings are dependent upon such articulation in all areas, and vocational education needs strengthening at all levels in this respect.

8. *The vocational and occupational teacher of the future will possess new and varied dimensions of skill and knowledge pertinent to his area of instruction.*

The teacher will be required to be competent at the level of the occupational scale he teaches. This implies a core of teachers operating at different levels within a given area of study. It also implies a differentiation in the background and skill requirement for the teacher at the various levels.

This principle grows out of a realistic observation that all students in a vocational machine shop are not going to be master mechanics. There are students in the vocational programs that will stretch their ability to attain occupational competency at the lowest level, and it is important that this group be given full concern and the fullest assistance in becoming what they can.

This range-of-skill concept has strong implications for the utilization of maximum teaching manpower in an age of great shortages. This same concept may also produce a greater degree of compatibility between the teacher and the students at the several levels.

9. *The vocational teacher of the future must assume a more positive attitude toward his opportunities and value in the total educational picture.*

His concept of himself should be that of a significant contributor

Donald Maley

to society. His actions and his belief in his work should demonstrate to his colleagues, his community, and the nation the high purpose and value of his work. This point is brought into focus in a statement made by Dr. Vernon Anderson, Dean of the College of Education at the University of Maryland:

> At times I hear a teacher of one of the specialized fields virtually apologize for the fact that his subject does not appeal to the intellect, in this day of stress on intellectual attainment. Scholarship does not reside in a subject. The study of a subject becomes alive, an adventure in research, an experience in discovery, a scholarly pursuit, if the teacher has the insight and understanding to make it so.

10. *The vocational teacher of the future will be required to undergo a constant process of self-renewal.*

This process of self-renewal is not something that automatically happens. Furthermore, certification and recertification requirements are not the answer to this problem. Self-renewal, to be effective, must stem from an attitude within the individual and should be the concern of teacher education, and ultimately of the whole of society.

The need for self-renewal in the individual becomes apparent as a rapidly changing society forces changes in the curriculum. Thus, the teacher as well as the substance of his actions (the curriculum) must undergo this constant process of renewal. The sensitivity to change in the curriculum is stressed by Smith, Stanley, and Shores (1965, p. 12) as follows:

> Since the curriculum is interwoven with the whole cultural fabric, it follows that as the culture undergoes serious modifications the curriculum will become an object of concern, especially among the more sensitive members of the teaching profession and of the society at large. The adequacy of the old curriculum for the new cultural circumstances will be searchingly questioned and changes in the curriculum proposed.

How can the teacher education process effectively deal with the behavior of the future teacher in the area of self-renewal? The previous ten points describing the general requirements for occupational and vocational teachers were an attempt to establish quality goals for a teacher education curriculum. The recognition or acceptance of such goals has numerous implications for curriculum development:

1. Teacher education must establish within the future teacher a sensitivity to the world about him and the impact of the social, economic, and the technological forces upon his area of instruction.

2. Teacher education will need to devote appropriate time and effort to the processes and procedures for community analysis, including the occupational, social, economic, and educational elements. This will entail experience with a wide range of research procedures and knowledge about the interpretation of research findings.

3. The disciplines dealing with human growth and development, psychology, and learning theory will require appropriate attention and emphasis.

4. The vocational teacher will need specialized courses in the areas of special education, sociology, economics, and communications to prepare for teaching assignments in groups with special needs. This may involve one or more forms of community study or work experience.

5. Practice and extended study in the area of learning experience design will need to be included in the professional sequence of courses. This may involve various forms of laboratory or cadet teaching experiences with the age groups to be taught.

6. The teacher should receive continuous exposure to the excellent use of the newer educational media as well as one or more courses in this area.

7. A number of public speaking and professional seminar experiences (courses or informal) should be included to develop articulation in the area. This also could include courses in philosophy and foundations of education.

8. The problem of skill development and skill evaluation may be accomplished through a broad range of processes including: credit by examination, special courses, technical and engineering credit transfer, as well as apprenticeship and other industrial training programs.

9. Professional leadership and internship experiences appear as other requirements. This could include participation in various levels of professional associations both in and out of vocational education, as well as internship in vocational administration.

10. Emphasis throughout the course work as well as in all assignments should be directed toward the self-sufficiency of the teacher in his ability to seek out answers, make use of resources, and develop satisfaction in the pursuit of knowledge.

THE preceding discussion centered around a projection of the general requirements for the specific vocational or occupational teacher. This phase of the discussion will deal with the continuum of teachers involved in the education of a disadvantaged student and some of their specific and related roles. This continuum of teachers spans the entire period of the individual student's education, reaching all levels and all teachers at each level. This section will attempt to examine the roles of some of these teachers as well as their relationships and competencies. It will also deal with the relationship of subject areas and methodology.

One of the problems that must be dealt with at the earliest school years and continuously thereafter pertains to the achieving of social effectiveness for every individual. It may be stated as a process of acculturation, which will permit young people to function in the broader arena of life as opposed to their deprived, socially starved, negative environment. For many of the disadvantaged, this may require the establishment of new goals, a new self-concept, a new sense of participation and contribution, and a desire to achieve at levels that add stature and dignity.

It would appear to be an act of considerable foolishness or even deception to proceed on the basis that learning the skills for a particular job or trade is sufficient for effective wage earning and citizenship. In many instances, the individual must be brought to a state of readiness for effective participation in the process of learning a trade or participating as a contributing member of society. It is a matter of taking the disadvantaged individual from his particular predicament and then providing the means for his maximum fulfillment as a human being in a dynamic and complex society.

Lundberg (1964, pp. 14–15) has stressed the need for this cultural base as follows:

> Society's central objective with the educationally disadvantaged is determined by the nature of their predicament. Their culture has failed to provide them with an adequate capacity for social functioning within their complex and personally damaging situation. Social effectiveness, the basic objective, is seemingly obtainable only through some new or strengthened processes of acculturation. The schools' educational objectives are likewise only realizable to the extent that schools and other social institutions succeed in building a cultural base that will support a more adequate social functioning.

This is a task that has significance for the individual from his first ventures into the school through every year to follow and through every teacher he has. It would naturally follow then that teachers at all levels be consciously pursuing the task of developing social effectiveness in each individual. The implication is simply that each teacher the student experiences is essentially a contributor to his vocational competence as such competence permits him to aspire and grow, to work and contribute.

This point is elaborated on by Grant Venn (1964, p. 159) in a conclusion that grew out of his study of vocational and technical education:

> Occupational education must become an integral part of total education. The importance of general education to the individual and his success in occupational preparation, as well as to the preservation of national values, cannot be overestimated; however, it is not enough for the great majority of youth and adults who work in today's society. To provide general education without occupational education is to ignore the facts of modern technological life; to attempt one without the other is to be totally unrealistic.

Thus, it appears obvious that all segments of the school that contribute to the general education of the student are involved in the process of preparing the individual for an occupation or vocation.

Vocational education and vocational teachers cannot be expected to compensate for the failures of the school during the first nine years of the child's education. Vocational education is not a panacea that can be turned on at the tenth or twelfth year to correct the shortcomings of the previous schooling. Much of the individual's possibility to become an effective worker and a contributor to society depends upon his ability to communicate, to calculate and reason, to secure information and organize it. The individual's realization of his potential will also depend upon his attitude toward learning and education as a process through which he may attain maximum development. Finally, and most importantly, the school should be a place where the individual can develop a positive attitude towards himself and his capabilities. He must develop a self-concept that will bring out the finest within him in his aspirations as well as his performance.

Barlow (1965, p. 13) in his discussion of disadvantaged youth made the following comment regarding the responsibility of the school to the individual:

If the student cannot acquire command of the three R's, something must change in his educational environment. If he cannot make his way with the masses in crowded classrooms and cannot keep pace with instruction, something must change so he can learn. If the student can find his way to the classroom by himself, he can most certainly learn something about the subject matter; but possibly the environment must change in order to enhance learning. The student failures of general education are not employable.

The changes and adaptations that the school makes to enhance the student's performance are manifestations of social and human awareness that will ultimately pay substantial dividends.

Education should be a building process. The builders include everyone associated with the school—the community, teachers, counselors, students, administrators, and the assisting staff. Every teacher that a student experiences throughout his formal education is a builder as each works in his unique way and subject area towards developing the student's capability. The teachers of the sciences, the social studies, and the arts provide other opportunities for the individual to grow and develop as a human in preparation for specific vocational instruction. This process would put every teacher in the role of a builder, and likewise the teacher of specific vocational or occupational areas would become a builder. This would be in opposition to the very prevalent use of the vocational teacher as a repairman attempting to mend the results of poor and inadequate instruction during the first nine or ten years of the student's education. If vocational education is to ever achieve its potential, the process of education at all levels from kindergarten upward must be strengthened and in this respect the continuum of teachers plays a most important role.

The vocational teacher usually finds his place near the end of the continuum. It is from his classes that the individual steps out into the world of work. Behind the student's entrance into the field of vocational education one may find extensive self-exploration, studies of occupations, counseling, visitations, and the development of intellectual readiness to select and pursue a vocation.

Furthermore, since the individual is involved in the preparation for a livelihood or an extended period of wage-earning capacity, one must assume that the particular student has developed a sensitivity to his needs, that he has well-founded aspirations and values, and that he has developed an awareness of his potential. These are some of the key factors upon which effective vocational election can be made.

It would appear to be chiefly the task of the earlier continuum of teachers to bring the individual to this point. The degree of their effectiveness would in turn influence the extent of accomplishment by the student in his vocation.

Since this discussion is related to the continuum of teachers with whom the student comes into contact, and to the continuum of educational program, it is imperative that one understand the impact and influence of each level and phase of the educational process. The school may be one of the few positive links between the disadvantaged and the world of work.

The elementary school teacher, in his ability (or inability) to deal with the pupil's unique characteristics, habits, and values, is contributing to or detracting from the individual's potential in his later vocational or occupational choice. Thus, the hypothesis governing this discussion is that every teacher with whom the student comes in contact is in essence a contributor to or a detractor from what that student may become regardless of his eventual occupational or vocational aspirations.

That this point is either ignored or neglected is demonstrated over and over again in all sections of the country in numerous ways. If there is a wave of unemployment or juvenile delinquency or low economic condition, one of the first solutions advocated will be to build a new vocational school, or to "beef up" the old program, or to train better vocational teachers. It is true that vocational education may be the pressing need of these people. But, to develop such a program without a serious and dedicated effort to build at the formative years of the primary, elementary, middle grades, and junior high school would be pure folly. It would be like attempting to build a sturdy brick structure high off the ground with only flimsy poles for a base support.

There must be strength in the continuum of teachers and program. However, as the school begins actually to deal with the realities and the problems of the disadvantaged, the average teacher of the usual middle-class educational program will not suffice. A new order of human values, of optimism and aspiration for such children, and of experiences will be required to bridge the gap between the worlds of the disadvantaged and the world of work and human contribution in a democratic society.

The relevance of the continuum of teachers and instructional programs in the education of the disadvantaged child is discussed in a particularly relevant series of four publications titled the *Disadvantaged Children Series* (Washington, D.C.: U.S. Government Printing Office). Their titles are as follows:

Donald Maley

No. 1. *Educating Disadvantaged Children Under Six* (Nursery and Kindergarten) OE-35060.

No. 2. *Educating Disadvantaged Children in the Primary Years* (Kindergarten through Grade 3) OE-35066.

No. 3. *Educating Disadvantaged Children in the Middle Grades* (Grades 4 through 6) OE-35068.

No. 4. *Administration of School Programs for Disadvantaged Children.* OE-35082.

In the education of the disadvantaged children under six years of age, Mackintosh, Gore, and Lewis (1965a, p. 16) offer the following teacher qualifications:

> She must understand biological and emotional characteristics and needs of all young children, must be observant and understand characteristics of the disadvantaged, and must identify particularly the differences that exist between these children and others. She must have faith that children can overcome these differences. . . .
>
> In addition, the teacher must understand how to work with parents to secure for children the reinforcement and support of the home.

Many failures in vocational education are germinated at this point in the educational ladder. However, the treatment of the individual must take precedence over the usual mass middle-class education.

The teacher qualifications for educating children in the middle grades have been identified by Mackintosh, Gore, and Lewis (1965b, p. 5) as follows:

> Necessary attributes of a teacher at any level are high regard for children, insight into what makes them "tick," and persistent faith that deep within each child lies the ability to respond if only he— the teacher—can be skillful enough to reach him. These attributes are particularly necessary for teachers of middle-grade disadvantaged children, especially those who have not made the best use of opportunities the school offers. Inspired with the feeling that where others have failed he will succeed, the teacher seeks new ways and goes the extra mile to interest these pupils.
>
> The teacher must be professionally equipped to detect strengths and weaknesses; to understand growth and learning; to make use of the powerful peer-group tendency characteristic of middle-grade children; to modify his approaches to find those which are successful with individuals or groups; to introduce activities which appeal to various avenues of learning; visual, auditory, motor, emotional, and intellectual; to provide for wide experiences in the sciences, humani-

ties, and the arts; to seek services for the physical, emotional, and intellectual needs of children in the class which require more help than he can give; to know and be able to enrich the curriculum with resources available both inside and outside the school; and to solicit the interest and cooperation of parents. He must show interest in and, if possible, take part in planning the after-school, Saturday, and summer opportunities extended to middle-grade children, coordinating these efforts with his own teaching.

It is quite clear that the teacher as described above possesses unusual attributes and that the demands upon the teacher education profession to produce such qualities will involve considerable thought and action. Similar qualities may also be identified for the junior high school teacher, along with an increasing awareness of the special developmental tasks that each student is attempting to master in a somewhat mixed and confused situation as he adjusts his hopes and aspirations for the future.

The continuum of educational *experiences* resulting from perceptive, imaginative teachers is likewise an important factor in the education of the disadvantaged. This is particularly true in the experiences the student has in the manual and mental learning processes. The central issue here is one of a greater degree of involvement by the student in whatever he studies. This point is discussed in the Massachusetts Institute of Technology report of *The Summer Study on Occupational, Vocational and Technical Education* (1965, p. 46):

> We should try to help pupils become familiar with the industrial world in which they live. Students must work with two- and three-dimensional materials, for manual and manipulative learning are as important as mental and textbook learning. Balancing these two elements of learning should also be the concern of teachers of science, social studies, mathematics, language arts, homemaking, business, music, art, and all other areas. Industrial arts offer practical and useful experiences for all students through the experiential laboratory, and in the upper levels (tenth, eleventh, twelfth grades) as well. It may contribute to prevocational as well as vocational objectives.

The preceding discussion of manual and mental learning experiences stresses the need for concern by a broad range of teachers (science, social studies, mathematics, language arts, homemaking, business, music, art, and industrial arts) for such activities. It also points up the role of different subject areas in the development of students for optimal vocational preparation.

Among the teachers that the student experiences throughout his school life there are some that have especially close relationships with certain areas of the vocational program. This is the case with the industrial arts teacher and the industrial-vocational area. The relevancy of industrial arts has special significance in the design of programs for those who are disadvantaged as well as those more privileged. Industrial arts in its study of the tools, materials, products, processes, and occupations of industry has been advocated for all levels from kindergarten to college and adult programs (M.I.T., 1965, p. 46):

> The study of industrial arts, encompassing materials, tools, processes, design, products, and social and economic problems of industry, will enrich the general education of each individual. Schools should offer this area of work to all levels from kindergarten through junior and senior high school, college, and adult programs.

The M.I.T. report (p. 46) makes a strong case for the experiential laboratory that exists in industrial arts and advocates this program for both boys and girls.

> These experiences should be an integral part of the general education program of all youth. Through experiential laboratories, industrial arts offer those learning experiences which assist boys and girls to understand the industrial and technical aspects of life today. This curriculum area makes a realistic contribution to education as a process and shares with other areas of the school the responsibility for promoting the continuing development of the good citizen.

This report also stresses the importance of all teachers in the accomplishing of certain educational goals (p. 46):

> Through the experiential laboratory, pupils would learn to appreciate the aesthetic qualities of industrial products and learn to utilize them to enrich their lives. This clearly makes imperative the cooperation of teachers, particularly the arts, homemaking, physical education, language arts, and music.

This last statement lends support to the notion that effective education is a team project and not a series of unrelated confrontations with teachers and subject matter. The continuum of teachers associated with the development of the vocational student has vertical lines stretching from the earliest of school years, and there must be at each year or level a horizontal association of teachers who have common goals related to each individual.

In summary, this discussion has centered around the mission of the total school and the contributions of every teacher to the individual child during his student life. Generalizations that grow out of the "continuum" analysis might be stated as follows:

1. The education of a vocational student is a continuing process that begins with his earliest association with the educational process.

2. The teachers of reading, writing, mathematics, social studies, art, music, economics, and industrial arts at all levels share a heavy responsibility for the effectiveness of the vocational program.

3. The developing of the disadvantaged person into a producing, contributing member of society is not a task that can be accomplished by the vocational teacher alone upon the student's arrival at the tenth, eleventh, or twelfth grades. The task can only be accomplished by an integrated team approach at each grade level and with strong lines of continuity between levels.

4. The education of the disadvantaged person requires a greater dedication on the part of all teachers to the ideal of education of the individual, regardless of his circumstances or differences.

5. The continuum-of-teachers concept as it pertains to the education of the disadvantaged is dependent upon the acceptance of the goal of maximum development of the human component and the fulfillment of the potential of each. Without such an acceptance, vocational education, academic, or any other curricular approach is doomed.

References

BARLOW, MELVIN L. "The Rationale for Vocational Education," *Vocational Education*. Sixty-fourth Yearbook of the National Society for the Study of Education. Chicago: University of Chicago Press, 1965.

LUNDBERG, HORACE W. "Some Current Problems in American Education," in *School Social Work,* ed. Horace W. Lundberg. Washington, D.C.: U.S. Government Printing Office, 1964.

MACKINTOSH, HELEN K., LILLIAN GORE, and GERTRUDE LEWIS. *Educating Disadvantaged Children Under Six.* Washington, D.C.: U.S. Government Printing Office, 1965 (a).

———. *Educating Disadvantaged Children in the Middle Grades.* Washington, D.C.: U.S. Government Printing Office, 1965 (b).

MASSACHUSETTS INSTITUTE OF TECHNOLOGY. *Final Report of the Summer*

Donald Maley

Study on Occupational, Vocational and Technical Education. Cambridge, Mass.: Massachusetts Institute of Technology, 1965.

PRESIDENT'S COMMISSION ON NATIONAL GOALS, *Goals for Americans.* Englewood Cliffs, N.J.: Prentice-Hall, 1961.

SMITH, B. OTHANEL, WILLIAM O. STANLEY, and J. HARLAN SHORES. *Fundamentals of Curriculum Development.* New York: Harcourt, Brace & World, 1965.

TYLER, RALPH. *Basic Principles of Curriculum Instruction.* Chicago: The University of Chicago Press, 1955.

VENN, GRANT. *Man, Education, and Work.* Washington, D.C.: The American Council on Education, 1964.

The Teacher in the Education of the Disadvantaged

Part Two

The Problem as Viewed by Educational Practitioners

7 Meeting the Needs of Disadvantaged Youth in a Disciplinary School

_____Marcus A. Foster*

Characteristics of the Disadvantaged Youth Who Constitute the Student Body of the O. V. Catto School

General Overview

THE O. V. CATTO SCHOOL is a disciplinary school in Philadelphia to which boys from approximately one-half of the geographic area of the city are sent. The district superintendent assigns a boy to Catto upon the recommendation of a principal. Most of the boys have engaged in disruptive behavior to the extent that it is not profitable to them nor their peers to attempt to meet their needs in the regular classroom.

The 400 boys who comprise the student body range in age from eight to seventeen. Eighty-seven per cent come from the junior and senior high schools. Their IQ range is from 55 to 130, the median being 90.

There is usually a 100 per cent turnover in the pupil population dur-

* This chapter was written while the author was principal of the O. V. Catto School, a remediation and disciplinary school in Philadelphia.

ing the course of the year. Some boys return to regular school, others are sent to custodial institutions, and others enter the world of work.

Some Characteristics of Catto Boys

Family Life. For the most part, Catto boys come from broken homes. The mother, aunt, or grandmother is usually the dominant figure. Where the male is present (the husband or paramour), he is often ineffective in guiding the boy. Sometimes the usually absent male is called upon to visit the home and administer corporal punishment, which is often harsh and excessive. The family is constantly plagued by chronic economic crises and frequently turns to the Department of Public Assistance and other agencies for help.

The homes are usually crowded, noisy, and totally lacking in facilities that are conducive to good study habits. There is a dearth of reading material and adequate study space.

Many of the parents manifest the symptoms of social and emotional disturbance that are prevalent among the boys, such as the inability to relate well to one's peers, inability to accept the consequences of one's actions, feeling of guilt, hostility, and inordinate aggressiveness.

Although the foregoing is an accurate description of most of the families served by Catto, there are many exceptions. Some of the boys have parents who are policemen, school teachers, and clergymen. They have brothers and sisters who are college students and who are doing well in school. Such background is much less predisposing toward emotional symptomatology than is a broken home.

School Progress. One of the most common characteristics of Catto boys is their lack of success in school. Some have been tested and labeled mentally retarded. All appear to be educationally retarded. This latter stems from many factors, including the acting out behavior; anti-intellectualism; the cumulative effect of not having mastered the basic skills; inability to set long-range goals and perform the necessary intermediate steps to reach them; the irrelevance of many school activities to life as the boys have come to know it; and the failure to accept the values of the culture, which they view as alien, hostile, and rejecting of them. Lack of proficiency in the communicating skills (listening, speaking, reading, and writing) is common. The most crippling deficiency is severe retardation in reading. The median instructional level as determined by an informal reading inventory is 2. These boys who have failed to learn after years of exposure in school begin to think

Marcus A. Foster

that they cannot learn. Some of their teachers develop this attitude about them.

Social and Emotional Development. Failure to have their needs met by the home, school, church, and other social institutions has caused many of the boys to turn to the gang for satisfaction. Boys who appear to be making a good adjustment in school succumb to the pressure of their peers to participate in delinquent acts.

Their acceptance of the standards of the gang finds expression in exaggerated hair styles and mannerisms and their willingness to commit antisocial acts rather than be thought of as lacking in courage.

An examination of psychological records revealed that about 65 per cent of the boys had been recommended for psychiatric evaluation because of emotional problems. Many boys are unable to secure this needed help because of the limited facilities available to them. Furthermore, most clinics are reluctant to invest their already overtaxed resources in cases that are at best unpromising. The absence of parents who are willing and able to utilize the service of Child Study Clinics prevents the boys from getting help.

Most of the boys have developed a negative self-concept. Those who have been unable to gain status through legitimate means turn to deviant behavior to bolster their ego. The absence of worthy models also hampers the development of a positive self-image.

_____A Description of the O. V. Catto Program and Its Objectives

THE objective of the Catto School is to help the boys become socially and emotionally adjusted so that they can return to regular school or enter the world of work, and concomitantly to help them develop as much proficiency in the basic skills as their abilities will permit.

For some boys, the shop program is a part of their general education. They are taught the care and use of tools, safety habits when working with machinery, etc. For other boys the shop emphasis is more vocational in nature. That is, the teacher seeks to develop saleable skills as a result of shop experiences. The following shop courses are offered:

1. Shoe Service and Leather Crafts.
2. Art Shop—Sign painting, silk screen process, mechanical drawing, and so on.
3. Tailoring—Power machine operating, steam pressing, hat blocking, alterations, and garment making.

4. Restaurant Practice—Short-order cooking, serving, menu planning, and related skills.

5. Gasoline Station Salesman—Lubrication, minor motor repairs, tire work, car care and cleaning.

6. Wood Shop—Use of power and hand tools, furniture refinishing.

The academic program emphasizes remediation and includes Social Studies, Mathematics, Science, Language Arts, Health and Physical Education, Remedial Reading, and Music.

The boys are grouped on the basis of chronological age and their vocational interests. Classes are small (fifteen) and the pupils are able to receive individual attention.

The work-program provides the opportunity for boys to earn money and to experience the dignity and self-esteem that flow from honest toil. For some boys, this the first time that they have learned that their services are valued. They soon discover that the service of experienced and skilled workers is more highly rewarded. They are therefore encouraged to stay in school. Some of the boys are employed in the federally funded programs, and others work on jobs located by the work-coordinators. They are supervised and are required to take the Occupational Practices course, which is designed to help them succeed on the job. They are also given help with money management in the Occupational Practices class.

Prevocational evaluation programs, which are financed by the Bureau of Vocational Rehabilitation, expose the boys to a variety of work experiences in a trade school and a nearby hospital.

Special projects are initiated to supplement the school's program. The Catto–University of Pennsylvania Reading Project is an example. Eighteen volunteers, after receiving thorough training and orientation, "contract" to tutor two boys each for a period of eighteen weeks. The results to date indicate that the boys are improving in their reading, but more importantly, the close relationship between the boys who have often experienced rejection and an interested college student has contributed to a positive change in attitude on the part of the boys.

A project to improve the language facility of problem boys through a cultural enrichment program has also been developed with the University of Pennsylvania.

A $20,000 grant from a private foundation will enable the school and the Child Study Center to provide psychiatric service for the boys who have not heretofore been able to get this help.

The recently opened O. V. Catto Community Evening Extension Center has enabled the school to provide training to residents of the community, parents of the boys, and selected pupils. This project has had a salutary effect on the attitudes of the parents and the community toward the school.

The approval of a proposal to operate the school in the summer gives assurance that boys will be able to receive the support of the school during a period when many who are left on their own get into difficulty.

_____The Needs of the Disadvantaged That the School Must Meet to Be Successful

IT HAS been pointed out that many of the pupils who come to Catto have experienced a lack of affection and understanding, major family problems, a lack of appropriate outlets for their energies, and limited success in school.

Some of the boys have met with the extremes of inordinate harshness or callous indifference as they have sought to gain recognition through a variety of means, both acceptable and unacceptable. In some cases, instead of receiving sympathetic guidance, offenders are unceremoniously dismissed from the regular school. Thus the children who need the help of regular school most are rejected, and the school, which is the one agency that is in continuous contact with all children, misses an opportunity to contribute significantly to the growth and adjustment of the problem child. The tendency of schools to relieve themselves of the inadaptive pupil is supported by those who cry for harsher punishment and stiffer penalties for offenders. This approach only deals with symptoms and may be damaging to the underlying causes of the deviant behavior. Therefore, whatever program is devised to help the disadvantaged child must take place in a climate that is supporting rather than oppressing and accepting rather than rejecting.

As a result of their experience, many boys who have been sent to Catto have come to view themselves as unworthy. Some have yielded to the subculture of the gang to find the esteem that was denied them in school and in the community. Some boys have selected unworthy models and have identified certain symbols of success (flashy car, fancy suits, money) as all important, without regard to how they have been acquired. Other boys have sought comfort through an unrealistic appraisal of their capabilities. Some boys have been overwhelmed by failure and cease to aspire; they are numbed by a sense of powerlessness and appear to be utterly unmotivated. Others strike out at society and authority figures, which they have come to identify as their enemies; thus fear, hostility, and hate are converted into aggressive behavior.

The Need to Develop a Positive Self-Image

The school must deal successfully with the problem of helping the boys develop a view of self that is positive. The therapeutic climate of the Catto School contributes to this. Everyone connected with the school—teachers, counselors, custodian, cafeteria workers, secretarial staff—realizes that the manner in which he performs his job has a direct bearing on how effective the school will be in achieving its objectives. There have been cases where the sympathetic understanding of the head dietitian or another member of the staff has contributed most significantly to the adjustment of a boy. This climate is established through staff development programs in which consultants are utilized. The case study approach contributes to sensitizing staff personnel to the needs of the pupils and increases their ability to view children as unique individuals.

A school-wide program to give the boys as many legitimate opportunities to gain a feeling of status contributes to building a view of self that is acceptable. This includes proper utilization of bulletin boards, assembly programs, awards convocation, honors day, and so on. Each person is urged to examine his interaction with the pupils and to avoid actions and words that tend to diminish a boy's self-esteem.

The faculty plans programs that are designed to help the pupils through a process of identity change. The boys are helped to select the identity features that need to be changed. These might be exaggerated styles and mannerisms, faulty speech patterns, public conduct, anti-intellectualism and so on. The boys are helped to see sense in making the change. This may be related to job opportunities, return to regular school, participation in special projects, and so on. The teachers and other staff personnel are helped to understand the importance of their role as hero models. The boys are given opportunities to make commitments to the new style of behaving through assembly programs. Teachers and others lend sympathetic support as the boys try to gain command of the new way of conducting themselves. Former pupils who have been successful return to lend their support to the program. Men from business and industry contribute their support through participation in career conferences and workshops. Everything that takes place in the school is measured against the criterion: Does this contribute toward helping the boy construct a positive self-image?

The Need to Convert Potential Intelligence into Operational Intelligence

It has been pointed out that the boys at Catto in many cases are pseudoretarded. A major contributing factor to this is their lack of school success. Many have interpreted their failure to learn as an innate inability to learn. To combat this, teachers are encouraged to plan a program that will at least maintain a balance between success and failure. This implies that the practice of placing social studies books that are written for capable ninth-grade pupils in the hand of boys reading with difficulty at the third-grade level must be eliminated. The teacher is called upon to prepare materials suited to the interest and reading levels of the pupils. The teacher is assisted in discovering materials that have been especially prepared to fit this need. Another factor is the problem of making the curriculum relevant to the learners. This does not mean watering down the course offerings or letting the boys pass without really learning the material. It does mean examining the present achievement level of the boy and being creative in providing experiences that will lead him to the next level.

All teachers must recognize their responsibility for helping to strengthen the weakest link in the school skills of disadvantaged children —the language arts. Through staff development programs, shop teachers, counselors, secretaries, and others must be led to see specific ways they can help children improve their ability to listen, speak, read, and write.

Occupational classes must always retain the flexibility for children to move back into the regular educational stream after they have been stimulated and motivated to aspire toward higher goals.

The Need to Utilize Available Resources

It is recognized that the disadvantaged child comes from multi-problem families. Some of the problems of Catto boys have their roots in the home, community, the school, the individual, and elsewhere. As in all human behavior, the causes are multiple and complex. The school working alone as an agent of change can seldom be entirely successful. Through counseling and the alertness of the staff, specific problems of the boys must be identified. One of the problems of disadvantaged families is their inability to use appropriate agencies in the most effective manner. Another aspect of this problem is the tendency of some families to develop the questionable skill of "conning" a living out of welfare agencies. The school has a role in coordinating and mobilizing available resources so that maximum benefit will accrue to the children under its care. It is recognized that the school can dissipate its energies in reaching too far beyond its primary responsibilities, but the school that deals only with the child views its task with myopic vision by considering only one aspect of the problem.

_____Personal Characteristics of Teachers of Disadvantaged Youth

THE teacher in the disciplinary school must possess certain personal characteristics if he is to be effective in contributing to the adjustment of problem boys. At Catto it is recognized that inadaptive school behavior is only partly the result of the attitude of the pupil. Of equal importance is the attitude of the teacher toward the pupil he is trying to help. There should be an acceptance of the boy with no prerequisite that he must be "good" to be acceptable. Children see through this superficiality and often reject the individual and the help he is offering, or they may play the game by pretending to measure up to what is expected of them.

The successful teacher at Catto manifests some of the following personal qualities:

1. Personality that permits him to deal with nonconforming behavior without damaging physical or psychological punitive measures.

In a treatment program, the boys must learn the lesson of accountability. There is, however, no place for vengeance or brutality. The necessity to punish at times is not questioned, nor is the need for authority that has this power questioned. The notion that punishment by itself is a sufficient approach to helping problem boys is rejected. This approach must yield to more constructive approaches. It is well known that coercive and repressive measures often turn the offender to more serious deviant behavior.

120
Marcus A. Foster

2. Disposition that permits continued support of the boy in spite of failures and obstacles.

Although the teacher is optimistic about the boy's potential for growth, he should not become discouraged if progress is slow or indeed if his most promising prospect becomes involved in serious difficulty with the police.

The thrust of the teacher's effort should be to help the boys discover and develop their strengths while diminishing those characteristics which tend to be degrading and detrimental. In this effort the successful teacher realizes that he is competing with a host of negative influences that are pulling the boy in a number of directions.

When confronted with apparent failure, the effective teacher continues his effort without diminution of enthusiasm and free of feelings of guilt or frustration.

3. Possession of a warm stable personality.

Disadvantaged pupils need the reassurance of a warm personality. The impersonal nature of large schools in the big cities makes this imperative. They need teachers who are capable of establishing a climate in which boys can develop what is a serious deficiency in most of them—self-esteem.

4. Possession of a sense of worth and ideals and values that are in consonance with the objectives of the school.

The importance of the teacher as a model has already been pointed out. However, it would be difficult to place too much stress upon this point. Much of what we wish to teach nonconforming youth is "caught" rather than "taught." Pupils are quick to identify discrepancies between practices and precepts.

_____Skills, Knowledge, and Understanding Needed by Teachers of Disadvantaged Youth

THE teacher of the disadvantaged pupil must have a thorough knowledge of child growth and development. He should be able to assess child behavior objectively and gain some insight into the problems confronting the pupils. He should be growing in his ability to ferret out the causes of deviant behavior. His knowledge of child growth and development should help him see each child as unique and of surpassing worth. This view should inspire the teacher to utilize all the resources at his command to help each child reach his full potential.

The teacher of disadvantaged boys should have knowledge of the conditions under which learning takes place best and most abundantly. This means that he is aware of the cognitive styles of the learner and is able to translate into practice the dictums of the theoretician. He knows how to capitalize upon his pupils' physical style of learning. His instructional procedures reflect his awareness of the importance of beginning with the concrete before moving to higher levels of abstract thinking. His classroom is a rich learning laboratory pregnant with possibilities for pupils to discover answers to their questions through their own activities.

The teacher of disadvantaged children should understand the environmental factors that contribute to the problems of disadvantaged youth. He must know that the slum is a profound educational institution that operates twenty-four hours a day. The many negative influences of the depressed community seek recruits for the evergrowing army of delinquents among the school failures, the undereducated, the poorly trained, the alienated, and the rejected. The successful teacher is able to identify the positive and negative factors in the community and guides his pupils accordingly.

Summary

THE O. V. Catto School serves pupils who have been assigned because of behavior problems. The school helps its boys to develop the inner controls that will enable them to function effectively in the regular school or the world of work. This is accomplished through a program that includes industrial arts, vocational education, academic subjects, and a variety of supplementary projects.

The boys served by the school have evidenced a need of help in achieving academic proficiency. This is related to their need of developing a positive self-image.

The successful teacher of Catto boys must have a sympathetic understanding of their problems. He knows how they grow and develop and is aware of the conditions under which they learn best.

By being a warm, stable person, the teacher of disadvantaged youth should, at least, give the child a sense of his own worth; and this may in some cases be the most that a teacher can give.

122
Marcus A. Foster

8 Job-Oriented Learning Experiences: A Partial Answer to the Needs of Disadvantaged Youth

Sidney N. Chernak

BALTIMORE CITY PUBLIC SCHOOLS

_____The Setting

B ALTIMORE, LIKE OTHER industrial centers has experienced a series of waves of emphasis on vocational education. The size of the waves has varied with each national crisis and if one were to write a local history of the vocational program, he would identify the height and characteristics of the crests and the depths of the troughs. The hand-me-down buildings and basements have all been and are still part of the mosaic of the program. Buildings that were condemned by a prominent survey team in the 1920s when the facilities were used for elementary schools still house some facets of the vocational program. On the other hand, two large specially designed building complexes house the vocational high school and technician programs. Another new building was designed particularly for a program for slow-learning girls.

Despite the handicaps that tired and worn-out physical surroundings

123

impose upon any program, dedicated staff members have developed a variety of effective curricula over the years on various levels of student ability in an attempt to meet the variety of needs and interests of this segment of the student population.

Currently, as our concerns mount over the needs of students in the lower 25 per cent of the ability group, we again turn to school experiences of vocational intent to form the backbone of programs that hopefully will motivate young people to remain in school long enough to acquire basic general knowledge in various academic disciplines plus enough skill training to enable them to become productive and self-sufficient as they take on the responsibilities of adult living.

Benjamin C. Willis, in his report on the President's Panel on Vocational Education, spoke up strongly in favor of vocational education for persons of all ability levels. He stated that "new programs of vocational education should be added to the school curricula which are occupationally oriented, which lead to employment in jobs known to exist and which can be successful educational experiences for youth who cannot profit from instruction in traditional programs."

This chapter has a three-fold concern: to delineate the characteristics of the disadvantaged youth and their needs; to describe the desirable personal characteristics of teachers who work with these students; and to describe several promising programs in the Baltimore City public schools. The programs described are intended as a sampling of the range of approaches taken to reach children on a continuum of abilities, motivations, and needs. Some of the programs are treated in depth in order to emphasize facets of planning and implementation that are unique.

Skill-centered Programs

ALL of these programs are designed to provide competency in the ability to communicate, understanding and skill in basic arithmetic operations, experiences in citizenship as well as an insight into the history and development of our country and the rest of the world. Exposure and participation in art and music activities round out what one student described as the "epidemic" subjects.

However, the major emphasis is upon the time spent in shops or laboratories where the student is "doing" and "handling."

124
Sidney N. Chernak

The Carrollton School

In this tired building is housed a program intended to redirect potential dropouts and returnees so that they will move toward responsible productive citizenship and away from the frustrations of unemployment and discomforts of failure.

THE PROBLEM

The unemployed out-of-school youth is the subject of increasing attention and concern to the political and educational leaders in large urban communities. Civic organizations, civil rights groups, and social welfare agencies are turning their spotlights on the problems that face a large segment of the youthful population of large cities. The lack of direction, inadequate preparation for living in our urban society, and apparent shrinkage in the capacity of expanding industry to absorb untrained workers is pictured as a serious threat to the sociopolitical economy of the metropolitan urban centers which constitute the megalopolis. Baltimore is sharing this concern.

AN APPROACH

The Carrollton School was established in September 1963, with the belief that a ₁roperly designed program with a job-oriented approach could redirect potential dropouts. The occupational training experiences were therefore selected with consideration for the ability and interest levels of the students who would in all likelihood be attracted by this program. The goal was employment following training. Classroom work was to be closely related to the shop and work experiences and would be functional. The educational leadership was chosen in such a way as to insure or at least promote creative approaches to teaching. Specific goals were identified to assist young people in the following ways:

1. To develop economic and vocational competence.
2. To acquire and use the basic skills.
3. To develop moral and ethical values.
4. To be effective citizens.
5. To be effective family members.
6. To develop and maintain sound mental and physical health.

PROGRAM OF STUDIES

GENERAL EDUCATION

1. Communication Skills
2. Mathematics
3. Social Studies
4. Physical Education
5. Music

JOB PREPARATION TRAINING

1. Custodial Service
2. Duplicating Services
3. Family Service Aide
4. Food Preparation and Service
5. Home Mechanics
6. Lawn and Garden Care
7. Painting, Decorating, and Furniture Refinishing
8. Shoe Repair
9. Small Appliance Repair
10. Valet Service

THE STUDENT BODY

There are approximately 550 boys and girls in attendance, distributed in a proportion of two boys to one girl. Their ages range from 15 to 20 years; the median age is 17.5 years. Mental abilities range from 55 IQ to 97 IQ. The average student performs at fourth grade level in reading and arithmetic.

All of these students have experienced failure in school; many have repeated two grades. The most recent educational experience of the majority of the student body was in a three-year program of Special Education in the junior high school.

Many of these young people come from large families; some are from broken homes; most have parents who are unskilled workers with a limited education; others live in foster homes because they have been neglected or completely abandoned by their parents. Often the only family income is that earned by the mother; in other cases, the family is supported by welfare funds.

Sidney N. Chernak

THE FACULTY

The nature of the student body with its history of failure and its background of family instability makes the selection of teachers a crucial decision. Personal qualities such as empathy, the ability to accept students as individuals, the desire to teach, and devotion to duty take on a greater importance than the more readily evaluated experience and professional background.

Teachers of the general education subjects are required to have a baccalaureate degree preferably in the area of Special Education. After appointment to teaching positions, they are required to participate in workshops designed to improve their teaching competence in the field of Special Education.

Vocational teachers must at least be high school graduates and must have a minimum of five years paid working experience in the occupation they hope to teach; or they must have a baccalaureate degree in vocational education with an area of specialization and two years of paid working experience in the occupation they hope to teach. All vocational teachers are required to take a minimum of eighteen semester hours in specified courses at the State University within two and one-half years of their appointment in order to meet city and state certification requirements. Biweekly meetings are held for newly appointed vocational teachers to give them direction and guidance in developing teaching competency.

FEATURES OF THE PROGRAM

Carrollton School operates on a basic 30-period schedule, not including lunch periods, from 9 A.M. to 2:30 P.M. During the course of a week, the student engages in approximately 15 periods of job preparation training and 15 periods of general education subjects.

The entering student follows a schedule that provides exploratory experiences in two job preparation areas. At the conclusion of a nine-week period, he may select two additional areas for exploration, or he may choose to specialize in one occupational field. The exploratory process continues until the student selects an area of interest in which he will specialize.

The vocational education offerings at Carrollton reflect the cluster concept of organization in which training is given for a family of related occupations in a single shop. Teachers attempt to develop skills in one job within a cluster before introducing the student to training in a related occupation. Thus, saleable skills are developed early in the program against the possibility of an early withdrawal by the student.

The use of the community as a laboratory illustrates the creative approach to education used by the faculty. The Lawn and Garden Care classes have assumed responsibility for the maintenance and beautification of a small neighborhood park. Custodial Service classes broaden their experience by traveling to other community schools to practice their maintenance skills on a variety of buildings. Students in the Family Service Aide classes provide volunteer services in a community nursing home.

In other shops students gain practical experience by servicing and repairing articles brought in by pupils and teachers. The school cafeteria is operated by the Food Preparation and Service classes under the guidance of their teacher.

Teachers search out work-study opportunities for their students and often use their own time to perform coordinating duties. Pupils' schedules are adjusted in a variety of ways to meet the demands of their work-study assignments. A coordinator is being assigned to the school.

JOB PREPARATION COURSE DESCRIPTIONS

CUSTODIAL SERVICES

The student in the Custodial course receives thorough training in the skills required to properly clean and maintain office buildings, industrial establishments, churches, and school buildings. His duties include sweeping, dusting, wall cleaning, window cleaning, floor sealing, waxing, buffing, metal polishing, maintenance of sanitary facilities, care of grounds, minor care of heating and ventilating equipment, and receiving supplies.

DUPLICATING SERVICES

The instruction in Duplicating Services covers a wide variety of skills used in the business and retail selling fields. Students develop competence in setting up and operating spirit duplicators and mimeograph machines, collating, hand binding, plastic binding, stitching, packaging, wrapping, labeling, shipping, receiving, and maintenance of stock inventory records.

Sidney N. Chernak

FAMILY SERVICE AIDE

This course was established to satisfy the need for properly trained people who can serve as day maids and mothers' helpers in private homes or assist in nursing homes, hospitals, and similar institutions. Instruction is given in care of the elderly, child care, meal planning and preparation, clothing construction and repairs, and housekeeping.

FOOD PREPARATION AND SERVICE

The Foods course provides training for students who wish to work in places where food is prepared and served in quantity. Employment opportunities are available in restaurants, cafeterias, hospitals, and nursing homes. Menu planning and using the cash register are included with the instruction in food preparation and service.

HOME MECHANICS

The purpose of the Home Mechanics course is to prepare students to perform a variety of home repairs. These activities include glazing, care and maintenance of screens and storm windows, floor sealing and refinishing, floor tile laying, door fitting, care and maintenance of window sash, and minor remodeling jobs in the home. The student completing this course should be able to find employment with a small firm engaged in the home remodeling business.

LAWN AND FLOWER CARE

Instruction in the Lawn and Flower Care course is geared to develop the skills usually associated with the functions of the paid gardener. Training is given in lawn cutting and edging, trimming and care of shrubbery, pruning, plant propagation, soil testing, and care and maintenance of equipment.

PAINTING, DECORATING, AND FURNITURE REFINISHING

Painting, Decorating, and Furniture Refinishing students receive instruction designed to prepare them for employment with small concerns involved in exterior and interior decorating or in furniture refinishing. The course emphasizes the use of various painting techniques, application of wallpaper and other wall coverings, and the basic skills of furniture refinishing.

SHOE REPAIRING

Students in the Shoe Repairing course can expect to obtain employment in shoe repair shops and shoe factories. They learn to replace heels and soles, mend uppers, dye shoes, and make minor orthopedic adjustments.

SMALL APPLIANCE REPAIR

A good appliance repairman can obtain employment in the serivce department of an appliance distributor or he can set up his own business with a very small investment. In the appliance shop students are taught to diagnose and repair domestic electrical appliances such as toasters, electric irons, broilers, waffle irons, and mixers.

VALET SERVICE

Students in the Valet Service course prepare for employment in cleaning and pressing establishments, small tailor shops, and large hotels. They are taught to use a variety of pressing machines, hand steam irons, and spotting equipment. They also learn to mend clothing and perform minor alterations.

GENERAL EDUCATION COURSE DESCRIPTIONS

COMMUNICATION SKILLS

Attention is focused upon a continuation of the developmental reading program, using basic textbooks. There is also an increased use of supplemental materials relating to job preparation.

Oral communication: Emphasis is placed upon developing self-expression through using the telephone teletrainer, conducting interviews, role playing, and good English usage.

Written communication: The correct form for writing business and social letters and notes of various kinds is stressed. Spelling is taught systematically in accordance with pupils' reading achievement levels and their job preparation areas.

MATHEMATICS

The fundamental processes are reviewed and practiced. Situational and meaningful arithmetic, including units on installment buying, bud-

Sidney N. Chernak

geting, banking and insurance, is taught. A thorough study of family finance is also included.

SOCIAL STUDIES

Units on government, driver education, public health services, adult education, elementary economics, and legal aid are taught. Citizenship and its responsibilities are emphasized.

Occupational information and guidance is stressed. *A Handbook for You, the Worker* is used as a text. Every effort is made to correlate the work in job training with the pupil's actual job preparation area.

SUMMARY

The Carrollton School was established to provide pre-employment training for youth with special needs. The major goal of the school is to produce responsible and vocationally competent citizens and all efforts of the faculty and administration are geared to this one purpose. Favorable student and community response give indications that Carrollton has been founded upon valid assumptions. Increased employment opportunities for these students, made possible by an enlightened public, can make this experiment an unqualified success.

Venable Junior High School

As a part of the secondary school program, the Baltimore School System maintains a number of schools known as Special Curriculum Schools. Slow-learning educable and trainable pupils who might be adversely affected in a large comprehensive junior high school are recommended for placement, with parental consent, in these school situations where one hundred to two hundred pupils are provided with a special program. Some of these schools are segregated by sex. The Venable School admits girls only and was especially designed for this program.

Typically the criteria applied are as follows:

1. An IQ range of 65–79 on an individual test.
2. Chronological age of 13 years and 8 months or above.
3. Reading and arithmetic levels at or above 3.0 on a standardized test.

4. Emotional stability.

5. Evident need for close supervision and assistance.

The Venable School is having singular success with a job preparatory program for girls. Occupational training is provided in two general areas—Commercial Food Service and Nursing Home Aides. The training is designed for a three-year sequence with the specific preparation in two broad areas of occupational information and the service skills.

OUTLINE OF PROGRAM

FIRST YEAR

OCCUPATIONAL INFORMATION

Why We Work
Kinds of Jobs Available
Ways of Getting a Job
Social Security Background Information
How to Fill Out a Social Security Number Application
How to Fill Out Job Applications
Waitressing
Preparation for an Interview
Coordination Program
Use of the Telephone—Personal and Business Use
    Resource—The Telephone and You
Background Information for Work
    Resource—Handbook for You, the Worker

COMMERCIAL FOOD SERVICE

Hygiene of the Food Handler
Preparation of Foods—Meats, Vegetables, Breads, Desserts, Salads
Use and Care of Restaurant Equipment

SECOND YEAR

OCCUPATIONAL INFORMATION

Review of Occupational Information
Elementary Economics

132
Sidney N. Chernak

COMMERCIAL FOOD SERVICE

(Continuation of work of previous year)
Serving of Food—Cafeteria and Restaurant Service

NURSING HOME AIDE

Home Nursing
Child Care
Grooming for Work
Nursing Home Aide

THIRD YEAR

OCCUPATIONAL INFORMATION

Review
Laws and Forms Young Workers Should Know
Office Girl—Simple Clerical Jobs
Filing
Cashiering
Use of Adding Machine
Department Store Wrapping

COMMERCIAL FOOD SERVICE

(Continuation of previous skills learned)
Meal Planning

NURSING HOME AIDE

Nursing Care (applied to care of older people)
Nursing Care (applied to care of children)
Nursing Home Aide Review
Nursing Home Aide Training at Red Cross Headquarters
Child Care (applied to work in nursery schools)

ON-THE-JOB-TRAINING

A work-study program is being conducted successfully at the following cooperating locations:

Hutzler's Department Store—Quixie Restaurant
Johns Hopkins Hospital—physicians' dining room

Union Memorial Hospital—diet kitchen
House in the Pines—convalescent home
Happy Hills—children's convalescent home

Following these experiences some girls take full-time employment and others become home managers and relieve their mothers who are employed.

Gompers General Vocational School

Five general vocational schools are situated in various quadrants of the city. The pupil population is relatively small in each building. One of the five is for girls only, two admit only male pupils, and two are coeducational. The Gompers School is the largest in terms of pupil population and admits boys only.

POINT OF VIEW OF THE PROGRAM

1. The general vocational junior high school provides promotional opportunities for the elementary school pupil completing the sixth grade.
2. Try-out programs in the various shop activities are provided for pupils entering the seventh grade from the elementary school.
3. The curricular offerings in these schools provide opportunities for boys and girls who:
   a. Are more interested in exploring educational opportunities offered in the general vocational curriculum than other junior high school curricula.
   c. Give evidence of characteristics that may lead to their dropping out of school.
   d. Are interested in obtaining basic vocational training that might lead to opportunities for advanced training at a higher educational level.

SUGGESTED CRITERIA FOR ADMISSION

Pupils recommended for the general vocational junior high school should have the following characteristics:

Sidney N. Chernak

1. Completion of the sixth grade.
2. Be at least 12 years and 8 months of age as of August 31.
3. IQ of 80 or better.
4. In general, achievement at a level of 4.5 or better in reading and arithmetic.
5. Interest in vocational preparation.

PHILOSOPHY

The general vocational curriculum at Samuel Gompers General Vocational School is designed for pupils who have an interest in exploring educational experiences inherent in vocational fields and acquiring occupational skills.

The term *general* in the title has a dual meaning. It implies educational development in skills general to various families of occupations as well as in the area of general education.

The trade courses are designed so that many of the skills developed can be applied to broad fields of employment as well as to specific occupations. These educational experiences are aimed at developing an individual who is adaptable and who possesses broad occupational skills that will be useful even if technological advances and the development of new materials outmode his old job.

This curriculum also makes a major contribution to the general education of its pupils. Equally important and complementary to the educational experiences that have been designed to develop the student's vocational competence and desirable attitudes are the educational experiences designed to develop his social and cultural background. This program also provides for the development of communication skills, for the development of appreciations, for the understanding of our democratic society, and for the development of good citizenship in that society.

In this curriculum, which for many may be terminal education, a major objective is maximum development of general skills in preparation for entrance into the world of work. It is not preparation for a specific occupation or job; it is rather a preparation for many jobs needing workers with training in *basic skills general to many operations and common to many occupations*. It is preparation in *attitudes* and *understanding* that will make for better citizenship, developed in classrooms and shops alike.

PURPOSES OF THE SCHOOL

To provide a friendly understanding, educationally productive atmosphere in which these boys will grow.

To provide a practical training program that will better prepare these young people for employment and living.

To instill in these boys the desire to put forward their best efforts to improve themselves.

THE FACULTY AIMS

To accept individual pupils for what they are and then to work with them on the causes of their maladjustment.

To give each boy an opportunity to succeed on his level.

To correct deficiencies and improve skills in reading, English, and arithmetic.

To develop practical skills in the use of materials, tools, and machines.

To develop self-confidence in the ability to get things done.

To get pupils to meet acceptable standards of work and conduct.

To train for citizenship by giving pupils accurate information and by providing opportunities for them to participate in school activities.

To develop an interest in and to provide opportunities to participate in desirable leisure-time activities.

To foster and maintain good health habits.

To develop wholesome habits and attitudes toward all people so that they may get along better.

To help each boy to better understand his environment.

To help each boy to be a better buyer and an intelligent consumer.

PROGRAM OF SHOP EXPERIENCES

Electrical Wiring and Repair
General Woodwork
Junior Business Occupations
Machine Shop
Mechanical and Automotive Assembly
Painting and Decorating
Printing
Shoe Repairing
Sign Painting and Show Card Writing—Commercial Art

136
Sidney N. Chernak

EXPLORATORY SHOP COURSES

During the seventh grade all pupils receive try-out experiences in all the shop courses given at Samuel Gompers General Vocational School. The emphasis in the try-out shop courses is to introduce the pupils to the role of that shop in the industrial world, to the common tools, machines, and materials used by that shop. In order for the pupil to understand what skills and aptitudes are required in the shop, the pupil uses some of the tools, machines, and materials. The shop try-out period consists of four periods per day, five days a week for five weeks. At the end of the first five weeks, the pupil moves to a second shop where he spends a like period of time. In all, during the seventh grade, the pupil will try out seven different shops. At the end of the seventh grade, the pupil will select the shop he wishes to make his major for the eighth through the twelfth grades. A pupil may request a change in his major after a conference with his counselor.

A TYPICAL WEEKLY PROGRAM

The typical weekly program in the general vocational junior high school consists of:

Shop Major	20 periods per week
English	4 periods per week
Social Studies	4 periods per week
Science (including Health)	3 periods per week
Mathematics	4 periods per week
Physical Education	2 periods per week
Art or Mechanical Drawing	2 periods per week
Music	1 period per week

WORK-STUDY PROGRAM

A limited number of pupils take part in the work-study program at the Samuel Gompers General Vocational School. The pupil spends part of his time in school and part of his time working for private employers on jobs related to his school shop major. The schedule for this program is flexible to suit both the school and the employer. Various schedules are used. For example, under one schedule a pupil may spend one week on the outside job and one week in school. Another possible schedule permits the pupil to attend school in the morning and work on the job in the afternoon. In selecting a schedule, consideration is given to travel time, nature of the job, and need for continuity.

The program is under the supervision of a counselor-coordinator who determines that the job is one that offers training as well as employment. The counselor-coordinator also relates the pupil's work experience to his school experience.

Jane Addams General Vocational School

This school is located in one of the buildings occupied by the Goucher College for many years as part of its campus. Its facilities are limited.

The Jane Addams School, as the name would suggest, is a girls' school. It has a specific objective—to equip its students to become effective homemakers and efficient employees. Girls from all over the city attend the school.

In this school the staff emphasizes personal counseling. Every effort is made to build pride in self and satisfaction in accomplishment.

PROGRAM OF STUDIES

JOB PREPARATORY

Business Education
Cafeteria—Tearoom Service
Dressmaking
Junior Sales
Power Machine Operation

GENERAL EDUCATION

Art
English
Mathematics
Music
Science
Social Studies

PERSONAL DEVELOPMENT

Child Care and Family Living
Personal Grooming
Physical Fitness

138
Sidney N. Chernak

Guidance
Library
Assemblies
Class Organizations
Excursions
Fashion Shows
Fireside Chats
Mother-Daughter Banquet
Student Council
Visitations
Yearbook

The William Patterson Junior High School

This special-curriculum school for boys houses only about two hundred students. The boys are typically overaged students who have been retained in the elementary school and have been recommended for transfer to this school in an attempt to give them a change of emphasis. However, students may also enter this school from the special-curriculum seventh or eighth grade classes of a comprehensive junior high school. Originally, the program was considered as terminal at the age of sixteen. However, boys are remaining on for longer periods of time.

Typically the criteria applied are:

1. An IQ range of 65–79 on an individual test.
2. Chronological age of 13 years and 8 months or above.
3. Reading and arithmetic levels at or above 3.0 on a standardized test.
4. Emotional stability.
5. Evident need for close supervision and assistance.

This school is being particularly successful in helping students attain a feeling of success and improving their feelings about themselves as individuals. The administrative and instructional staff members are working together to expand the experiences of their students in order to avail themselves of employment opportunities being opened up through the Work-Study Program that has been introduced in this school.

For example, they have introduced Driver Education in order to teach boys to drive light delivery trucks used generally by retail establishments such as drug stores, grocery stores, and meat markets. The driver education course is being used to stimulate interest in reading. Because they need reading skills to understand directions, merchandise orders, street signs, and so on, the students are "taking to" reading instruction with greater zest.

In another direction, the school has entered into an agreement with a large meat packer for a short training program in meat cutting. The packing house is supplying the meat, tools, and instructor. The skills to be developed are those that are repetitive but useful and job-oriented.

The school is currently exploring the need for low level skill opportunities for boys in hospitals.

_____Characteristics of Disadvantaged Youth

Environmental Setting

In seeking to characterize disadvantaged youth in a student body of a particular school or community one cannot separate the students from their individual and community environments.

The culturally deprived students are native-born youth or recent immigrants who have had few opportunities to adjust to or take on urban mores and values that could promote personal growth. A high mobility rate has frequently resulted in patchwork education and a reduction in motivation for acquiring the necessary skill and knowledge to cope with life's problems. Mobility does not necessarily mean interstate movements. A teacher, by examining the permanent records of a class, can discover instances when the frequent shifting of the family may have had its effect on learning.

The effect of such upheavals on parents frequently is to reduce their desire to assume community responsibility or to participate in PTA and other neighborhood activities. These parents frequently lack the time, energy, knowledge, patience, and understanding needed to provide the necessary out-of-school learning experiences that are so valuable and that have shown their value in programs like Headstart and Early Admissions.

Fractured home groups, uncared-for physical ills, emotional and social disturbances, economic pressures translate themselves into indif-

Sidney N. Chernak

ference, low aspirations, and eventually below average achievement in the several areas of learning. The physical environment presents a picture of overcrowded homes, deterioration, lack of any semblance of privacy, minimum requirements of sanitation and safety. Thus, teachers who expect home study to supplement classroom work are unrealistic in their expectations, which may be geared to warm, quiet, compatible, comfortable environments conducive to learning.

So, we need to visualize the possessions of culturally disadvantaged children as including disappointments, unsatisfied needs, myriads of hates.

Educational and Physical Manifestations

Studies generally disclose a high frequency of hearing defects, speech impairment, diseased tonsils, dental decay and neglect, as well as dietary deficiencies in inner-city children.

Although hospital out-patient clinics appear to be crowded with indigent patients, home-visitors, nurses, and social workers report that parents of the inner-city students do not seek or do not have the knowledge of where to go for needed assistance. Consequently, schools undertake to provide information and advisory services to parents concerning health matters. A group of five Baltimore City hospitals have just received a grant that will enable them to study and provide health services for 20,000 school-connected children up to the age of 18. The Health Department, hospital, and schools will all cooperate on this project. This should be a big step forward in the direction of reducing one of the handicaps that affect the rate of learning of disadvantaged students.

These students are easily disturbed and upset by changes in their school environment and frequently feel secure in a well-ordered situation. Although they may turn to displays of aggression in relationships with their peers and teachers, underneath this manifestation one finds a shyness and fear in dealing with new teachers who must sell themselves before they are accepted.

What may be interpreted as absence of drive and ambition can be traced to lack of praise by former teachers and parents for achievements that merited commendation in the past. Consequently, these deprived students may react in an oversensitive manner to the exposure of their weaknesses. The writer recently saw a film, "Going to School," produced for the College Entrance Examination Board. The young people were not actors but were secondary school students in unrehearsed situations in one of our major cities. One of the most unforgettable scenes is one where a boy of 15 just cannot come up with the answer to his teacher's question after three tries. Probably only the presence of the cameraman prevented an explosion as this teenager's inadequacy was brought into focus.

A. Harry Passow, in a paper presented at a seminar at Ohio State University, (1964) states:

> How to concoct a climate in which teachers genuinely believe in the potential ability of disadvantaged children, are committed to its nurture, and convey this respect through their relationships with pupils and parents is part and parcel of the curriculum problem. What the teacher expects or does not expect and how the disadvantaged student perceives those expectations can influence significantly the child's aspiration level and involvement in the educational process.

_____Needs of Disadvantaged Youth

Identification and Belonging

The disadvantaged student, more than any other, needs and desires to become identified with at least one teacher. Every student wants to be known as an individual and recognized as a person. He wants to belong, to "make a team." The high school football player who makes the team has a coach to go to with problems or for advice on matters other than athletics.

At the 1964 Pacific Regional Conference of the National Rehabilitation Association, Richard E. Farson of the Western Behavioral Sciences Institute advanced the thought that "counseling at its best seems to be a series of occasional moments of humanness—moments and hours characterized by defensiveness and evasion, intellectualization and abstraction, game playing and role playing with both client and counsellor trying to be something they are not." It is the human moments rather than the defensive, evasive hours that are to be striven for.

Identification with a faculty member can well provide the humanness in guidance that could make the big difference when a student needs help in making up his mind about such important matters as drop-

Sidney N. Chernak

ping out or continuing in school, selecting a "stiff" course or a soft one. Such a contact needs to be initiated by a faculty member who is sincere but discreet. A few available minutes each day or each week is all that is needed to make a counselor out of every teacher.

Understanding of Self

Students are troubled by their self-assessments, particularly when they have met with academic failure one or more times. They consequently need some means by which in an unthreatened environment they can ask questions and receive answers and direction that will help them honestly appraise their strengths and weaknesses. They need to be helped to understand that successes are balanced by failures, which do not herald the end of all things. Evaluation instruments and techniques need to be explained to students as they are employed as springboards to improvement.

Motivation

Students, just like other people, see the importance of what is ordered for them in terms of their own goals as expressed by their dreams and hopes. Richard H. Turner in his comments about the Turner-Livingstone Readers (1964, p. 3) points out that in these texts there is a ray of hope implanted in the minds of the underprivileged student. "Not pie-in-the-sky hope. But realistic hope. Implicit in the text are ideas like these: you can learn to read, you can get a part-time job, you can ride a taxi, you will be able to lead a better life, you can do something." This is the kind of motivation that makes the most sense to young people. The activities of schools need to be planned to create this positive, meaningful approach to the concerns of young people who seek utilitarian and immediate goals for learning.

Realistic Learning Situations

We recognize that automation will continue to disrupt the balances in labor, but we must still realize that skill training in various fields for many young people represents the entrance ticket to adolescent security.

With a large number of young people employment-bound after their high school years, school systems with flexible vocational programs that include a wide variety of skill training opportunities will present the realistic educational opportunity sought by many students and their parents.

Exercises with tools, equipment, and materials can provide student experiences that will build self-confidence. Such experiences can and should be differentiated according to the ability levels of students in a large school system. Vocational educators need to be careful to avoid the situation described by Melvin L. Barlow (1962, p. 9) when he said that "Vocational educators have joined the rest of education in avoiding the slow learner by making him unacceptable in vocational classes as he is in other classes."

_____ Behavioral Characteristics of Teachers

Empathy for Disadvantaged Youth

Teachers who reject children either overtly or by default will not stimulate any warmth in their student-teacher relationships. Some teachers who themselves have come from the ranks of the disadvantaged are among the most outspoken rejectors of the disadvantaged.

In the ASCD Yearbook for 1964 DeHann and Doll (pp. 15–16) beseech teachers "to be interested also in making, for themselves, discoveries of the talents and abilities of learners. We believe that teachers should be surprised and delighted at the potential they see in children and youth and we expect teachers to communicate their surprise and delight to their pupils. In this way teachers can participate in the discovery of human potential."

Understanding

Students, with few exceptions, do not want any grownups to feel sorry for them. But, they do want teachers to take seriously what they say and do; to be sympathetic to their problems of growing up; to display patience in helping them eliminate or reduce the causes and discomforts of educational disability; to show respect for them even if they

144
Sidney N. Chernak

disagree with the outward manifestations of youth in transition. This all adds up to warmth as a dimension in teaching.

Skill in Teaching

Teachers must be able to demonstrate a high level of skill in anything they wish to teach or freely admit the absence of such skill without sacrificing their own position of respect. It is not unusual for a student to possess information or skill that can enhance the learning at hand. A demonstration of this kind by a student may well be the very thing that can give him the motivational lift he needs to find his place in the sun.

Commitment to Teaching the Disadvantaged

To be successful in teaching disadvantaged children a teacher must be free from bias to the extent that he accepts each student and his parents and receives personal satisfaction from the observable growth that takes place as a result of his teaching. Such evidences as they accumulate give teachers the self-confidence and enthusiasm that catches fire with students. Of the many ways a teacher can display faith in young people, none is more effective than placing before them a challenge to attain higher goals that ordinarily would be considered out of reach.

Inventiveness

Edmund W. Gordon (1966, p. 23), in discussing desired teacher behavior in the area of psychoeducational processes, gives high priority to the following skills, among others:

> Skill in utilization of knowledge and experience in an infinite variety of ways to achieve maximal learning styles and learning strengths. . . .

> Skill in relating knowledge of physical, mental, psychological, social and educational status and of capacity and readiness for learning to the design of learning experiences and to the guidance of pupil development.

> Skill in the utilization and development of materials and procedures leading to the use of appropriate aspects of the environment and in

the use of oneself to influence and modify individual and group learning.

Thus to be effective in this sense teachers need to plan effectively only to set plans aside when a change of direction is dictated by the conditions or interests that appear.

Eagerness to Learn

Every student is different, every class is different, and each time a teacher becomes involved with the same unit of work, his approach, the receptivity of the pupils, and the centers of interest will vary if the atmosphere is attuned to such differences and permits them.

Thus a teacher must constantly be seeking improved approaches and techniques. A program of intervisitation of teachers to other schools and school systems can produce a few transferable ideas. But a teacher can acquire ideas without moving out of the school building in which he teaches. All a teacher needs to do is visit one or two classrooms, or the library, or a departmental office and he will learn something. In addition, teachers should search out the current literature in their fields of interest as well as the areas of concern. Teachers need to realize that all ideas in the business of education are not original and may and indeed should be borrowed, revamped, adapted, and used if they show promise of enhancing the learning process.

_____Skills, Knowledge, and Understanding Needed by Teachers

Classroom Organization

There are many routines connected with the activities in the classroom which in the interest of time and general orderliness need to be reduced to the lowest denominator. For example, the distribution of books and other materials, preparation and operation of visual aid equipment, ventilation, lighting; all of these and others can be made routine at the opening of the semester and distributed among students so that they feel a part of the organization and at the same time learn to assume responsibility. The delegation of such matters serves two

Sidney N. Chernak

additional purposes: it provides the teacher with the necessary freedom of time for working with individuals and groups and gives a sense of security to a large number of students who appreciate and need the order of such an environment.

What is being suggested here is the consistency of certain portions of the school environment without ruling out the exciting elements of surprise and stimulation in other areas. Miriam Goldberg (1963) has expressed it this way:

> The successful teacher meets the disadvantaged child on equal terms, as person to person, individual to individual. He sets clearly defined limits for his pupils and will brook few transgressions. He is aware that, unlike middle-class children, they rarely respond to exhortations intended to control behavior through invoking feelings of guilt and shame. He, therefore, sets the rules, fixes the boundaries, establishes the routines with a minimum of discussion. Here he is impersonal, undeviating, strict, but never punitive.

Knowledge of the Community

Exploration is good for the teacher as well as the student. In order to really understand the environment a teacher can walk and drive through the living, shopping, and working areas in which his students spend most of their time. Visits to homes with the permission of parents and children is an insightful experience. Teachers should extend the same courtesy to students and parents that they themselves expect and not walk into homes unannounced. It is important that a specific purpose be identified for the visit. Such visits to homes and other areas in the neighborhood should result in understanding of the conditions of life in the student community.

Motivation

Armed with the knowledge about students acquired through observing them, studying their previous records, both formal and anecdotal, and planned brief interviews, a teacher comes into possession of the raw material for motivation. Motivational devices aimed at the interests of students become an important instructional stock in trade. The approaches need to be selected carefully through screening sessions in which some are rejected as inappropriate or ineffective in terms of the group and the conditions.

Going Beyond the Call of Duty

Although the tendency in some circles is toward measuring the expenditure of time and energy, there is hardly an enthusiastic, effective teacher alive who does not devote time and energy beyond the call of duty in order to see that his students receive the full measure of his instruction and guidance. Typically, these are the teachers who appear to gain the greatest amount of personal satisfaction from their work.

Accompanying students to activities in the community or attending student events of an athletic, dramatic, or other nature provides insights that cannot be gained as readily in the classroom. Student-teacher relations take a big step forward when a teacher of English congratulates a student for an outstanding performance that he witnessed over the weekend. "Oh, were you there?" The interpretation of this question takes on a great deal of meaning and importance.

Diagnoses and Remediation

The teacher must become an expert in discovering the causes for non-learning symptoms and then know how to select, invent, or research the effective remedy. Strong bridges are built every day by teachers who can say to children, "I know what the trouble is and I feel that I can help you." Several successes like this and you are "in," not only with the one student you helped but with the dozen who learn that "you know your stuff."

It is not anticipated or expected that teachers will know all of the answers instantaneously. So it is important to know where to look or, lacking such knowledge, to seek it from experienced teachers, supervisors, principals, references, in-service courses, or college professors.

Communication Skills

Have you ever asked someone to repeat a direction that you have just given them? If you have, then you know what happens. There is no reason for us to believe that students and parents do not have the same

Sidney N. Chernak

difficulty in interpreting the many things we say or write or do. Consequently, teachers must be alert to the possibilities of misinterpretation and develop a series of checks to test the effect of their own teaching.

The following point of view seems relevant: Any specialist living in a democratic republic who has had the privilege or opportunity to collect information that is uniquely different from and potentially useful to others has the obligation to present such information so that anyone can and will understand it.

In the sense that a teacher is a specialist he should also meet this criterion.

Conclusion

The Problem

Many students who are disadvantaged drop out of school because they can see no immediate rewards for continued attendance. Many of them have a history of failure throughout their school careers. Lack of ability, little regard for the value of education, disinterested parents, unstable home conditions, poverty, physical disability, and a low level of aspiration are but a few of the factors contributing to their lack of progress in school.

Most of these dropouts are confident that they will easily obtain employment, but they quickly become disillusioned by the scarcity of jobs available to people with little education and no saleable skills. Employment trends indicate that there can be expected a continuing decrease in jobs for the unskilled and undereducated.

Causes

We generally have not provided adequately for the lower 25 per cent of the student population and the average students. Educators as well as the general public feel strongly about this lack.

In 1965 Denver conducted an opinion survey on the programs that the school system was offering for pupils of different levels of accomplishment. The responses indicated that 19 per cent of the parents felt that too little attention was being given the students in the superior category, 24 per cent felt the same way about the average students, and 59 per cent felt that too little attention was being given to the less able students.

Although a high level of professional competence is necessary for teaching disadvantaged children, neither the teacher training institutions nor the public school systems have developed particular teacher training programs in depth. All over the country, under the prodding and financing of the U.S. Office of Education, the Ford Foundation, and other groups, programs are taking shape. In Baltimore City, Project Mission is being carried on over a three-year period in cooperation with three teacher preparation institutions. Now in its second year, this program has shown some promising results.

Many people are inclined to define disadvantaged students as delinquent or neglected children. There is no question that these students have cultural handicaps, but many of them have hidden talents, latent abilities, and interested parents. Such projects as the Higher Horizons program in New York City and the Mott Project in Flint, Michigan, have demonstrated the possibilities of discovery when the proper all-out approach is used to provide meaningful experiences and opportunities for these children.

A Partial Solution

No one should have any difficulty in supplying evidence to support the contention that it is far more wholesome and economical to educate people for their own economic competence and well-being than it is to distribute charity and through this act deprive people of their self-respect.

School and our society must unite to make this solution for some of our students work effectively. The AASA Yearbook of 1966 calls attention to this concern in the following manner: It is imperative that dignity be attached to all socially useful labor. One of the first obligations of educators is to raise the prestige of all socially useful labor and to place education for the professions in its proper perspective. At the outside, only 12 in every 100 individuals in the average community will find their occupational futures in medicine, law, teaching, nursing, dietetics, engineering, or other professions.

Three examples from my own experience are relevant here. Each example concerns a man who dropped out of the regular secondary program and subsequently enrolled in a general vocational school as a last resort. All three had a series of tryouts in a number of activities until

Sidney N. Chernak

they settled as follows: J. S., painting and decorating; J. P., business education; R. T., electrical repairs. At the present writing, J. S. is using his decorating skills in painting lifelike figures for a wax museum; J. P. is an assistant buyer in the furniture department of a well-known chain store; R. T. comes to the central office as a permanent maintenance person whenever electrical repairs are needed.

Students and parents will come to see if our programs show promise and will give support and remain to learn if they are convinced that we are on the right track.

An example of this took place in Warren, Ohio, a community of 60,000. The educators in that city believe in ability grouping. At the lower end of the learning rate scale they have developed a special occupational junior-senior high school. When it was first opened, it was designed as a junior high school with no thoughts of a senior high school program. It was thought that when the students reached age sixteen, they would leave school. However, many of the students wished to continue their education. So a suitable program was developed and the school has now been chartered as a first-rate high school by the Ohio State Board of Education.

Thus with the struggle against poverty and the emphasis on education, job training becomes a major possible solution for many of our students of high school age.

References

AMERICAN ASSOCIATION OF SCHOOL ADMINISTRATORS. *Imperatives in Education,* 1966, Section 3.

BARLOW, MELVIN L. "Vocational Education in the Fabulous Future," *American Vocational Journal,* 37 (1962), 9–11.

DeHANN, ROBERT F., and ROBERT C. DOLL. "Individualizing Instruction," *ASCD Yearbook,* 1964, Section 1.

"DENVER LOOKS AT ITS SCHOOLS." Highlights from the Opinion Survey, 1965.

FARSON, RICHARD E. Pacific Regional Conference of the National Rehabilitation Association, 1964. (Unpublished paper.)

GOLDBERG, MIRIAM. "Adapting Teacher Style to Pupil Differences." Unpublished paper presented at Columbia Teachers College Conference on Disadvantaged Children, 1963.

GORDON, EDMUND W. "Desired Teacher Behavior in Schools for Socially Disadvantaged Children." In *Teachers for the Disadvantaged,* eds. Michael D. Usdan and Frederick Bertolaet. Chicago: Follett Publishing Co., 1966, 23–30.

PASSOW, A. HARRY. "Instructional Content for Depressed Urban Centers: Problems and Approaches." Unpublished paper presented at Ohio State University, 1964.

TURNER, RICHARD H. *A Letter to Teachers of America's Cultural Victims.* Chicago: Follett Publishing Co., 1964.

WILLIS, BENJAMIN C. "Vocational Education in the Years Ahead," *American Vocational Journal,* 38 (1963), 18–19.

152
Sidney N. Chernak

9 Manpower Development Training— Rochester Style

Paul K. W. Springer DIRECTOR,
MANPOWER DEVELOPMENT TRAINING CENTER,
ROCHESTER, NEW YORK

The City and Its Problem

ROCHESTER IS a typical city which looks upon itself as progressive. It is a light-industry city using a notably large amount of technical know-how. The industrial scene, largely coordinated by an Industrial Management Council, has been remarkably tranquil. Its labor unions have taken a moderate and enlightened viewpoint. The unemployment rate has varied from 1.3–2.0 per cent. There are currently more than 4,000 unfilled jobs, mostly in the skilled areas. Its social agencies are coordinated into a Council of Social Agencies, the catalog of which furnishes a rather sophisticated approach for help to unfortunate persons who, for one reason or another, cannot be self-sufficient. Its school system is progressive; it believes in research; it has excellent leadership; it works rather closely with community ties. In addition, there are six institutions of higher learning in Greater Rochester. In the arts, Roch-

153

ester can point proudly to the Eastman School of Music, the Art Gallery, the Public Library System, and the Museum. All of these contribute to a fuller life and to enriched education.

This is the surface portrait of Rochester, the city. Behind this picture there is yet another, more disturbing portrait:

1. *The dropout problem.* Approximately 900 students (6 per cent) drop out from Rochester's schools during a single academic year. The indication is that although the proportion of dropouts may be decreasing, the total number is rising owing to population increase. In a decade this means there are some 9,000 youths who have failed to complete traditional school programs.

2. *The influx of the southern Negro.* In the decade 1950–1960, Rochester's nonwhite population rose 208.8 per cent (Table 9–1). This was the highest of any community in New York State.

TABLE 9–1. Nonwhite Population of Rochester, 1950–1970

Year	Nonwhite Population	Per Cent
1950	7,937	2.4
1960	24,184	7.6
1965 (estimate)	35,000	10.9
1970 (projection)	60,000	19.0

The increase of the nonwhite population has been largely southern Negro. A significant number of nonwhite population has immigrated from Puerto Rico and Cuba. Both the Puerto Rican and Cuban nationals usually present a linguistic problem. The Bureau of Municipal Research identifies 54 per cent of the nonwhite population as being born outside the State of New York.

3. *Youth unemployment.* If Rochester's overall unemployment rate of 1.3–2.0 per cent is considered by age groups, one finds that the 17–21-year-old group has a 13 per cent unemployment rate. The unemployment rate for the nonwhite teenager is almost double that of the white teenager—at the present time, about 28 per cent.

It is this background of unemployment and undereducation that feeds the pool of idle youth walking the streets of Rochester.

The stirring was beginning to reach the surface in 1961. The United States Census was beginning to make its message clear. The New York State Division of Youth conducted a study in Rochester, published in

Paul K. W. Springer

May 1962, which rather clearly delineated the dropout picture. In September 1963 a group of executive leaders in the area of Youth Service in Rochester went to a neighboring city, Syracuse, where they would be free of business pressure, telephones, secretaries, and wives to brainstorm youth's problems. These were busy people who found it difficult to either get together or at least to do so for any profitable length of time.

_____The Manpower Training Program

As ONE of the outcomes of this seminar the Rochester Umbrella Manpower Training Project for Youth was born. It was to focus on the disadvantaged, the unemployed, the undereducated youth of Greater Rochester. The aim—to get them off the street and into entry jobs.

In reality there was to be a considerable time lapse before the Youth Program could be implemented. The planning of the complex project began in November 1963. It was not until April 1964 that the project obtained federal approval. It was not until June 9, 1964 that funds in the amount of $1,487,847 were actually released to fund the project. In this frame of reference it is important to point out that the Rochester Manpower Center began operation on July 6, 1964 with minimum staff equipment, and supplies because of the pressure of time. It is also significant to point out that just less than three weeks later, on July 24, 1964, the racial disturbance began which had such wide news coverage. The Manpower program was thus able to play a significant role in a community attempting to put the pieces back together again.

The Rochester Multi-Occupational Manpower Project for youth makes provision for the training of 1,000 youth in seven broad vocational areas or job families. There are thirty-two specific occupations in these broad areas.

Youths are referred to the Training Center weekly by the New York State Employment Service. In most cases the referral is made to a broad area that has been predetermined through testing and interview activities by the New York State Employment Service. On arrival the trainee is placed under the direct control of a Broad Training Instructor. A significant portion of the activities during the first week will, however, be focused around the Manpower Counselor with whom the trainee will relate during his stay at the Center. A typical orientation program presented to new trainees during the first week is as follows:

Monday

1. Welcome and introduction to staff members (counselor, attendance interviewer, instructor).
2. Discussion
   a. What trainees want in life (values).
   b. Life stages (Buehler—Growth, Exploratory, Establishment, Maintenance, Decline).
   c. Identification and discussion about the major decision areas of life.
   d. Clarification and discussion of vocational objectives:
      (1) Why we work.
      (2) What we want in a job.
      (3) How we can increase the chance of getting what we want.
3. Introduction to MDT Center
   a. Background of MDTA—its purpose and function.
   b. Information about the areas of training (Broad and Specific, Mathematics, Reading, Communication Skills, High School Equivalency).
   c. Clarification of:
      (1) Instructor's role.
      (2) Counselor's role.
   d. Explanation and interpretation of the first week's program.
   e. Standards and regulations pertaining to behavior, attendance, grooming, smoking, breaks, parking, and so on.
4. New York State Employment Service—role and function
   a. Regulations pertaining to allowance.
   b. Filling out forms.
   c. Outlook of employment opportunities in Monroe County.
5. Exploratory functions
   a. Tour of the facilities (in groups of 6–10 trainees, a tour is made of the entire building).
   b. Trainees introduced to the instructor and the vocational area where the trainee will be functioning.

Tuesday, Wednesday

1. SRA Testing program—(6–9) Form B. Two parts are given each day.

Thursday

1. Cornell Survey of Worker Attitudes.
2. Viewing and discussing a film covering obtaining and holding a job.

Paul K. W. Springer

3. Further clarification of the counselor's role and his relationship to each training area.
4. Reading and optional completion of the Mooney Problem Check List (its purpose and usage clarified).
5. Discussion of the routine for Friday when the counselor assigned for each area plans a group or individual session with the trainee.

Beginning the first week and continuing for as long as necessary the trainee is involved in a prevocational program. This prevocational phase, for which the Broad Area Instructor has prime responsibility, works to develop within each trainee a knowledge of what his particular choice of job family is like, what its possibilities are, what its specific requirements are. The trainee has an opportunity to get some vocational experience in the job family, to determine whether he is adapted to and challenged by its opportunities. At the same time the instructor is interested in determining the probable capability of each trainee. During this stage the counselor also plays a part. If there are problems or doubts the trainee-instructor-counselor relationship makes it possible for the trainee to apply for a change to another job family that seems a more realistic choice.

At some time before the trainee can leave the prevocational phase, a decision must be made that the area chosen is one in which the trainee has a reasonable chance for success. Obviously, if a girl has third grade reading ability it would be rather unwise to agree to stenographic training. Working as a team, the instructor, the counselor, and on occasion the psychologist must help the trainee develop an understanding so that he may begin training at a point commensurate with his ability to achieve. Aspiration must also be developed so that the trainee will accept remedial education. By so doing the trainee gives evidence of acceptance that lack of educational factors will limit later success.

The Manpower Center believes strongly in the right of the individual to fail. Although the team will do its best to ensure realistic choices, the decision will always be made in the trainee's favor. If, in fact, the trainee does fail in his selected vocational goal, it will be used as a part of the vocational counseling program for him. The remarkable point is that a significant number who have made choices above their apparent capacity do not fail. The high-aspiration factor allows them to succeed.

As many of the trainees have educational lack, basic education and remedial education are extremely important. Although the Center is aware that education has been an unpleasant experience for many, it feels that basic and remedial education must be provided to bring the trainee up to minimum educational competence so as to function adequately in his vocational area. For this same reason high school equivalency is also offered. There is this difference: high school equivalency is not forced. It must come as a result of guidance and counseling. It is felt that the decision to take on this program falls within the aspiration-development function of counselors with their trainees.

The program can be summarized as being a rather sophisticated vocational experience with supporting services and one that also places great emphasis on the work of a counseling team.

The Trainees

PERHAPS it is easier to understand the plan and its objectives by examining a cross section of the youth who are served by the Manpower Center.

Without researching the two populations, efforts to set forth a list of significant characteristics that would distinguish Manpower trainees from pupils of a typical urban high school would be almost fruitless. Even the fact that the point of emphasis of the Center is on "disadvantaged" youth cannot limit the strong similarity that still exists between these two groups. The term *disadvantaged*, as the counseling team views it, has reference to many conditions. A person may be economically disadvantaged, geographically disadvantaged, and so on. Manpower trainees tend to have a greater degree of disadvantage than the rest of the population in the following ways: more Manpower trainees experience more acute financial difficulties; there is a greater incidence of unwed mothers; there are a greater number on probation from the courts; there are more persons with academic deficiencies; there are more who have short-term and unrealistic goals; there are many who tend to manifest attitudes and behavior that are unrewarded by society.

Experience at the Center shows that these trainees need acceptance. Most of them perform better in vocational and related basic education areas than test scores would tend to predict. Many need to be freed at first from direct challenges that would demand an absolute and correct answer, attitude, or approach. A significant number feel out of their natural environment and very uncomfortable at first. Immaturity is a common attribute. There is a tendency to tardiness and absence in the initial phases; many refuse to accept responsibility.

On the other side of the ledger it may be offered that Manpower

Paul K. W. Springer

trainees appear to have a stronger desire to improve occupational and educational status. They have benefited to a degree from those lessons of life which in many instances they have experienced during the interim between school departure and Manpower entry.

The IQ levels of these students run the gamut from the 60s to the 130s. Roughly one-quarter are high school graduates or equivalency graduates by the end of their training period. The trainee enrollment is approximately 50 per cent male and 50 per cent female. The trainee population is approximately 50 per cent white and 50 per cent non-white—the latter mainly Negroes. The Negro enrollment percentage is increasing.

The identification of needs for these trainees is approached with the same reservation as was necessary in enumerating their distinguishing characteristics. This reluctance is not at all to denigrate the efficacy and wisdom of attempting to know better the individual with whom the team will work. The concern is that a skewed picture, such as is often envisioned of the early school leaver, shall not be fostered. Efforts have been made, all too often from without, to analyze, dichotomize, and editorialize the disadvantaged. A strong need is felt at the Man-power Center to listen to this youth in order to realize what *he* is saying, what *he* feels and wishes for himself. This approach of seeing the trainee from within seems to have been met. A popular adage is echoed by a Rochester Manpower Administrator, "A mind convinced against its will is a mind uncommitted still." These young people manifest a need to have someone genuinely interested in them—as one trainee put it, "To care enough to give me hell."

Many have a history of failure. Their need is for success—actually on a day-by-day basis. The desire to postpone rewards, such as is entailed in a four-year apprenticeship, is anathema to many.

The need to see the relevance of any instruction, vocational or aca-demic, or any admonition regarding punctuality, grooming, attitudes with others, is keen among these trainees. The style of the training center differs from the traditional school for this major reason. The en-tire concept at the Manpower Center is on-the-job, not at-school; train-ing hours, not class hours; instructors, not teachers; Applied Mathematics, not Mathematics I; Communication Skills, not English II.

THE attributes of an "ideal teacher" possibly should not vary much, whether the practitioner is involved with the disadvantaged or with traditional groups of youth. This statement is based on the premise that if an instructor has competence in his subject area, he will do the best work in whatever environment he is placed. It must be noted that an instructor with less than ideal characteristics begins to show the limitations of his effectiveness quite quickly when he works with the disadvantaged.

In *Improving English Skills of Culturally Different Youth,* Jewett and Gunderson (1964, p. 4) have listed eleven guidelines which distinguished an effective teacher. He should:

1. Dare to be creative and imaginative.
2. Allow students freedom from pressures, whatever the source.
3. Appear relaxed and informal.
4. Be firm but understanding.
5. Maintain a sense of humor in the most trying and humorless situations.
6. Approach all problems honestly, in absolute control of the emotions; be shock-absorbent.
7. Prepare to work consistently with individuals in a group situation and accept varied responses on a wide range of grade levels.
8. Seek insight to the pupil's problems and interests.
9. Continue to work with enthusiasm for prolonged periods without the encouragement generated by discernible student progress.
10. Demonstrate a sincere concern for the student's welfare.
11. Stimulate through encouragement and sincere praise.

Most of these guidelines are equally applicable whether exhibited by teachers of the disadvantaged or by teachers of traditional groups. There are some added guidelines, however, which seem important in dealing with youth at the Manpower Center. The teacher:

1. Must be able to communicate at the trainee level.
2. Must understand the environment and conditions of deprivation and poverty.
3. Must believe in the value of the Manpower program.
4. Must have a knowledge of employment and trends in his vocational area.

Paul K. W. Springer

5. Must be able to relate all facets of his teaching to the world of work.
   a. Necessity for related mathematics, reading, and communication skills.
   b. Necessity to teach for transfer of skills within a family of occupations.
6. Must have a knowledge of the cultural and emotional framework which directs the attitudes of his trainees.
7. Must have a vital interest in and adequate knowledge of his own role in the total counseling process.

Perhaps as good a way to summarize the "ideal" instructor for working with disadvantaged youth is to say that he must possess a high degree of flexibility. He must be a study in contrasts for he must be loose but firm; patient but persistent; able to teach and be taught; a friend and a foreman; empathetic but not sympathetic.

Problems and Rewards

As USUAL, it is the teacher who possibly can express best the problems and the rewards of teaching. The following is a spontaneous treatise written by an excellent remedial teacher at the Manpower Center. It is cited below just as it was written, including the title, which seemed rather expressive.

This I Believe
(And Try to Remember!)

To contend that each of us is here through choice is a fallacy. We have strange rites to perform and unusual demands are placed upon our time and resources. It is not *our* time. We come here with doubt and misgiving, although the surface seems unruffled, and we do not know whether we are "welcome in the church or if the church will welcome us." If we learn with time to believe more fully in our work, it is only because "our work" believes more fully in us.

I have asked myself many times why the work done here has become increasingly important and why it should be considered a valuable part of our time during the race for space. Each question splinters into a thousand more, until I find myself dealing with individuals, all different, each in his own right demanding knowledge, patience, and understanding. We live in a demanding society—one in which the demanding tone is usual and the polite request a rarity.

I have not tried to concern myself with "IQ." We don't hear the term much around here. The unwritten law does not belong in the printed ritual. Once, anyway, "IQ" was just another working term, never meant to be exact, and meant always to be used with tact and understanding. The new text I picked up the other day worked the term to excess. I had the feeling that the team had run away when the driver lost control of the reins.

There are so many "demands." Here the student may (1) lack the skills of writing, speaking, and listening; (2) often understand more than he is able to express orally or in writing; (3) forget quickly; (4) require twice the number of repetitions as an average pupil for successful retention; (5) be less imaginative; (6) lack curiosity; (7) frequently be unable to see consequences and "be covered by the ashes"; (8) reach conclusions without adequately considering alternatives; (9) be unable to follow prolonged discussions; (10) have difficulty with abstractions; and (11) fall behind the average pupil at an increasing rate.

He may also be:
1. Success starved.
2. Need a balance between success and failure as much as any pupil.
3. Have limited motivation.
4. Enrolled in school (any school), convinced he cannot write or speak correctly.

To my surprise, I found all kinds of learners. I am convinced that there should have been no reason for some of my students to drop out of school (if they did) in the first place. They have the abilities necessary for almost any work they might care to do *but they do need proof that these abilities exist in the first place.* One of my students has a deep understanding of the beauty to be found in poetry and the written word in general. To be sensitive and receptive to complex ideas, it is necessary, first of all, to have a fairly logical mind. It is not necessary to go off the deep end. Coupled to and consistent with this idea there is a dynamic conviction, always present, that we must be practical in our approach to the solutions for practical problems—every day.

If I have been forced to provide practical answers to many questions and to forget many of the lessons of the past, it is not always my students who are to blame. Often, in this situation, more than

Paul K. W. Springer

in any other, it has been necessary to provide some of the imagination, the curiosity, the material for the start of the discussion, some of the logic, and a retracing of the conclusions.

I am not in the least interested in the winner in "the battle of wits," as long as my students find some solid ground on which to stand in the future.

Conclusion

IT IS not a simple process to evaluate a special program such as a Multi-Occupational Manpower Project. As yet, no yardstick exists with which to measure. However, facts and impressions are available that lead one to believe that there has been some success.

The Manpower Center worked with 1,450 young people during the 1964–65 year: 90 per cent of these were early school-leavers, 74 per cent of those enrolling completed the training program for which they registered, 70 per cent of those finishing training actually entered the labor market.

These young people have been seen arriving at the Manpower Center nondescript, insecure, pessimistic, dejected, angry, undereducated, and without marketable skills. They have been seen coming to the realization that Manpower Training is a chance for success, perhaps their last chance. They have been seen blossoming in the joy of their own success and entering society as gainfully employed workers.

Practitioners have learned that there is excellent potential in the Multi-Occupational Manpower Project, with its focus on counseling and emphasis on meeting the needs of youth for employment. Youth responds positively to the atmosphere of opportunity with its aura of sensitized friendship.

Youth can be helped to help themselves.

Reference

JEWETT, A., and DORIS V. GUNDERSON. *Improving English Skills of Culturally Different Youth in Large Cities.* Bulletin No. 5. Washington, D.C.: Office of Education—30012, 1964.

Part Three

Approaches to Teacher Education

10 A Master's Degree Program for the Preparation of Teachers of Disadvantaged Youth

John L. O'Brian
RUTGERS UNIVERSITY

The Setting

THOSE READING this volume have by now come to realize that our traditional teacher training programs at the undergraduate and graduate levels cannot prepare teachers to work effectively with disadvantaged youth. Such programs, through their liberal arts, subject matter, and methodology offerings, are doing an outstanding job of preparing teachers to work with students identified with the middle-class culture. But these teachers are not adequately prepared to work with disadvantaged youth. Generally speaking, the teacher has come from, or had acquired, the value system of the majority culture. He is not prepared cognitively or emotionally to accept the value system, the culture, or the world of the disadvantaged. Without this as a frame of reference, the teacher of the disadvantaged becomes a *disadvantaged teacher*.

The teacher of the disadvantaged must be competent in the subject to be taught; he must possess all the skills and knowledge of pedagogy; he must be receptive to new innovations—in the technology of education, in new patterns of staff utilization, and in new school organizational patterns, as must all teachers; but in addition, he must be introduced to and gain an understanding of the world and the culture of the disadvantaged. This is a process of acculturation. When we look at the job of the teacher of the disadvantaged, we realize that an important aspect of this job will be to introduce the disadvantaged pupil to the expectations and goals of the majority culture, which in our country is the white middle-class culture. This again is a process of acculturation.

It is extremely difficult to describe in a few words the population on which the writings in this book is focusing. A review of the literature shows that such terms as *disadvantaged, culturally disadvantaged, culturally different, socioeconomically disadvantaged, academically disadvantaged, socially disadvantaged, the poor, and the poverty stricken,* among others, are used interchangeably when referring to this segment of the population. We must understand that not all of these labels can be applied to any one of those we are considering but that all apply to the population as a whole, and all are so inextricably interwoven that they cannot be separated. The import of this state of affairs for a teacher training program is that we must develop in the teacher an understanding of the implications of these labels in the eyes of youth so affected, and rely on the teacher to make individual evaluations and adjustments in his daily contact with each student.

In an attempt to overcome the cumbersome explanations associated with the various labels attached to these youth, the Panel of Consultants in their report *Education for a Changing World of Work*[1] used the descriptive phrase *youth with special needs* when referring to this population. In this chapter the terms *disadvantaged* or *youth with special needs* will be used interchangeably and as a blanket expression taking into account the considerations set forth above.

A cliché that is relevant when programs for youth with special needs are being pondered is that *the teacher is the most important factor.* Although this is true in all educational endeavors, it is especially true when we are working with the disadvantaged. This point has been

1. U.S. Department of Health, Education, and Welfare. *Education for a Changing World of Work. Report of the Panel of Consultants on Vocational Education.* Washington, D.C.: Government Printing Office (OE–80021), 1963.

John L. O'Brian

emphasized in the preceding chapters. There are few in the educational community—particularly those from areas where there is a high concentration of Negroes, Puerto Ricans, Appalachian whites, Mexican-Americans, American Indians, Cubans, and migrant workers—who would not agree that providing realistic educational programs for teachers of today's youth (and adults) is the greatest and perhaps the most difficult challenge facing education. There are many who believe that only limited success has been attained in many federally supported training programs because of a lack of teachers trained to work with the disadvantaged and a limited understanding on the part of the program administrators of the students who were to be educated.

_____A Needed Teacher Training Program

CONCERNING the problem that existing teacher education programs of the traditional type cannot prepare teachers to successfully work with youth with special needs, a key aspect that is missing is an understanding of the youth to be served. This understanding must go beyond an introduction to the culture. These youth need allies with unlimited commitment; they do not want pity, sympathy, and censure. If a single word is desired to describe what is needed, *empathy* perhaps fills this need best. The teachers of youth with special needs must understand and appreciate the special needs that these youth possess and their bases. They must be willing to accept these youth as they are and be dedicated to providing unlimited help.

An effective way in which the teacher can gain insight into the world of youth with special needs is to become involved in their world. Reading and discussion alone cannot bring about the understanding that is needed; experiencing is a vital link that must be included. To read, study, experience, live, and become involved is the road to understanding, appreciation, and empathy. What is being said by those presenting the previous chapters is that a teacher of the disadvantaged must build a frame of reference upon which to base and from which he can project his expertise. His expertise must be projected from a base that is representative of understanding. Sympathy is repulsive to the disadvantaged —they do not desire it and they cannot benefit from it.

A fact of life that must be understood by the teacher of youth with special needs is that the value system of these youth differs from that

*A Master's Degree Program for the Preparation of Teachers
of Disadvantaged Youth*

of the middle class. The value system of the world of the youth with special needs has been developed over the years as a means of survival. We must understand too that the value system that has been developed in the inner city of the large urban centers, which is predominately Negro, differs from that of the Appalachian white, the American Indian, the Mexican-American, the southern Negro, the Puerto Rican, the Cuban, and the migrant worker. The teacher of these groups must become familiar with the culture of those with whom he proposes to work.

The problems of the disadvantaged are complex. They cannot be adequately evaluated or diagnosed, nor can adequate solutions be prescribed, if a monolithic approach is utilized. In professional circles we have isolated the disciplines of sociology, psychology, social psychology, and anthropology. Furthermore, specializations have developed within these disciplines. The problems of the disadvantaged cannot be looked at from the point of view of a single discipline. They must be considered in their complex whole. A mix or a blending, a concerted effort by a team cognizant of the role of all behavioral sciences must focus on the problem.

If the plight of the disadvantaged is to be solved, then education must also be included in the mix. Education is the key to open the door, it is the vehicle of progress. It is at this point that even the best plan can bog down. The teacher, more than any other member of the mix, bears the heaviest responsibility. The classroom becomes a miniature society with all its inherent complex problems. The teacher is called upon repeatedly hour after hour, day after day, to analyze and prescribe. If he is to be effective in this responsibility to the degree necessary to be successful with his students, he must have a working knowledge of concepts spanning all the behavioral sciences. Compounding his problem is the fact that such decisions must be made without the privilege of time to consider the facts or time to plan. It can be concluded that the teacher of the disadvantaged must have at least a working knowledge of the basic concepts of these disciplines as they relate to the problems of the disadvantaged and a knowledge of how they consort with one another. If education is to fulfill its mission, if preventive programs are to replace remedial programs, this goal must be realized.

The teacher training curriculum proposed in the remaining portion of this chapter is based on this axiom. It was developed through the joint efforts of an interdisciplinary group actively interested in and associated with meeting the needs of the disadvantaged youth in our schools. The

170
John L. O'Brian

disciplines of sociology, anthropology, social psychology, vocational education, special education, educational psychology, and guidance were represented.[2]

The Curriculum—Background

THE proposed curriculum evolved out of the collective thinking of an interdisciplinary team. The objective of this joint effort was to produce a program at the Master's level that would provide the teacher with a repertory of skills, knowledge, understanding, and attitudes that would enable him to work successfully with youth with special needs.

The Master's level program was selected for a number of reasons. To build the experiences necessary to develop an effective teacher of disadvantaged youth into the baccalaureate program would necessitate deleting a large segment of the existing curricula. These curricula have been studied and evaluated and have withstood much examination. A decision would have to be made as to whether or not such deletions should come from subject matter content, from methodology and pedagogy, or from other liberal and broadening aspects of the curriculum. To weaken any of these would be difficult to justify. Many critics of teacher education programs are currently advocating the strengthening of these areas and recommending a five-year program.

Maturity is another factor to be considered. The curriculum incorporates several practicums involving actual contact and first-hand experience with the world of the disadvantaged. Such exposure demands maturity of judgment that is usually associated with a more adult person.

Teaching youth with special needs will be a challenging and trying experience. Classroom generalship will be a prime factor in the day-to-day contact with these youth. There is much to be said in favor of experience, which is necessary for learning many of the "tricks of the

2. The author would like to acknowledge the members of the Curriculum Committee, who, as a team under the direction of the author, developed the curriculum that is described in detail in this chapter. They are Drs. Arnold Buchheimer, William Carriker, Donald Maley, William Phillips, Jr., Lawrence Plotkin, Bruce Tuckman, and Mr. Leonard Zeitz. As you will note, these individuals expressed their position on the problems of teaching the disadvantaged in the first section of the book. The author would also like to acknowledge the support of the U.S. Office of Education, Division of Comprehensive and Vocational Education Research under Grant OE 6–85047.

trade." Every person must discover the techniques that work best for him. This is only emphasizing the well-known fact that there are many different solutions to the same problem. There is no guarantee that what will work for teacher A will also work for teacher B. Teaching experience, maturity, "tricks of the trade," a desire to work with youth with special needs (a desire that often grows out of experience) seem to substantiate the position that the Master's program is the appropriate level on which to offer this program. A final justification for this position, and one easily understood, stems from the curriculum itself. The content and level of the seminars, courses, and workshops demand a basic level of background and understanding that would not be available in a baccalaureate program, which, in itself, would have to be revised and limited in order to incorporate the proposed curriculum.

In setting forth these recommendations a number of assumptions were made. It was assumed that the candidate (1) would hold the baccalaureate degree and have teaching experience, (2) be competent in his subject matter specialty, (3) have a desire to teach the disadvantaged, and (4) generally would come from the middle class (based on primary teacher source rather than choice). In addition, since the greater portion of youth with special needs will come from the inner portions of urban communities, the specific application given should reflect this reality. The concepts presented, however, are closely related to other populations and need only a change of emphasis to become valid.

A study of the curriculum will show that it has a progression and integrity of its own consistent with educational theory and current interdisciplinary thinking regarding the disadvantaged. A premise upon which these efforts are based is that vocational teachers, as well as academic teachers, trained in our traditional programs, have neither the conceptual understandings of teaching the disadvantaged nor the background and experiences to understand the milieu in which these youth grow up, live, and survive. The curriculum is designed to give the prospective teacher of the disadvantaged the following content:

1. An orientation experience that will sensitize him to the world of youth with special needs.

2. An understanding of the characteristics of the population to be taught.

3. Basic sociological, psychological, educational, anthropological, and literary concepts dealing with the disadvantaged.

4. Direct experiences to develop an understanding of the culture of the disadvantaged.

5. An integrating experience that is composed of selected educational processes such as teaching methodology, program development, curriculum development, and evaluation—all with special emphasis on teaching the disadvantaged.

6. A supervised teaching experience with a student population that is disadvantaged in some way—for example, socially, culturally, economically—and whose educational achievement has been limited.

7. A supervised work experience under the direction of a professional worker. The purpose of this experience is to give the student an understanding of agency structure and agency programs dealing with the poor and the disadvantaged.

8. A seminar that will provide an opportunity to integrate and relate issues that have grown out of the experiences of the curriculum.

9. An opportunity (a) to investigate a problem related to the youth with special needs and to report this in a Master's Paper, or (b) to evaluate the total experience received in the Master's program and to report this in an Evaluation Paper. Both of these experiences provide the student with a vehicle to integrate his experiences and knowledge gained and to apply them to his own professional improvement.

Thus the curriculum to be presented is based on a progression from *orientation to conceptualization* and from *experiencing to integration and application* of experiences.

The structure and scheduling of the components of the curriculum are very important. The curriculum when offered in coordinated units becomes greater than the sum of the individual parts. It is highly recommended that persons pursuing this educational objective be free to concentrate on the program and be able to devote full time to it. The courses, seminars, and field experiences are designed to be given in units that consider the problems of the disadvantaged in their complex interrelationships. To achieve this, interplay must be possible. Theory must be put to the test of reality if it is to become truly meaningful. Reinforcement cannot wait until next year or some other distant point in time. Learning based on the principle of discovery is meaningful and lasting. Such discovery is possible when students are faced with actual problems and opportunity is provided to "discover" theory and solutions in the environs of the seminar. As it will be seen, a team approach is recommended as the mode of instruction. This is in agreement with the thesis that the problems of the disadvantaged should be considered in their complex entirety.

One final word, the curriculum recommended should prove appropriate for the teacher whatever his subject matter specialty is: whether it is English, social studies, mathematics, vocational (all areas), technical, language, and so on.

_____The Curriculum—An Overview

THE curriculum consists of four blocks that have been developed to be compatible with an administrative pattern utilizing two sixteen-week semesters and two summer sessions. Institutions operating on a trimester or quarterly basis will have to make necessary adjustments. Efforts should be made to maintain the integrity of the blocks. An inspection of the offerings within these blocks will demonstrate the feasibility of this recommendation.

A cursory examination of the curriculum depicted in Figure 10–1 shows the rationale upon which the curriculum is built. In the first summer the teacher candidate is oriented to the curriculum and to the world of the disadvantaged. In the fall semester the relationship and dependence of the three programs are obvious. While the student is engaged in finding out what the world of youth with special needs is all about through actual contact with this world, he is also finding out about this world through vicarious experiences provided in the other two courses. This will better enable him to understand what he is experiencing. In addition, he will be able to relate the theories of the behavioral sciences to actual experiences, and in many instances discover for himself theories that explain the phenomena he is living and studying. At this point in the curriculum the teacher trainee will have been exposed to numerous experiences that will provide background for the next block or phase of his program—that of working with disadvantaged youth in an educational setting.

In the spring semester a series of three courses have been developed that supplement each other in numerous ways. An educational practicum within the environs of a school serving youth with special needs will be set up. Currently, the teacher trainee will be engaged in a Seminar in Learning, Development, and Measurement and a course entitled Educational Processes for Teaching the Disadvantaged. These two courses, plus the prior educational experiences of the curriculum, have as

174
John L. O'Brian

I. Summer Session

   A. Orientation Workshop (Three Credits)

II. Fall Semester

   A. The Social Psychology of the Disadvantaged (Four Credits)
   B. Seminar in Urban Society (Four Credits)
   C. Field Experience (Four Credits)

III. Spring Semester

   A. Seminar in Learning, Development, and Measurement (Four Credits)
   B. Educational Processes for Teaching the Disadvantaged
     (Four Credits)
   C. Educational Practicum for Teaching Disadvantaged Youth
     (Four Credits)

IV. Summer Session

   A. Professional Issues Seminar (Three Credits)
   B. Integrating Option
     1. Master's Project (Three Credits) or
     2. Evaluative Paper (No Credit)

Figure 10-1. Master's degree program for teachers of disadvantaged youth.

their objective the preparation of the individual for his educational practicum. Once again the trainee will have an opportunity to experience, and while experiencing he will be able to obtain continuous professional consultation. As in the fall semester, there is also provided opportunity for interaction with fellow classmates. The sharing of experiences, the discussion of avenues of action, the application of hypotheses developed in the supporting educational activities will provide a unique educational program.

The fourth major block of the curriculum, which takes place in the second summer session, involves two separate functions, yet each contributes to a common objective. The objective is to provide a means of integrating and relating the total individual and collective experiences of the curriculum into a meaningful pattern. The first of these is the Professional Issues Seminar. This seminar will focus on issues germane to the broad topic of teaching youth with special needs. It will not be until this point in the program that the student will have both the practical and cognitive experiences necessary to fully consider and come to grips with the problems of this population.

The second aspect of this fourth block of the curriculum has two options—the Master's Project or the Evaluative Paper. Each of these will contribute to the integrating objective of this block, the main difference being that this is an individual effort as contrasted to the Professional Issues Seminar, which involves group processes. The differences between the Master's Project and the Evaluative Paper are described fully in a later section.

_____The Curriculum—The Component Parts

Orientation Workshop

The workshop serves as an orientation medium for the curriculum. Its primary functions are to introduce, sensitize, and orient the student to the culture of the disadvantaged and to provide a self-exploratory experience in terms of personal reactions. To achieve this general objective a combination of practical experiences conducted in the environment of the disadvantaged along with opportunity for reading, listening to records, and viewing films and plays are incorporated in the plans for the orientation workshop. Opportunity is provided for the students to meet in small groups, under the direction of a workshop supervisor, to discuss their experiences, emotions, and attitudes that will grow out of the workshop activities. The model for such a workshop is anthropological in structure. The need for the teacher of the disadvantaged to understand the culture of those he will teach has often been stated as a need by those who work in disadvantaged settings.

Objectives. The orientation workshop aims to achieve a number of specific objectives, which support and supplement the general objectives stated above:

1. To sensitize the student to the culture of the disadvantaged.
2. To explore personal attitudes in relation to this culture.
3. To understand and appreciate the life of the disadvantaged.
4. To break down stereotypic thinking about the disadvantaged.
5. To develop an appreciation of the variety of life among the disadvantaged.
6. To develop an appreciation of the resourcefulness of the disadvantaged.
7. To understand and appreciate the cultural gap between the middle class and the disadvantaged.

176
John L. O'Brian

8. To narrow the cultural gap between the student and the disadvantaged.

9. To gain a direct insight of and experience with the structure of the life of the disadvantaged.

10. To provide background experience upon which appropriate learning methods can be developed.

General Comments. The workshop will be offered on the time equivalency of a three-credit course. Because of the nature of the activities and the desired outcomes, it is recommended that the responsibility for the program be held jointly by an anthropologist and a counselor (who may be a clinical psychologist, a counseling psychologist, or a psychiatrist). These workshop supervisors will be responsible for identifying and establishing the "living--in" experiences in which the students will become involved, as described in Unit I. The student will be responsible for activities relating to his reading, viewing films and plays, and obtaining and listening to appropriate records. The discussion groups will be organized and conducted on an informal basis by the supervisors.

Unit I will be followed by three other units. These will be conducted concurrently since they are related and supplementary.

The overall objective of the workshop is to introduce, sensitize, and orient the student to the culture of the disadvantaged and to provide a self-exploratory experience in terms of personal reactions. If the student is to achieve this objective he must establish a rapport with the culturally disenfranchised and indigenous community life. The contact should be with indigenous persons rather than with professional persons so that the experience will be differentiated from later field and practicum experiences.

COURSE OUTLINE

UNIT I   GENERAL ORIENTATION

Purpose: The first week of the Orientation Workshop will be utilized to give the student an overview of the curriculum and the workshop.

    A. The following are typical of the activities that should take place during Unit I:

        1. General introduction of staff and class members.

        2. Overview of the curriculum-objectives, purposes, evaluation, anticipated outcomes.

3. Overview of the workshop-objectives, purposes, evaluation, anticipated outcomes.
4. Assignment of initial living-in experience.
5. Explanation of the student's responsibility for Unit III—Sensitizing Experiences.
6. Preparations for the living-in experience.

UNIT II   EXPERIENCE IN LIVING

Purpose: The Experience in Living unit is intended to provide opportunity for guided and supervised participation and observation of the world of the disadvantaged. This is in the nature of a full living-in experience. It is not desirable or intended that the trainee be placed in a world that could be alien or hostile without proper supervision. This supervision should be a joint responsibility of the university and a community leader. *Suggested Experiences:* The settings for the experiences enumerated below should be in communities where the disadvantaged predominate. Involvement in one experience does not preclude involvement in the other experiences; indeed it is hoped that the trainee will participate in as many activities as possible.

1. Reside in a local YMCA or YWCA, housing development, or other local dwelling.

2. Do volunteer work with local churches, mission societies, or other indigenous community improvement agencies.

3. Attend political meetings, rallies, and so on, so as to gain knowledge of the local political structure.

4. Attend community meetings, rallies, and so on.

5. Be a participant-observer of informal local activities, such as bowling, attending local theaters, taverns, boys' clubs, church meetings, grange hall activities (informal activities will vary from community to community).

6. Obtain employment as a clerk in a retail store, or engage in diverse commercial enterprises of the community on the indigenous level.

7. Acquire knowledge of local police and juridical activities through court attendance, police hearings, probation sessions.

UNIT III   SENSITIZING EXPERIENCES

Purpose: This unit has as its objective the furthering of a sensitivity toward and understanding of the culture of the disadvantaged through the vehicles of literature, films, records, and plays.

John L. O'Brian

A. The readings are nonacademic in nature and the emphasis will be on fiction, personal experiences of the authors, and essays. The plays will be of a similar nature.

1. A suggested bibliography of readings, films, records, and plays is given in the Suggested Reading List that follows Unit IV. This list should be used as a guide.

UNIT IV DISCUSSION

Purpose: The Discussion unit is the seminar aspect of the workshop and is designed to provide opportunity for students to discuss their feelings, emotions, and attitudes that emerge as a result of the living-in experiences and from the readings, films, records, and plays.

A. Twice a week the students will meet in small groups under the guidance of the workshop supervisors—an anthropologist and a counselor.

1. The supervisors may be aided and the discussions supplemented by indigenous surrogates defined as persons residing in the community. These persons should be those who hold the community's trust and who act as guides, gate-keepers, and alter egos to the students.

2. The nature of the discussions should be informal.

3. The function of the supervisors, who will be the group discussion leaders, should be to act as clarifying agents of feelings, emotions, and attitudes. The supervisors should help the student to develop an appreciation of the cultural dimensions of his experience as well as to clarify his personal attitudes.

4. It is not intended that the student become a member of the disadvantaged group, but rather that he develop an understanding and acceptance of his own adjustment difficulties to the world of the disadvantaged.

5. Supervisors should be available to the students for personal consultation.

SUGGESTED READING LIST

A. Books

1. Agee, James, and W. Evans. *Let Us Now Praise Famous Men.* Boston: Houghton Mifflin, 1960.

2. Baldwin, James. *Notes of a Native Son*. Boston: Beacon Press, 1955.

3. ———. *Nobody Knows My Name*. New York: Dial Press, 1961.

4. ———. *The Fire Next Time*. New York: Dial Press, 1963.

5. ———. *Going to Meet the Man*. New York: Dial Press, 1965.

6. Brown, Claude. *Man-Child in the Promised Land*. New York: Macmillan Co., 1965.

7. Caldwell, Erskine. *Tobacco Road*. New York: New American Library, 1932.

8. Caudill, Harry. *Night Comes to the Cumberland*. Boston: Little, Brown and Co., 1963.

9. Clark, Kenneth. *Dark Ghetto*. New York: Harper & Row, 1965.

10. Davis, Sammy, Jr. *Yes I Can*. New York: Farrar, Straus & Giroux, 1965.

11. Ellison, Ralph. *Invisible Man*. New York: Random House, 1952.

12. Gregory, Dick. *Nigger*. New York: E. P. Dutton & Co., 1964.

13. Griffin, J. Howard. *Black Like Me*. Boston: Houghton Mifflin Co., 1961.

14. Harrington, Michael. *The Other America*. New York: Macmillan Co., 1962.

15. Killens, John. *And Then We Heard the Thunder*. New York: Alfred A. Knopf, 1962.

16. La Farge, Oliver. *Laughing Boy*. Boston: Houghton Mifflin Co., 1963.

17. Lewis, Oscar. *Five Families*. New York: Basic Books, 1959.

18. ———. *Children of Sanchez*. New York: Random House, 1961.

19. Steinbeck, John. *Grapes of Wrath*. New York: Viking Press, 1958.

20. ———. *Tortilla Flat*. New York: Bantam Books, 1965.

21. Wright, Richard. *Native Son*. New York: New American Library, 1962.

B. PLAYS

1. Baldwin, James. *Blues for Mister Charlie*. New York: Dial Press, 1964.

2. Genet, Jean. *The Blacks: A Clown Show*. New York: Grove Press, 1960.

John L. O'Brian

3. Jones, Le Roi. *Baptism and the Toilet*. New York: Grove Press, 1967.
4. Odets, Clifford. *"Waiting for Lefty,"* in Clifford Odets, *Six Plays*. New York: Modern Library, 1963.
5. Rice, Elmer L. *"Street Scene,"* in Elmer L. Rice, *Three Plays*. New York: Hill & Wang, 1965.

Note: Many plays are available in print, either as separate plays or as collections and anthologies.

C. FILMS

Note: Many of the following return as "film classics"; hence failure to see them when they first appear does not mean that they are lost forever to the viewer.

1. *David and Lisa*
2. *The Forgotten Village*
3. *The Grapes of Wrath*
4. *Home of the Brave*
5. *The Leather Boys*
6. *The Mark*
7. *Mornings for Jimmy*
8. *Nothing but a Man*
9. *One Potato, Two Potato*
10. *The Pawnbroker*
11. *The Pearl*
12. *The Quiet One*
13. *Sallah*
14. *The Southerner*
15. *West Side Story*
16. *The Wild Ones*

D. RECORDS

1. Anderson, Marian
   He's Got the Whole World in His Hands (Victor LM-2032)
2. Bibb, Leon
   Oh Freedom and Other Spirituals (Washington 701)
   Tol' My Captain (Vanguard 9058)
3. Dylan, Bob
   Bob Dylan (Columbia CL-1779)
4. Guthrie, Woody
   Ballads of Sacco and Vanzetti (Folkways 5485)
   Dust Bowl Ballads (Folkways 2011)
   Sing with Leadbelly (Folkways 2483)
5. Holliday, Billie
   Blues Are Brewin' (Decca 8701)
   Lady Sings the Blues (Verve 8099)
6. Leadbelly
   Last Sessions (Folkways 2941-2)
7. Robeson, Paul
   Spirituals (Columbia ML-4105)

8. White, Josh

      Chain Gang Songs (Elektra 158)

      Empty Bed Blues (Elektra 211)

Note: To be comprehensive such a list would include such individuals as: Pete Seeger, John Jacob Niles, Odetta, Big Bill Broonzy, Brownie McGhee, Sister Rosetta Tharpe, Sonny Terry, and Cisco Houston. Folkways Records also includes in its catalogue albums of regional folk music and American Indian folk music, by tribe and/or by area.

E. TELEVISION DOCUMENTARIES

1. Many TV documentaries have chronicled the plight of the poor. The faculty should be aware of such future programming. Requests can be made for loans of earlier documentaries from broadcasting sources.

The Social Psychology of the Disadvantaged

This course involves an analysis of the personal, educational, and vocational characteristics of the poverty stricken. Empirical information and theories on racial differences, prejudice, and attitude change are an integral part of the course. The unique role of the Negro in American history as well as in the present is traced as a model. Novels, essays, and plays are used to present the human aspects of poverty to the student.

Academic courses in the behavioral sciences usually do not treat the issues of poverty nor do they systematically integrate their facts and theories with material from other social sciences. This course is an attempt to utilize the relevant aspects of social psychology for an understanding of the problems posed for society by the urban poor. Material from sociology, anthropology, history, and literature is integrated with that of psychology.

Objectives: The overall purpose of this seminar is to prepare teachers of disadvantaged youth to teach more effectively. Subsidiary objectives include the following:

1. To provide relevant information from social psychology and related disciplines so that the problems posed by the disadvantaged for society can be understood.

2. To influence the attitudes of the teacher trainees so that their work will be marked by zeal and empathy.

John L. O'Brian

3. To make meaningful the problems of poverty raised in other courses of the curriculum.

4. To provide a better understanding of the contemporary United States.

General Comments: The course in The Social Psychology of the Disadvantaged should be offered on the time equivalency of a four-credit course. It is recommended that the course be conducted on a combined lecture and seminar basis with specialists from other disciplines invited to participate as much as possible. A social psychologist will have the primary responsibility. Teachers from the following disciplines will participate in the units designated: Anthropology—Units I, II, and III; Sociology—Units I, IV, and VII; Education—Units I and VII; Civil Rights—Unit VII; History—Unit VIII; and, Literature—Unit IX.

Because the Negro is a large element of the disadvantaged population in most cities, emphasis has been placed on this group as a model. Where minority groups such as the Mexican-American, the Indian, the Puerto Rican, or the Appalachian white constitute a significant proportion of the disadvantaged to be taught, Units VII, VIII, and parts of IX can be changed to fit the particular need.

It is suggested that the course instructors be alert to the treatment of the problems of the disadvantaged by the mass media (television, weeklies, and dailies) and by the arts (movies, plays, and novels). They can then make timely assignments that will make the course relevant for contemporary issues.

COURSE OUTLINE

UNIT I   THE CHARACTERISTICS OF THE URBAN POOR: THE PROBLEM AND ITS TERMINOLOGY

Purpose: This unit is designed to acquaint the student with the psychological, educational, and vocational characteristics of disadvantaged youth.

TOPICS FOR DISCUSSION

A. Definitions of disadvantaged youth.
1. Functional failure to adapt.
2. Socioeconomic class.
3. Family and neighborhood constellation.
4. Psychological characteristics.

B. Problems posed for society by large pockets of urban poor.
1. Family disruption.
2. Delinquency.
3. Drug addiction.
4. "Social dynamite."
C. The role of education in dealing with disadvantaged youth.
1. Historical role of acculturation.
2. Contemporary approaches.
3. General education for general employment.
D. A critique of the concept of cultural deprivation as an explanatory concept for educational retardation.

UNIT II RACIAL AND ETHNIC DIFFERENCES (GENERAL)

Purpose: This unit is designed to analyze the problems posed when a "difference" is found in the measurement of psychological characteristics between races.

TOPICS FOR DISCUSSION

A. The anthropological approach.
1. The concept of race.
B. The biological approach.
1. Arguments concerning "racial superiority."
a. Physical and physiological characteristics.
b. Refutation.
C. The cultural argument.
1. Contributions to culture.
2. Level of development.
3. Refutation.
D. The evidence from scientific studies of intellectual and non-intellectual traits.
E. The role of environmental factors.

UNIT III RACIAL AND ETHNIC DIFFERENCES IN MEASURED INTELLIGENCE

Purpose: The objective of this unit is to develop the points made in Unit II as they are applied to the specific problem of intellectual differences.

TOPICS FOR DISCUSSION

A. Measured differences in intelligence (the experimental literature related to the topic is to be summarized).

184
John L. O'Brian

B. An analysis of the role of environmental factors.
   1. Language.
   2. Education.
   3. Socioeconomic class.
   4. Speed.
C. The test instrument's role in producing differences.
D. The effect of changed environment on measured intelligence.

UNIT IV   RACIAL PREJUDICE

Purpose: The objective of this unit is to make the student aware that a central social issue, racial prejudice, can be studied as a sociopsychological process. This will enable him to understand the phenomenon in himself and others in the community.

TOPICS FOR DISCUSSION

A. Theories of racial prejudice.
   1. Economic: historical emphasis (exploitation theory).
   2. Urbanization: sociocultural emphasis (mass culture and urban traits).
   3. Atmosphere: situational emphasis.
   4. Frustration: psychodynamic emphasis (reactions to frustration).
   5. Phenomenological emphasis (man's perceptions and beliefs).
   6. Emphasis on earned reputation: group differences that provoke hostility.
B. The learning of prejudice.
C. The functional role played by prejudice in the life of the individual.
D. Stereotypes and prejudice.
E. The role of the school.

UNIT V   ATTITUDES AND OPINIONS:
THEIR MEASUREMENT AND CHANGE

Purpose: The purpose of this unit is to make the student aware of the dynamic qualities of attitudinal systems and the conditions under which changes occur.

TOPICS FOR DISCUSSION

A. The psychological structure of attitude.
   1. Direction.

A Master's Degree Program for the Preparation of Teachers of Disadvantaged Youth

2. Degree.
3. Intensity.
4. Salience.
B. The development of attitude.
C. Changing attitude.
   1. Interpersonal contact.
     a. In military.
     b. In housing.
     c. In school desegregation.

Note: The student's experiences in the program will be discussed in terms of the above.

UNIT VI   RELATIONSHIP BETWEEN ATTITUDINAL PATTERNS AND PERSONALITY

Purpose: This unit is designed to show the relationship between belief systems and the personality structure of the believer.

TOPICS FOR DISCUSSION

A. The generality of prejudice.
B. The relationship between personality factors and generalized ethnocentricity.
C. The authoritarian personality.

UNIT VII   NEGRO REACTION TO PREJUDICE

Purpose: To analyze the way in which contemporary minority groups respond to prejudice so that the wide range of adjustment visible in the behavior of Negroes is made understandable.

TOPICS FOR DISCUSSION

A. The emergence of various viewpoints and leaders in the Negro's movement toward equality is analyzed by reading and writing two book reports on current issues.

UNIT VIII   THE NEGRO IN THE UNITED STATES: THE HISTORICAL BACKGROUND

Purpose: To develop an understanding of the historical roots of current problems, the Negro's role in American history is treated in detail.

A. Slavery.

B. The Civil War.

C. Reconstruction.

D. The post-Reconstruction period.

E. Contemporary issues.

UNIT IX READING IN THE LITERATURE OF THE POOR

Purpose: To make understandable the lives of the poor in flesh and blood characterization.

TOPICS FOR DISCUSSION

A. Readings from literature dealing with the poor will be assigned for review.

B. The student is to write two book reviews. Two different authors from the Suggested Reading List given for Unit IX are to be used.

SUGGESTED READING LIST

UNIT I. THE CHARACTERISTICS OF THE URBAN POOR: THE PROBLEM AND ITS TERMINOLOGY

1. Clark, K. B. "Clash of Cultures in the Classroom," *Integrated Education,* 1, No. 4 (1963), 7–14.

2. Cleft, V. A. "Factors Relating to the Education of Culturally Deprived Negro Youth," *Educational Theory,* 14 (1964), 76–82.

3. Deutsch, M. "Minority Group and Class Status As Related to Social and Personality Factors in Scholastic Achievement," *Social and Applied Anthropological Monograph,* 2 (1960).

4. Havighurst, R. J. "Who Are the Socially Disadvantaged?" *Journal of Negro Education,* 33 (1964), 210–218.

5. Landers, J. "The Responsibilities of Teachers and School Administration," *Journal of Negro Education,* 33 (1964), 318–332.

6. Lipton, A. "Cultural Deprivation," *Journal of Educational Sociology,* 36 (1962), 17–19.

7. Mackler, B., and M. G. Gidding. "Cultural Deprivation; A Study in Mythology," *Teachers College Record,* 66 (1965), 608–613.

8. National Education Association. *Education and the Disadvantaged American.* Report of the Educational Policies Commission, 1962.

9. Perry, J. "The Preparation of Disadvantaged Youth for Employ-

ment and Civic Responsibilities," *Journal of Negro Education,* 33 (1964), 275–281.

10. Riessman, F. "Cultural Styles of the Disadvantaged," *Integrated Education,* 1 (1963), 9–15.

11. Wolf, E. P., and L. Wolf. "Sociological Perspective on the Education of the Culturally Deprived Children," *School Review,* 70 (1962), 373–387.

SUPPLEMENTARY READINGS

12. Clark, K. B. *Dark Ghetto.* New York: Harper & Row, 1965.

13. Passow, A. H. (ed.). *Education in Depressed Areas.* New York: Teachers College Bureau of Publications, 1963.

14. Sexton, P. *Education and Income.* New York: Viking Press, 1961.

UNIT II. RACIAL AND ETHNIC DIFFERENCES (GENERAL)

1. Klineberg, O. *Social Psychology.* 2nd ed. New York: Holt, Rinehart & Winston, 1954, pp. 291–327.

SUPPLEMENTARY READINGS

2. _____. *Race Differences.* New York: Harper & Row, 1935.

3. Pettigrew, T. F. *A Profile of the American Negro.* Princeton, N.J.: D. Van Nostrand Co., 1964, pp. 59–159.

UNIT III. RACIAL AND ETHNIC DIFFERENCES IN MEASURED INTELLIGENCE

1. Brown, F. "An Experimental and Critical Study of the Intelligence of Negro and White Kindergarten Children," *Journal of Genetic Psychology,* 65 (1944), 161–175.

2. Dreger, R. M., and K. S. Miller. "Cooperative Psychological Studies of Negroes and Whites in the U.S.," *Psychological Bulletin,* 57 (1960), 361–402.

3. Deutsch, M., and B. Brown. "Social Influences in Negro-White Intelligence Differences," *Journal of Social Issues,* 20 (1964), 24–36.

4. Els, K., et al. *Intelligence and Cultural Differences.* Chicago: University of Chicago Press, 1951, pp. 3–57.

5. Jackson, E. R. "The Impact of Environment on Racial Achievement," *Journal of Human Relations,* 6 (1958), 47–53.

6. Lee, E. S. "Negro Intelligence and Selective Migration," *American Sociological Review,* 16 (1951), 227–233.

7. McCord, W. M., and N. J. Demerath. "Negro vs. White Intelligence: A Continuing Controversy," *Harvard Educational Review,* 28 (1958), 120–135.

John L. O'Brian

8. McQueen, R., and B. Churn. "The Intelligence and Educational Achievement of a Matched Sample of White and Negro Students," *School and Society,* 88 (1960), 327–329.

9. Osborn, R. T. "Racial Differences in Mental Growth and School Achievement: A Longitudinal Study," *Psychological Reports,* 7 (1960), 233–239.

10. Pasamanick, B., and H. Knoblock. "Early Language Behavior in Negro Children and the Testing of Intelligence," *Journal of Abnormal and Social Psychology,* 50 (1955), 401–402.

11. Plotkin, L. "Racial Differences in Intelligence," *American Psychologist,* 49 (1959), 526–527.

12. Rohrer, J. H. "The Test Intelligence of Osage Indians," *Journal of Social Psychology,* 16 (1942), 99–105.

13. Sherman, M., and C. B. Key. "The Intelligence of Isolated Mountain Children," *Child Development,* 3 (1932), 279–290.

SUPPLEMENTARY READINGS

14. Haggard, C. A. "Social Status and Intelligence; An Experimental Study of Certain Cultural Determinants of Measured Intelligence," *Genetic Psychology Monograph,* 49 (1954), 141–186.

15. Hunt, W. A. "Negro-White Differences in Intelligence in World War II—A Note of Caution," *Journal of Abnormal and Social Psychology,* 42 (1947), 254–255.

16. Klineberg, O. *Negro Intelligence and Selective Migration.* New York: Columbia University Press, 1935.

17. ———. *Characteristics of the American Negro.* New York: Harper & Row, 1944.

18. Machover, S. "Cultural and Racial Variations in Patterns of Intellect," *Teachers College Contributions to Education,* No. 875, 1943.

19. Tumin, M. M. (ed.). *Race and Intelligence.* New York: Anti-Defamation League, 1963.

UNIT IV. RACIAL AND ETHNIC PREJUDICE

1. Allport, G. *The Nature of Prejudice.* Cambridge, Mass.: Addison-Wesley Publishers, 1954, pp. 3–81, 189–205, 206–220, 243–260.

2. Clark, K. B. *Prejudice and Your Child.* Boston: Beacon Press, 1963, pp. 17–94.

3. Krech, D., and R. S. Crutchfield. *Theories and Problems of Social Psychology.* New York: McGraw-Hill Book Co., 1948, pp. 443–531.

189

4. Dollard, J. *Caste and Class in a Southern Town.* New Haven, Conn.: Yale University Press, 1937.

5. Marrow, A. J. *Changing Patterns of Prejudice.* Philadelphia: Chilton Books, 1962.

6. Montagu, A. M. F. *Man's Most Dangerous Myth.* New York: Columbia University Press, 1945.

UNIT V. ATTITUDES AND OPINIONS: THEIR MEASUREMENT AND CHANGE

1. Alsop, S., and O. Quayle. "What Northerners Really Think of Negroes," *Saturday Evening Post,* 238 (1964), 17–21.

2. Deutsch, M., and M. E. Collins. "The Effect of Public Policy in Housing Projects Upon Interracial Attitudes," in *Readings in Social Psychology,* eds. E. E. Maccoby, T. M. Newcomb, and E. L. Hartley. 3d ed. New York: Holt, Rinehart & Winston, 1958.

3. Hartley, E. L. "Development of Attitude Toward Negroes," in *Readings in Social Psychology,* eds. T. M. Newcomb and E. L. Hartley. 2d ed. New York: Holt, Rinehart & Winston, 1952.

4. ———— and R. E. Hartley. *Fundamentals of Social Psychology.* New York: Alfred A. Knopf, 1955, pp. 651–740.

5. Hyman, H. H., and P. B. Sheatsley. "Attitudes Toward Desegregation," *Scientific American,* 195 (1956), 35–39.

6. Katz, D., and K. W. Braly. "Verbal Stereotypes and Racial Prejudice," in *Readings in Social Psychology,* eds. E. E. Maccoby, T. M. Newcomb, and E. L. Hartley. 3d ed. New York: Holt, Rinehart & Winston, 1958.

7. Krech, D., and R. S. Crutchfield. *Theory and Problems of Social Psychology.* New York: McGraw-Hill Book Co., 1948, pp. 149–273.

8. MacKenzie, B. "The Importance of Contact in Determining Attitude Toward Negroes," *Journal of Abnormal and Social Psychology,* 43 (1948), 417–441.

9. "How Whites Feel About Negroes: A Painful American Dilemma," *Newsweek,* 62 (October 21, 1963), 44–57.

10. Starr, S. A., R. M. Williams, and S. A. Stouffer. "Negro Infantry Platoons in White Companies," in *Readings in Social Psychology,* eds. E. E. Maccoby, T. M. Newcomb, and E. L. Hartley. 3d ed. New York: Holt, Rinehart & Winston, 1958.

11. Stember, C. H. *Education and Attitude Change; The Effect of Schooling on Prejudice Against Minority Groups.* New York: American Jewish Congress, Institute of Human Relations, 1961.

12. Banks, W. R. "Changing Attitudes Toward the Negro in the U.S.," *Journal of Negro Education,* 30 (1961), 87–93.
13. Boas, F. *Race and Democratic Society.* Locust Valley, N.Y.: J. J. Augustin Publishing Co., 1945.
14. Klineberg, O. *Social Psychology,* 2d ed. New York: Holt, Rinehart & Winston, 1954.
15. Lindzey, G. (ed.) *Handbook of Social Psychology,* II. Cambridge, Mass.: Addison-Wesley, 1954, pp. 1021–1062.
16. Rose, A. M. *Studies in Reduction of Prejudice,* 2d ed. Chicago: American Council on Race Relations, 1948.

UNIT VI.   RELATIONSHIP BETWEEN ATTITUDINAL
           PATTERNS AND PERSONALITY

1. Adorno, T. W., et al. *The Authoritarian Personality.* New York: Harper & Row, 1950, pp. 971–976.
2. Bettelheim, B., and M. Janowitz. *Dynamics of Prejudice.* New York: Harper & Row, 1950, pp. 7–31.
3. Himmelhock, J. "Tolerance and Personality Needs; A Study of the Liberalization of Ethnic Attitudes Among Minority Group College Students," *American Sociological Review,* 15 (1950), 79–88.
4. Milner, E. "Some Hypotheses Concerning the Influence of Segregation on Negro Personality Development," *Psychiatry,* 16 (1953), 291–297.
5. Protho, E. T. "Ethnocentrism and Anti-Negro Attitudes in the Deep South," *Journal of Abnormal and Social Psychology,* 47 (1952), 105–108.
6. Smith, C. W., and J. W. Protho. "Ethnic Differences in Authoritarian Personality," *Social Forces,* 35 (1957), 334–338.

UNIT VII.   NEGRO REACTION TO PREJUDICE

Note: The student is to write two book reviews from the following:

1. Brink, W., and L. Harris. *The Negro Revolution in America.* New York: Simon and Schuster, 1964.
2. Burns, W. H. *The Voices of Negro Protest in America.* New York: Oxford University Press, 1963.
3. Clark, K. B. (ed.). *The Negro Protest: James Baldwin, Malcolm X and Martin Luther King Talk with K. B. Clark.* Boston: Beacon Press, 1963.
4. ———. *Dark Ghetto.* New York: Harper & Row, 1965.
5. Killens, J. O. *Black Man's Burden.* New York: Trident Press, 1965.

6. Lincoln, C. E. *The Black Muslims in America.* Boston: Beacon Press, 1961.
7. Lomax, L. E. *The Negro Revolt.* New York: Harper & Row, 1962.
8. Silberman, L. E. *Crisis in Black and White.* New York: Random House, 1964.

UNIT VIII. THE NEGRO IN THE UNITED STATES: THE HISTORICAL BACKGROUND OF CONTEMPORARY PROBLEMS

A. GENERAL HISTORY

1. Franklin, J. H. *From Slavery to Freedom.* 2d ed. New York: Alfred A. Knopf, 1965.
2. Tanenbaum, F. *Slave and Citizen: The Negro in the Americas.* New York: Alfred A. Knopf, 1946.

SUPPLEMENTARY READINGS

3. Aptheker, H. *The Negro People in America.* New York: International Publications, 1946.
4. Frazier, E. F. *The Negro in the United States.* New York: Macmillan Co., 1957.
5. Herskovitz, M. J. *The Myth of the Negro Past.* Boston: Beacon Press, 1958.
6. Myrdal, G. *An American Dilemma.* New York: Harper & Row, 1944.
7. Redding, J. S. *They Came in Chains.* New York: J. B. Lippincott Co., 1950.

B. SLAVERY

8. Aptheker, H. *American Negro Slave Revolts.* New York: International Publications, 1963.
9. Botkin, B. *Lay My Burden Down—A Folk History of Slavery.* Chicago: University of Chicago Press, 1945.
10. Davidson, B. *Black Mother: The Years of the African Slave Trade.* Boston: Little, Brown and Co., 1961.
11. Elkins, S. *Slavery.* Chicago: University of Chicago Press, 1959.
12. Stampp, K. M. *The Peculiar Institution: Slavery in the Ante-Bellum South.* New York: Alfred A. Knopf, 1956.

C. RECONSTRUCTION AND POST-RECONSTRUCTION

13. Franklin, J. H. *Reconstruction After the Civil War.* Chicago: University of Chicago Press, 1961.
14. Woodward, C. V. *The Strange Career of Jim Crow.* New York: Oxford University Press, 1957.

John L. O'Brian

15. Du Bois, W. E. B. *Black Reconstruction in America, 1860–1880.* New York: Meridian Books, 1966.
16. Shenton, J. P. *The Reconstruction: A Documentary History of the South.* New York: G. P. Putnam's Sons, 1963.
17. Wharton, V. L. *The Negro in Mississippi, 1865–1890.* Chapel Hill, N.C.: University of North Carolina, 1947.
18. Woodward, C. V. *Tom Watson, Agrarian Rebel.* New York: Macmillan Co., 1938.

UNIT IX. READINGS IN LITERATURE OF THE POOR

Note: The student is to write two book reviews. Two different authors from the following list are to be used.

1. Baldwin, James. *Notes of a Native Son.* Boston: Beacon Press, 1955.
2. ———. *Nobody Knows My Name.* New York: Dial Press, 1961.
3. ———. *Another Country.* New York: Dial Press, 1962.
4. ———. *The Fire Next Time.* New York: Dial Press, 1963.
5. ———. *Blues for Mister Charlie.* New York: Dial Press, 1964.
6. Ellison, R. *The Invisible Man.* New York: New American Library, 1964.
7. Gold, M. *Jews Without Money.* New York: Liveright Publishing Corp., 1935.
8. Gregory, Dick. *Nigger.* New York: E. P. Dutton & Co., 1964.
9. Killens, J. O. *Youngblood.* New York: Dial Press, 1954.
10. ———. *And Then We Heard the Thunder.* New York: Alfred A. Knopf, 1962.
11. Lewis, O. *Children of Sanchez.* New York: Random House, 1961.
12. Marshall, P. *Brown Girl, Brownstones.* New York: Random House, 1959.
13. Wright, R. *Native Son.* New York: New American Library, 1962.
14. ———. *Black Boy.* New York: Harper & Row, 1963.
15. ———. *Lawd Today.* Chicago: Walker and Co., 1963.

Seminar in Urban Society

This seminar deals with urban social organization, stratification, and change; the organizational context of work and industry; the culture of youth; with racism, racial conflict, and tension; with deviancy and conformity; and with the social system of community life.

The assumption is made that the quality of instruction, as well as other pertinent goals, can be increased or attained by providing teachers and other related personnel with systematic knowledge and appreciation of the irrealities and realities of the American societal system. Teachers of adolescents and young adults, in particular, must be made aware of the practices and the system of contemporary American societal life. All of the other elements or components of the proposed curriculum must ultimately make sense within this context. This crucial need applies specifically to each of the six units comprising the seminar. *Objectives:* The specific objectives of the seminar include the following:

1. To determine the ways that the members of American society really behave.

2. To determine the ideologies, goals, and values (actual and professed) that members of American society hold.

3. To determine the main social structures into which members of American society organize themselves, the nature of the connections between such structures, and the consequences of such structure.

4. To determine the principal agents, agencies, and channels of change that exist among members of American society.

5. To determine the persistent and recurrent problems or failures of American society.

6. To identify models or patterns of deviance and conformity observed among members of American society.

General Comments: The Seminar in Urban Society will be offered on a time equivalency of a four-credit course. It is recommended that this seminar be interdisciplinary in form and content. It is also strongly recommended that the instructor of primary responsibility be a sociologist interested in theory and/or urban problems; he should utilize representatives from the other behavioral sciences (for example, anthropology, economics, geography, history, political science, and social psychology) as well as representatives from literature, the arts, and philosophy. Discussion, dialogue, and conversation should be the heart of the dynamics of the seminar. These activities should be supplemented with lectures, guided reading, supervised small-group thinking periods, films, and field visits. To be truly successful the participants must engage in extensive reading from the wealth of material available.

Evaluation should not be of the traditional type. It should be based upon a terminal personal conference with the seminar director. Another aspect that should receive consideration would be the submission of a written critique of the Seminar and the Orientation Workshop as they relate to the educational system and learning.

COURSE OUTLINE

UNIT I   THE NATURE OF SOCIETY

Purpose: The purpose of this unit is to provide the student with an analytical tool useful for the objective and accurate understanding of the contemporary group life of man. It will provide a set of concepts and propositions about associative life and an introductory application of them to the major processes, structures, and dynamic conditions of contemporary American society.

TOPICS FOR DISCUSSION

A. The approach: society, sociology, and social systems analysis.
B. Social power, tension and conflict: processes and structures.
C. Stratification: the legitimacy and illegitimacy of inequality.
   1. Topdog and underdog.
D. Ideology.
   1. Sources.
   2. Causes.
   3. Functions.
E. Social movements and social change.
   1. Dissent.
   2. Conformity.

UNIT II   URBANISM AS A WAY OF LIFE

Purpose: The purpose of this unit is to provide the student with a "case" for the analysis and interpretation of the social processes, structures, and consequences of associative life in urban and nonurban community systems.

TOPICS FOR DISCUSSION

A. The urban community: structure and processes.
   1. Ecological and demographic correlates.
   2. Rural and urban social systems.
B. Urbanization and industrialization.
   1. The metropolitan region.
C. Slum and suburb communities.
D. The city: the transformation of power.

A Master's Degree Program for the Preparation of Teachers of Disadvantaged Youth

1. Problems.
2. Prospects.

UNIT III   RACISM, TENSION, CONFLICT, AND POWER RELATIONS

Purpose: The purpose of this unit is to provide the student with knowledge about and understanding of the tensions and conflicts, especially in urban areas and educational systems, arising out of intergroup contacts and relations. Attention will be given especially to racial, religious, and ethnic group processes. The structure, process, costs, and consequences of the American system of racism will be emphasized.

TOPICS FOR DISCUSSION

A. The nature of the problem: intergroup relations.
    1. Prejudice, discrimination, and segregation—an American system.
B. Causes of the problem.
    1. Inferiority and superiority.
C. Functions of the problem.
    1. Superordination and subordination.
D. Consequences of the problem.
    1. Educational.
    2. Economic.
    3. Political.
    4. Psychological.
    5. Moral.
    6. Social.

UNIT IV   THE WORLD OF YOUTH

Purpose: The purpose of this unit is to provide the student with knowledge about and insight into the social worlds of adolescents and young adults. Emphasis will be placed upon both conformity and deviancy within community (urban and nonurban) settings, educational systems, and in the world of work.

TOPICS FOR DISCUSSION

A. Socialization, role, and reference group theory.
B. Social mobility and intergenerational conflict.
C. Colonialism, authority, conformity, and dissent.

196
John L. O'Brian

D. Sex, aggression, and violence.
E. Education and miseducation.
F. The labor market.
   1. Powerlessness of youth.

UNIT V COMPLEX ORGANIZATIONS: BUREAUCRACY AND INSTITUTIONAL SYSTEMS; SOCIAL CONTROL AND DECISION-MAKING

Purpose: The purpose of this unit is to provide the student with knowledge about the organization and functions of work in our industrial and urban society. The structural contexts of work, and the principles underlying the processes of conflict within community settings will be stressed. The ramifications of variables of youth, minority status, and education for work and leisure will be explored.

TOPICS FOR DISCUSSION

A. The world of work.
   1. Authority and discipline.
   2. Myths and reality.
B. The labor market and the work force.
C. Unions and management.
D. Education and job.
E. Work and leisure.

UNIT VI SOCIAL CHANGE: EQUILIBRIUM AND DISEQUILIBRIUM

Purpose: The purpose of this unit is to enhance the student's insight into the dynamics of societal alteration and transformation. The goals, agents, vehicles, functions, and consequences of social change will be examined, with special attention being given to the practices and the system of education in contemporary American society.

TOPICS FOR DISCUSSION

A. The status quo.
   1. Ideology and Utopia.
B. Reform, rebellion, and revolution.
C. Who gets what, when, and how?

D. Power and powerlessness: the poor.

E. Deviance and pathology.

SUGGESTED READING LIST

UNIT I. THE NATURE OF SOCIETY

1. Berger, Peter L. *Invitation to Sociology.* Garden City, New York: Anchor Books, 1963.

2. Bredemeier, H. C., and R. M. Stephensen. *The Analysis of Social Systems.* New York: Holt, Rinehart & Winston, 1965.

3. Bremmer, R. *From the Depths.* New York: New York University Press, 1956.

4. Brim, Arville G., Jr., and S. Wheeler. *Socialization After Childhood.* New York: John Wiley & Sons, 1966.

5. Centers, R. *The Psychology of Social Classes.* Princeton: Princeton University Press, 1949.

6. Coser, L. A. *The Functions of Social Conflict.* New York: The Free Press, 1956.

7. Durkheim, E. *Education and Sociology.* New York: The Free Press, 1956.

8. Goldstein, Bernard. "The Culture of Poverty: Implications for Education." Unpublished paper presented before Annual Meeting of the American Montessori Society, 1965.

9. Harrington, M. *The Other America.* New York: Macmillan Co., 1962.

10. Homans, G. *The Human Group.* New York: Harcourt, Brace & World, 1950.

11. Hunter, Floyd. *The Big Rich and the Little Rich.* New York: Doubleday and Co., 1965.

12. Keller, Suzanne. *The American Lower Class Family.* New York: New York State Division for Youth, 1965.

13. Kolko, G. *Wealth and Power in America.* New York: Frederick A. Praeger, Inc., 1962.

14. Lipset, S. M., and R. Bendix. *Class Status and Power.* New York: The Free Press, 1953.

15. Miller, S. M. "The American Lower Class," *Social Research,* 34 (Spring 1964), 1.

16. Mills, C. W. *Power, Politics and People.* New York: Oxford University Press, 1963.

17. Toch, Hans. *The Social Psychology of Social Movements.* New York: Bobbs-Merrill Co., 1965.

198

John L. O'Brian

UNIT II. URBANISM AS A WAY OF LIFE

1. Bell, Robert R. *Marriage and Family Interaction*. Chicago, Ill.: Dorsey Press, 1963.
2. Clark, K. B. *Dark Ghetto*. New York: Harper & Row, 1965.
3. Cox, Harvey. *The Secular City*. New York: Macmillan Co., 1965.
4. Elias, C. E., Jr. *Metropolis: Values in Conflict*. Belmont, Calif.: Wadsworth Publishing Co., 1964.
5. Hoover, E. M., and R. Vernon. *Anatomy of a Metropolis*. Garden City, N.Y.: Anchor Books, 1962.
6. Hunnicutt, C. W. (ed.). *Urban Education and Cultural Deprivation*. Syracuse: Syracuse University, School of Education, 1964.
7. Jacobs, Jane. *The Life and Death of Great American Cities*. New York: Random House, 1961.
8. Nisbet, Robert A. *The Quest for Community*. New York: Oxford University Press, 1953.
9. Passow, A. H. (ed.). *Education in Depressed Areas*. New York: Columbia University Press, 1963.
10. Rossi, P. *The Politics of Urban Renewal*. New York: The Free Press, 1961.
11. Schnore, Leo F. *The Urban Scene*. New York: The Free Press, 1965.
12. Weber, M. *The City*. New York: The Free Press, 1958.

UNIT III. RACISM, TENSION, CONFLICT, AND POWER RELATIONS

1. Anonymous. "The Worldwide Plague of City Riots: A British View," *Harper's Magazine,* November 1965.
2. American Academy of Arts and Sciences. "The Negro American," *Daedalus,* 94 (1965), 743–1164.
3. Frazier, E. F. *The Black Bourgoisie*. New York: Collier Books, 1962.
4. Glazer, Nathan. "Negroes and Jews—The New Challenge to Pluralism," *Commentary,* 38 (December 1964), 6.
5. _____ and D. P. Moynihan. *Beyond the Melting Pot*. Cambridge, Mass.: M.I.T. Press, 1963.
6. Goffman, E. *Stigma*. Englewood Cliffs, N. J.: Prentice-Hall, Inc., 1963.
7. Pettigrew, T. *The Profile of the Negro American*. New York: D. Van Nostrand Co., 1964.
8. Rustin, Bayard. "From Protest to Politics: The Future of the Civil Rights Movement," *Commentary,* 39 (February 1965), 2.
9. Sexton, P. C. *Spanish Harlem*. New York: Harper & Row, 1965.

A Master's Degree Program for the Preparation of Teachers of Disadvantaged Youth

10. Simpson, G. E., and J. M. Yinger. *Racial and Cultural Minorities.* New York: Harper & Row, 1964.
11. Woodward, C. Vann. *The Strange Career of Jim Crow.* New York: Oxford University Press, 1957.
12. Yinger, J. Milton. *A Minority Group in American Society.* New York: McGraw-Hill Book Co., 1965.

UNIT IV. THE WORLD OF YOUTH

1. Erikson, E. H. *Childhood and Society.* New York: W. W. Norton & Co., 1950.
2. Friedenberg, Edgar Z. *The Vanishing Adolescent.* Boston: Beacon Press, 1959.
3. ————. *Coming of Age in America: Growth and Acquiescence.* New York: Random House, 1965.
4. Goldstein, B., and H. Stark. *Entering the Labor Force.* New York: Holt, Rinehart & Winston, 1964.
5. Goodman, P. *Growing Up Absurd.* New York: Random House, 1960.
6. Gottlieb, D., and Charles E. Ramsey. *The American Adolescent.* Chicago, Ill.: Dorsey Press, Inc., 1964.
7. ———— and J. Reeves. *Adolescent Behavior in Urban Areas.* New York: The Free Press, 1963.
8. Hare, Paul, et al. *Small Groups.* New York: Alfred A. Knopf, 1955.
9. Riessman, Frank. *The Culturally Deprived Child.* New York: Harper & Row, 1962.
10. Ritchie, O. W., and M. R. Koller. *Sociology of Childhood.* New York: Appleton-Century Crofts, 1964.
11. Strom, Robert D. *Teaching in the Slum School.* Columbus, Ohio: Charles E. Merrill Books, 1965.
12. Whyte, W. F. "A Slum Sex Code," *American Journal of Sociology,* 49 (July 1943).

UNIT V. COMPLEX ORGANIZATIONS: BUREAUCRACY AND INSTITUTIONAL SYSTEMS; SOCIAL CONTROL AND DECISION-MAKING

1. Anonymous. "Why White Collar Workers Can't Be Organized," *Harper's Magazine,* 215 (August 1957).
2. Barnett, Lawrence J. "Does Education for Work, Work?" *The Urban Review* (May 1966), 6 pages unnumbered.
3. Becker, H. S. "The Career of the Chicago Public School Teacher," *American Journal of Sociology,* 57 (1952).

200
John L. O'Brian

4. Bierstedt, Robert, et al. *Sociology and Contemporary Education.* New York: Random House, 1964.

5. Blau, P. M. *Bureaucracy in Modern Society.* New York: Random House, 1956.

6. Brookover, W. B., and D. Gottlieb. *The Sociology of Education.* New York: American Book Co., 1964.

7. Caplow, T. *The Sociology of Work.* Minneapolis: University of Minnesota Press, 1954.

8. Dahrendorf, R. *Class and Class Conflict in Industrial Society.* Stanford: Stanford University Press, 1959.

9. Etzioni, A. *Complex Organizations.* New York: Holt, Rinehart & Winston, 1964.

10. Gouldner, Alvin W. *Patterns of Industrial Bureaucracy.* New York: Harper & Row, 1954.

11. Hollingshead, A. B. *Elmtown's Youth.* New York: John Wiley & Sons, 1949.

12. Hughes, E. C. *Men and Their Work.* New York: The Free Press, 1958.

13. "Educational Planning for Socially Disadvantaged Children and Youth," *The Journal of Negro Education,* 33 (Summer 1964).

14. Parkinson, John N. *Parkinson's Law.* London: John Murray, 1958.

UNIT VI. SOCIAL CHANGE: EQUILIBRIUM AND DISEQUILIBRIUM

1. Becker, Howard. *Outsiders.* New York: The Free Press, 1963.

2. Barzun, J. *Teacher in America.* Garden City, N. Y.: Anchor Books, 1954.

3. Cloward, R. A., and L. E. Ohlin. *Delinquency and Opportunity.* New York: The Free Press, 1960.

4. Miller, S. M., and Martin Rein. "Poverty and Social Change," *The American Child,* (March 1964).

5. Turner, R. H., and L. M. Killian. *Collective Behavior.* Englewood Cliffs, N. J.: Prentice-Hall, Inc., 1957.

Field Experience

This experience provides the student with an opportunity to observe and participate in a variety of professional settings involving disadvantaged populations. The student will be placed in public and private organizations and agencies having responsibility for employment, community service, and welfare. In addition, it provides an opportunity to enlarge upon the orientation experiences and to integrate concepts learned in the Seminar in Urban Society and The Social Psychology of the Disadvantaged with the real problems faced by the social agencies and their clients. The process of professional intervention and its effects upon minority group problems will also be studied. Through such experiences the student can become aware of the variety and magnitude of the problems of the disadvantaged and the effects of professional intervention.

Objectives: The Field Experience aims to provide insights and skills different from those of the Orientation Workshop and the Educational Practicum. These goals are enumerated below:

1. To provide a knowledge and awareness of the helping agencies that exist, their philosophies, techniques, and their success or lack of it.

2. To provide an understanding of how the disadvantaged get jobs and the effects on them of their failure to get jobs.

3. To provide an understanding of community action programs and processes.

4. To provide an understanding of programs available and supported at different levels by federal, state, and local governments (as well as private institutions and volunteer groups), and the interactions and opportunities fostered by these sources.

5. To provide the student an opportunity to apply and validate the concepts acquired in the Seminar in Urban Society and The Social Psychology of the Disadvantaged.

6. To provide a setting in which the student will be able to learn something about himself when confronted with the problems of the disadvantaged and as related to the notion of the helping hand.

7. To develop knowledge of the processes used to interview and place people into semiskilled and unskilled (entry level) jobs.

8. To gain insight into the needs of industry, the kinds of jobs available for those with limited skills, the training, education, and personality traits needed by those employed in such jobs.

9. To gain knowledge of the various private and public programs available to help the disadvantaged.

General Comments: The Field Experience should be offered on the time equivalency of a four-credit course. It should be run concurrently with the Seminar in Urban Society and The Social Psychology of the Disadvantaged.

Each student should be placed in two settings during the Field Ex-

202
John L. O'Brian

perience. One of these should be an industrial setting; the other should be selected from among community, social, and welfare agencies.

The industrial setting should be in an industrial concern that employs large numbers of persons in low-level skilled jobs. Students placed in such situations will observe and participate in the process of induction of employees into the labor force. They will: (1) meet and interact with applicants; (2) see, use, and interpret application forms; (3) observe people working at all levels of employment including semiskilled and unskilled jobs; (4) add to their knowledge of the demands of the jobs by actually working at some of the jobs; (5) gain knowledge of the testing programs used by industry in the selection of employees; and (6) gain knowledge of union and labor organization grievance procedures.

In the majority of cases, entrance to the world of work for the disadvantaged will come through the personnel offices these students will be attached to in their Field Experience. The teacher with breadth and, to some degree, depth of experience, will be more effective in helping the disadvantaged prepare themselves to become employable. A goal that will make it possible to satisfy biological as well as social needs is extremely important for the disadvantaged. Employment as a terminal educational goal is realistic for the disadvantaged.

The second experience should have as a setting those agencies and institutions that have been organized to aid the disadvantaged. The teacher of the disadvantaged will also be confronted, through the students, with a variety of personal and family problems concerning social needs, financial needs, and the like. Unless these needs can be satisfied, the probability of the educational program's being successful is doubtful. To deal with this the teacher must also function as a coordinator of community services. It is necessary that he be aware of the community services that exist, the manner in which one obtains these services or takes advantage of them, the nature of the services rendered, and the likely outcome.

Field coordinators, under the direction of a field experience supervisor, should be responsible for placement and guidance of the student. Students should meet with the field coordinators once a week to discuss common and unique experiences and to relate these experiences to concepts examined in the seminars.

To facilitate placement procedures the class may be divided into two groups—one group in an industrial setting and the other in an agency setting. At the midpoint in the semester the groups will rotate their assignment. The order of the units that follow, therefore, does not have chronological implications.

COURSE OUTLINE

UNIT I   THE INDUSTRIAL SETTING

Purpose: This unit will provide an opportunity for the student to acquire first-hand experience in an industrial setting so as to better prepare him to aid the disadvantaged in obtaining employment.

SUGGESTED ESTABLISHMENTS

A. Manufacturing industries.
B. Service industries.
    1. Food and beverage preparation.
    2. Lodging and related services.
    3. Amusement and recreation.
    4. Health occupations.
C. Occupations in processing industries.
    1. Food, tobacco, paper, petroleum, coal, chemicals, plastics, synthetics, rubber, paint, wood, stone, wood products, clay, leather, and textile products.
D. Transportation occupations.
E. Packaging and materials handling.
F. Distribution and sales.

UNIT II   THE COMMUNITY, SOCIAL, AND WELFARE AGENCY SETTING

Purpose: To provide the student with an opportunity to be confronted by the problems of the disadvantaged; to see the dynamics and the bases of these problems, as well as the effects of intervention on their outcomes.

SUGGESTED AGENCIES

A. Division of employment security.
    1. The students will be expected to participate in the tasks of the agency, to interview candidates, review job applications, classify jobs, and to become aware of the outcomes of attempted placements and recommendations. These activities

will be under the guidance of experienced agency personnel. This agency, in particular, is utilized frequently by individuals seeking low-level skilled jobs.

B. Welfare departments.
  1. Students will be assigned to participate in the activities of city or state welfare departments. This would entail consideration of applications, interviewing applicants, and following up problems associated with failure to receive welfare.

C. Programs funded under the Economic Opportunity Act (and other social legislation).
  1. This includes Community Action Programs, Job Corps, VISTA, and other such sponsored programs. The student will engage in participation and observation of federally sponsored community programs where such are available, interact with the clientele for whom they provide services, and observe the effects of such services that are provided.

D. Privately financed volunteer programs.
  1. Programs that are referred to include such programs as the Ford Foundation grant projects. Again the student will participate and observe the management of these programs, the clientele served, and the effects of the services rendered.

E. Public health agencies.
  1. Students will be assigned to hospitals, clinics, emergency wards, and other public health facilities for which remuneration is not required for services rendered. Individuals will participate as far as possible and observe the clientele served and the effects of the services provided, both in terms of their adequacy and inadequacy.

F. Recreational facilities in slum areas.
  1. This includes playgrounds, community centers, parks, and other play and athletic facilities that have been provided for the community. Individuals will participate on an informal basis, observe the individuals, and observe interactions taking place at such community centers.

UNIT III THE SEMINAR

Purpose: The purpose of the seminar aspect of the Field Experience course is to discuss issues of common concern.

A Master's Degree Program for the Preparation of Teachers of Disadvantaged Youth

A. The students will meet once a week with the Field Experience supervisor and the field coordinators to discuss problems, critical incidents, unusual happenings, and so on, that arise out of their field experiences. The following are given as typical examples of topics that might arise out of the seminar phase of the Field Experience:

1. Establishing rapport with clients.
2. Determining reasons why those attempting to aid the disadvantaged are often rejected.
3. Factors that lead to the disadvantaged person's resenting or attempting to exploit the helping hand.
4. Methods of selling oneself to the disadvantaged person.
5. Inadequacies, fears, prejudices, and misconceptions felt by the student when working with the disadvantaged.
6. The responsibility of the disadvantaged person for his own condition.
7. The adequacy of society's attempt to fulfill its responsibility to the disadvantaged.
8. Evaluation of training at the unskilled and semiskilled level to provide a permanent solution for the problems of the disadvantaged.
9. Industry's responsibility in solving the problems of the disadvantaged.
10. Feasibility of the poor participating in the administration of programs aimed at helping the poor.

Note: The field coordinator will serve primarily as a model for those students in his charge. Insofar as he is exemplary in his functioning as a field coordinator, students will learn through contact with him how such a coordinator can function effectively. Specifically, the field coordinator must be a resource man, a contact man, a teacher, and a counselor. As a resource man, he is aware of opportunities that exist, the agencies and the services they provide. As a contact man, he is able to place the student in the agencies by having acquaintance with the appropriate persons and having gained their confidence through prior contacts. As a teacher, the coordinator must attempt as much as possible to structure the learning experience of the student and familiarize him with basic principles and sources of information appropriate to his experience. As a counselor, the field coordinator must help the student work out personal problems that may have been created from this experience.

Seminar in Learning, Development, and Measurement

This seminar is designed to provide an introduction to the basic theories and concepts of the psychology of learning, human development, and educational tests, measurement, and evaluation, along with the application of these basic theories and concepts to existing learning problems prevalent among culturally disadvantaged youth.

In order to teach culturally disadvantaged youth, one must understand their basic learning problems. Such problems stem from learning experiences and particular aspects of development which are common in a disadvantaged environment; furthermore, these problems have definite implications for testing and measurement with this population. To understand the particular learning problems of disadvantaged youth, students have a need to know the basic concepts of learning, development, and measurement which help to understand the dynamics of a specific population.

Objectives: The seminar will be directed toward achieving the following:

1. Knowledge of some basic concepts in the psychology of learning.
2. Knowledge of some basic concepts in human development.
3. Knowledge of some basic concepts in educational measurement.
4. Awareness of some of the special learning problems of the disadvantaged.
5. Understanding of the dynamics of these learning problems and their causes based on learning, development, and measurement concepts.

General Comments: This seminar dealing with learning, development, and measurement will be offered on the time equivalency of a four-credit course. It is recommended that the seminar be conducted by three individuals—one who has a familiarity with and a commitment to the principles of learning theory, one who has a familiarity with human development including emotional as well as intellectual development, and one who has a familiarity with measurement, testing, and evaluation in an educational context. The instructor with primary responsibility should be a psychologist with an awareness of and commitment to the problems of education.

This seminar should be closely coordinated with the seminar on Educational Processes for Teaching the Disadvantaged and the Educational Practicum, all three will be taken concomitantly. Theory that will be generated in this seminar should be clearly tied in with practice as discussed in the Educational Processes for Teaching the Disadvantaged seminar and as carried out in the Educational Practicum. Experiences in Processes and Practicum should be cited in the Seminar in Learning, Development, and Measurement in order to bring the applicability of the conceptual approach into sharper focus.

COURSE OUTLINE

UNIT I BASIC CONCEPTS OF LEARNING

Purpose: The purpose of this unit is to provide the student with a knowledge of some of the essential concepts used to explain learning phenomena as a prerequisite to applying these concepts to specific learning problems. Basic concepts will be presented in such a manner that their general implications for education will be constantly highlighted.

TOPICS FOR DISCUSSION

A. Parameters of learning.
1. Conditioning and associative learning.
2. Extinction, generalization, discrimination.
3. Reinforcement.
4. Forgetting.
B. Types of learning and conditions under which they occur.
1. Signal learning.
2. Stimulus-response learning.
3. Chaining.
4. Verbal association.
5. Multiple discrimination.
6. Concept learning.
7. Principle learning.
8. Problem-solving.
C. Some selected learning phenomena from a theoretical point of view.
1. Drive, habit strength, inhibition, goal gradient, delay of reinforcement, secondary drive and reinforcement (Hull).

John L. O'Brian

2. Laws of effect, exercise, readiness (Thorndike).
3. Learning of meaning, latent learning (Tolman).
4. Intermittent reinforcement (Skinner).

UNIT II BASIC CONCEPTS OF HUMAN DEVELOPMENT

Purpose: The purpose of this unit is to provide the student with a knowledge of some of the essential concepts used to explain developmental phenomena as a prerequisite to applying these concepts to specific developmental problems engendered by the environment. Basic concepts will be presented in such a manner that their general implications for education will be constantly highlighted.

TOPICS FOR DISCUSSION

A. Development is *not* genetically preordained (nor intelligence fixed by genetic factors).
   1. The case for genetic predeterminism.
   2. The case against genetic predeterminism.
B. Phases in the development of the intellect.
   1. Early motor development.
   2. Preverbal and preoperational thought.
   3. Stage of concrete operations.
   4. Stage of formal operation.
C. The development of the ego and moral development.
   1. Infantile sexuality.
   2. The emergence of identity.
   3. The emergence of morality.
D. Career development.
   1. Adolescence as exploration.
   2. The transition from school to work.
   3. The trial process.
   4. Period of establishment.
   5. Maintenance stage.
   6. Years of decline.

UNIT III THE ESSENTIALS OF MEASUREMENT

Purpose: This unit is designed to provide the student with a knowledge of some of the essential concepts upon which tests and measurements on human beings are based, along with a knowledge of test construction both for individual and program evaluation. The use of these

A Master's Degree Program for the Preparation of Teachers of Disadvantaged Youth

concepts and their limitations in actual situations will be dealt with later.

TOPICS FOR DISCUSSION

A. The parameters of measurement evaluation and interpretation.
   1. Item analysis: technique and purpose.
   2. Reliability (of tests and of human beings used as measuring instruments).
   3. Validity: content, concurrent, predictive, construct (emphasis on content validity).
   4. Norms, standard scores, and standardizing population.
B. The development of a test for evaluating students or programs.
   1. Stating educational objectives.
   2. Construction of test items.
   3. Evaluation of test items.
   4. How to use the test to evaluate student's performances.
   5. How to use the test to evaluate the effect on the program or curriculum (the content validity approach).
C. Standardized tests.
   1. Individual and group intelligence tests (verbal and non-verbal).
   2. Tests of aptitudes and abilities.
   3. Tests of achievement.
   4. Other types of tests.
   5. How to find and assess a standardized test.

UNIT IV   THE LEARNING OF THE CULTURALLY DISADVANTAGED: COMPETING REWARDS AND THEIR IMMEDIACY

Purpose: This unit has been developed to present the view that culturally disadvantaged students are often biologically disadvantaged as well and therefore will apply their efforts to earn rewards that will satisfy their biological needs; they will also be inclined more toward immediate reinforcement rather than working toward long-term goals. These phenomena will be treated as learning phenomena.

TOPICS FOR DISCUSSION

A. The nature of the problem.
   1. The effect of hunger on classroom performance (Breckenridge; Vincent; Schorr).

John L. O'Brian

2. The applicability (or lack of it) of present learning to the immediate future.

3. The desire to earn money as a factor in the education of the disadvantaged.

B. Applicable learning principles.
   1. Delay of reinforcement and goal gradient (Hull; Hilgard).
   2. Law of effect (Thorndike).
   3. Learning based on drive reduction (Hull); notion of competing reinforcements (Hilgard).

C. Supporting evidence relating to the culturally disadvantaged.
   1. Orientation toward immediate reward—some findings (LeShan; Mischel).

D. Reasons for the existence of the problem.

E. Solutions for the problem.
   1. The effect of quick feedback on the student.
   2. The effect of relating school experiences to real life experiences.

UNIT V   THE DEVELOPMENT AND
         MEASUREMENT OF INTELLIGENCE
         IN THE CULTURALLY DISADVANTAGED

Purpose: This unit has as its primary purposes the development of an understanding of why culturally disadvantaged youth often score lower on conventional intelligence tests; why a culturally impoverished environment often leads to a less developed intelligence; emphasizes the limitations in intelligence testing, and seeks some remedies for this situation.

TOPICS FOR DISCUSSION

A. Lower measured intelligence among the disadvantaged as a function of experience.
   1. Inapplicability of intelligence test scores (Klineberg; Pettigrew).

B. The effect of limited experiences.
   1. The importance of stimulation (Ausubel; Bloom; Hunt; Wolf; Deutsch).
   2. Developmental problems and language learning (John; Bernstein).
   3. Problems in conceptual development (Siller).

C. Reversibility of the effects of early experience.
   1. General statement (Hull).

2. Work with the mentally retarded (Dennis; Skeels and Dye; Wellman).
3. Work with the disadvantaged (Boger).

D. Cumulative nature of the learning deficit.
1. Reasons for the cumulative deficit. (Deutsch; Krugman; Osborne).
2. Implications.

E. Techniques available to the classroom teacher for counteracting the deficit.
1. Teaching at the perceptual level.
2. Conversing with students.
3. Relating concepts to student's experiences.
4. Field trips—new experiences.

F. Kinds of programs needed.
1. Early enrichment (Head Start).
2. Educational television (Brazziel and Terrell).
3. Remedial services (Krugman; Schreiber; Shaw).

G. The implications for intelligence measurement.
1. Need for culture-free instruments.
2. Validity of intelligence measurement.
3. Assessment of potential for learning.
4. IQ information as a source of teacher bias.

UNIT VI ACHIEVEMENT MOTIVATION AND LEARNING AMONG THE CULTURALLY DISADVANTAGED

Purpose: This unit is aimed at introducing the student to the concept of achievement motivation; to discuss where it comes from; to consider why it is often low among the disadvantaged and how their experiences may account for this; and to discuss what can be done about it.

TOPICS FOR DISCUSSION

A. A definition and description of achievement motivation.
1. Presentation of the concept (McClelland; Atkinson).
B. Environmental bases of achievement motivation.
1. Middle-class cultural experience (McClelland; Rosen).
2. Rewarding success and punishing failure (McClelland).
3. Parental training (Winterbottom; Rosen and D'Andrade).
4. Parental attitudes (Kahl).

C. Bases for limited achievement motivation among the disadvantaged.
  1. Class ethic.
  2. Opportunities for success.
  3. Frequency of punishments by parents (Bronfenbrenner).
  4. Lack of appropriate models.
D. Techniques to increase achievement motivation.
  1. The use of successive approximations to shape behavior (Skinner).
  2. Frequent use of rewards for even minimal successes, utilizing successive approximations technique (these youth are success starved).
  3. Avoidance of punishment.
     a. Punishment does not lead to extinction of punished behavior (Estes).
     b. Punishment often leads to fear of failure (Atkinson).
  4. Presentation of tasks of graded degree of difficulty in sequence from easy to difficult.
  5. Use of tangible rewards (Zigler and DeLabry).
  6. Use of objective criticism (Lewin et al.).

UNIT VII   THE LEARNING OF ATTITUDES AMONG THE CULTURALLY DISADVANTAGED

Purpose: This unit is designed to acquaint the student with the nature of the attitudes of culturally disadvantaged youth toward self, others, and society and their bases; and, to discuss ways in which such attitudes can be altered through learning intervention.

TOPICS FOR DISCUSSION

A. Attitudes of the culturally disadvantaged toward self, others, and society.
  1. Negativism, fatalism, and cynicism.
  2. Psychopathic, antisocial, and delinquent behavior.
  3. Low aspiration and self-expectation; low self-concept.
B. The bases for these attitudes—how they are learned.
  1. Social status and social experiences (Hieronymus).
  2. Rejection (Ausubel and Ausubel; Goff).

A Master's Degree Program for the Preparation of Teachers of Disadvantaged Youth

C. Techniques available to the classroom teacher for changing attitudes.
 1. The teacher as a model (Witty).
 2. Student participation and the development of involvement and responsibility (Lewin; Lewin, Lippitt and White; Coch and French).
 3. Role-playing as a basis for learning new attitudes (King and Janis; Brehm).
 4. The use of praise and approval: rewards as the basis for learning new attitudes.
 5. Programmed success as the basis for elevating level of aspiration: rewards as the basis for new learning (Sears).
 6. Approach-avoidance conflict with regard to education: its reduction through reducing avoidance tendencies and fear (Dollard and Miller; Brown).
 7. The differential treatment technique: a reaction to individual differences (Hunt).

SUGGESTED READING LIST

UNIT I.   BASIC CONCEPTS OF LEARNING

1. Bugelski, B. R. *The Psychology of Learning Applied to Teaching.* Indianapolis: Bobbs-Merrill Co., 1964.
2. Deese, J. *The Psychology of Learning.* 2d ed. New York: McGraw-Hill Book Co., 1958.
3. Gagne, R. M. *The Conditions of Learning.* New York: Holt, Rinehart & Winston, 1965.
4. Hilgard, E. R. *Theories of Learning.* 2d ed. New York: Appleton-Century-Crofts, 1956.

UNIT II.   BASIC CONCEPTS OF HUMAN DEVELOPMENT

1. Bloom, B. S. *Stability and Change in Human Characteristics.* New York: John Wiley & Sons, 1964.
2. Church, J. *Language and the Discovery of Reality.* New York: Random House, 1961.
3. Erikson, E. H. *Childhood and Society.* New York: W. W. Norton Co., 1950.
4. Flavell, J. H. *The Developmental Psychology of Jean Piaget.* Princeton, N. J.: D. Van Nostrand Co., 1963.
5. Hunt, J. McV. *Intelligence and Experience.* New York: Ronald Press, 1961.

John L. O'Brian

6. Piaget, J. *The Moral Judgment of the Child.* New York: The Free Press, 1932.

7. Super, D. E. *The Psychology of Careers.* New York: Harper & Row, 1957.

8. Werner, H. *Comparative Psychology of Mental Development.* New York: International University Press, 1940, esp. Part V.

UNIT III. THE ESSENTIALS OF MEASUREMENT

1. Adams, Georgia S. *Measurement and Evaluation in Education, Psychology, and Guidance.* New York: Holt, Rinehart & Winston, 1965.

2. Buros, O. K. *The Sixth Mental Measurements Yearbook.* Highland Park, N. J.: Gryphon Press, 1965.

3. Remmers, H. H., N. L. Gage, and J. F. Rummel. *A Practical Introduction to Measurement and Evaluation.* 2d ed. New York: Harper & Row, 1965.

4. Smith, F. M., and S. Adams. *Educational Measurement for the Classroom Teacher.* New York: Harper & Row, 1966.

5. Thorndike, R. L., and Elizabeth Hagen. *Measurement and Evaluation in Psychology and Education.* 2d ed. New York: John Wiley & Sons, 1961.

UNIT IV. THE LEARNING OF THE CULTURALLY DISADVANTAGED:
          COMPETING REWARDS AND THEIR IMMEDIACY

1. Breckenridge, Marian E., and E. L. Vincent. "Nutrition and Growth," in *The Adolescent—A Book of Readings,* ed. J. M. Seidman. New York: Holt, Rinehart & Winston, 1962.

2. Hilgard, E. R. *Theories of Learning.* 2d ed. New York: Appleton-Century-Crofts, 1956.

3. LeShan, L. L. "Time Orientation and Social Class," *Journal of Abnormal and Social Psychology,* 47 (1952), 589–592.

4. Mischel, W. "Preference for Delayed Reinforcement and Social Responsibility," *Journal of Abnormal and Social Psychology,* 62 (1961), 1–7.

5. Schorr, A. L. "The Non-Culture of Poverty," *American Journal of Orthopsychiatry,* 34 (1964), 220–221.

UNIT V. THE DEVELOPMENT AND MEASUREMENT OF
         INTELLIGENCE IN THE CULTURALLY DISADVANTAGED

1. Ausubel, D. P. "How Reversible Are the Cognitive and Motivational Effects of Cultural Deprivation? Implications for Teaching the

Culturally Deprived Child." (Paper read at a conference on the teaching of the culturally deprived child, Buffalo, N. Y., 1963.)

2. Bernstein, B. "Linguistic Codes, Hesitation Phenomena and Intelligence," *Language and Speech,* 5 (1962), 31–46.

3. Bloom, B. S. *Stability and Change in Human Characteristics.* New York: John Wiley & Sons, 1964.

4. ———, A. Davis, and R. Hess. *Compensatory Education for Cultural Deprivation.* New York: Holt, Rinehart & Winston, 1965.

5. Boger, J. H. "An Experimental Study of the Effects of Perceptual Training on Group IQ Scores of Elementary Pupils in Rural Ungraded Schools," *Journal of Educational Research,* 46 (1952), 43–53.

6. Brazziel, W. F., and Mary Terrell. "An Experiment in the Development of Readiness in a Culturally Disadvantaged Group of First-Grade Children," *Journal of Negro Education,* 31 (1962), 4–7.

7. Dennis, W. "Causes of Retardation Among Institutional Children," *Journal of Genetic Psychology,* 96 (1960), 47–59.

8. Deutsch, M. "The Disadvantaged Child and the Learning Process," in *Education in Depressed Areas,* ed. A. H. Passow. New York: Teachers College, Columbia University, 1963.

9. ———. "The Role of Social Class in Language Development and Cognition." New York: Institute for Developmental Studies, 1964. (Mimeographed.)

10. Hunt, J. McV. *Intelligence and Experience.* New York: Ronald Press, 1961.

11. ———. "The Psychological Basis for Using Pre-School Enrichment as an Antidote for Cultural Deprivation," *Merrill-Palmer Quarterly,* 10 (1964), 209–248.

12. John, Vera P. "The Intellectual Development of Slum Children: Some Preliminary Findings," *American Journal of Orthopsychiatry,* 33 (1963), 813–822.

13. Klineberg, O. "Negro-White Difference in Intelligence Test Performance: A New Look at an Old Problem," *American Psychologist,* 18 (1963), 198–203.

14. Krugman, M. "The Culturally Deprived Child in School," *National Education Association Journal,* 50 (1961), 22–23.

15. Osborne, R. T. "Racial Differences in Mental Growth and School Achievement: A Longitudinal Study," *Psychological Reports,* 7 (1960), 233–239.

John L. O'Brian

16. Pettigrew, T. "Negro American Intelligence: A New Look at an Old Controversy," *Journal of Negro Education,* 33 (1964), 6–25.
17. Schreiber, D. "Identifying and Developing Able Students from Less Privileged Groups," *High Points,* 40 (1958), 5–23.
18. Shaw, F. "Educating Culturally Deprived Youth in Urban Centers," *Phi Delta Kappan,* 45 (1963), 91–97.
19. Siller, J. "Socio-Economic Status and Conceptual Thinking," *Journal of Abnormal and Social Psychology,* 55 (1957), 271–365.
20. Skeels, H. M., and H. B. Dye. "A Study of the Effects of Differential Stimulation on Mentally Retarded Children," *Proceedings of the American Association for Mental Deficiency,* 44 (1939), 114–136.
21. Wellman, Beth L. "Iowa Studies on the Effects of Schooling," *Yearbook of the National Society for the Study of Education,* 39 (1940), 377–399.
22. Wolf, R. M. "The Identification and Measurement of Environmental Process Variables Related to Intelligence." Unpublished doctoral dissertation, University of Chicago, 1964.

UNIT VI. ACHIEVEMENT MOTIVATION AND LEARNING AMONG THE CULTURALLY DISADVANTAGED

1. Atkinson, J. W. (ed.). *Motives in Fantasy, Action and Society.* Princeton, N. J.: D. Van Nostrand Co., 1958.
2. Bronfenbrenner, R. "Socialization and Social Class Through Time and Space," in *Readings in Social Psychology,* eds. Eleanor E. Maccoby, T. M. Newcomb, and E. L. Hartley. 3d ed. New York: Holt, Rinehart & Winston, 1958.
3. Estes, W. K. "An Experimental Study of Punishment," *Psychological Monographs,* 57, No. 263 (1944).
4. Kahl, J. A. "Educational and Occupational Aspirations of Common Man'Boys," *Harvard Educational Review,* 23 (1953), 186–203.
5. Lewin, K., R. Lippitt, and R. K. White. "Patterns of Aggressive Behavior in Experimentally Created 'Social Climates,'" *Journal of Social Psychology,* 10 (1939), 271–299.
6. McClelland, D. C., et al. *The Achievement Motive.* New York: Appleton-Century-Crofts, 1953.
7. ———. *The Achieving Society.* Princeton, N. J.: D. Van Nostrand Co., 1961.
8. Rosen, B. C. "The Achievement Syndrome: A Psychocultural Dimension of Social Stratification," *American Sociological Review,* 21 (1956), 203–211.

9. ———— and R. D'Andrade. "The Psycho-Social Origins of Achievement Motivation," *Sociometry,* 22 (1959), 185–218.

10. Skinner, B. F. *The Behavior of Organisms: An Experimental Analysis.* New York: Appleton-Century-Crofts, 1938.

11. Winterbottom, Marian R. "The Relation of Need for Achievement to Learning Experiences in Independence and Mastery," in *Motives in Fantasy, Action, and Society,* ed. J. W. Atkinson. Princeton, N. J.: D. Van Nostrand Co., 1958.

12. Zigler, E., and J. DeLabry. "Concept Switching in Middle-Class, Lower-Class and Retarded Children," *Journal of Abnormal and Social Psychology,* 65 (1962), 267–273.

UNIT VII. THE LEARNING OF ATTITUDES AMONG
THE CULTURALLY DEPRIVED

1. Ausubel, D. F., and Pearl Ausubel. "Ego Development Among Segregated Negro Children," in *Education in Depressed Areas,* ed. A. H. Passow. New York: Teachers College, Columbia University, 1963.

2. Brehm, J. W. "A Dissonance Analysis of Attitude Discrepant Behavior," in *Attitude Organization and Change,* ed. M. J. Rosenberg. New Haven: Yale University Press, 1960.

3. Brown, J. S. "Gradients of Approach and Avoidance Responses and Their Relation to Level of Motivation," *Journal of Comparative and Physiological Psychology,* 41 (1948), 450–465.

4. Coch, L., and J. R. French. "Overcoming Resistance to Change," *Human Relations,* 1 (1948), 512–532.

5. Dollard, J., and N. E. Miller. *Personality and Psychotherapy.* New York: McGraw-Hill Book Co., 1950.

6. Goff, R. M. "Some Educational Implications of the Influence of Rejection on Aspiration Levels of Minority Group Children," *Journal of Experimental Education,* 23 (1954), 179–183.

7. Hieronymus, A. N. "Study of Social Class Motivation: Relationships Between Anxiety for Education and Certain Socio-Economic and Intellectual Variables," *Journal of Educational Psychology,* 42 (1951), 193–205.

8. Hunt, D. E. "Conceptual Systems Assessment in Planning Differential Educational Treatment and in Measuring Developmental Change." (Paper presented at the meeting of the American Psychological Association, Chicago, Ill., 1965.)

9. King, B. T., and I. L. Janis. "Comparison of the Effectiveness of

Improvised Versus Non-Improvised Role-Playing in Producing Opinion Changes," *Human Relations,* 9 (1956), 177–186.

10. Lewin, K. "Group Decision and Social Change," in *Readings in Social Psychology,* eds. G. E. Swanson, T. M. Newcomb, and E. L. Hartley. 2d ed. New York: Holt, Rinehart & Winston, 1952.
11. ———— R. Lippitt, and R. K. White. "Patterns of Aggressive Behavior in Experimentally Created 'Social Climates,'" *Journal of Social Psychology,* 10 (1939), 271–299.
12. Sears, Pauline S. "Levels of Aspiration in Academically Successful and Unsuccessful Children," *Journal of Abnormal and Social Psychology,* 35 (1940), 498–536.
13. Witty, P. A. "The Teacher Who Has Helped Me Most," *Elementary English,* 34 (1947), 345–354.

Educational Processes for Teaching the Disadvantaged Youth

This course is designed to provide the educational framework in which the previous psychological, sociological, and behavioral experiences are brought into the context of the school program and the individual laboratory.

The course embraces selected educational processes such as teaching methodology, program development, curriculum development, and evaluation with special emphasis on the teaching of the disadvantaged youth. It is an integrating experience in teacher education that draws upon the disciplines of psychology, sociology, anthropology, economics, and educational pedagogy for its content, basic educational procedures, and organizational structure. This integration is achieved in the processes used in the conduct of the class.

The basic need for the course is one of establishing a background for the teachers of the disadvantaged in the ordering of and planning for educational experiences that provide for maximum effectiveness in teaching and programming for the student. Specific needs are as follows:

1. A broad range of understanding and capability in a number of instructional methods.

2. A broad and integrated perception of curriculum organization, curriculum development processes, and factors related to curriculum change.

3. An understanding of the program potentials that exist in vocational and occupational education.

4. Broader and deeper capability in the areas of program and curriculum evaluation.

Objectives: The Educational Processes course will be directed toward the following objectives:

1. To broaden the teacher's understanding in the area of curriculum development.

2. To broaden the teacher's understanding in the area of program planning and execution.

3. To enable the teacher to use effectively a number of different methods of teaching as appear appropriate for students of varying backgrounds and abilities.

4. To enable the teacher to use a wide range of instructional media as appear appropriate for the teaching of the disadvantaged.

5. To enable the teacher to design learning experiences as required for a wide range of student abilities as well as social differences.

6. To enable the teacher to use effectively a number of evaluation and measurement techniques in appraising educational progress.

7. To enable the teacher to use community (sociological and economic) data in the establishment of direction for educational experiences of the disadvantaged.

8. To articulate the nature, function, and processes involved in the education of the disadvantaged.

General Comments: The Educational Processes course will be offered on the time equivalency of a four-credit course. It is recommended that the course be conducted on a seminar basis with a multidisciplinary faculty involvement. Such an approach will involve the disciplines of psychology, sociology, anthropology, and special education. These disciplines will be used as the particular topics under discussion warrant their involvement.

The instructor of primary reponsibility should be an educator with expertise in the areas of curriculum and methodology. Special consultants and guest speakers who are practitioners in the schools for the disadvantaged should be called into the seminars to provide a perspective in direct association with the central problems involved with the handling of such youth.

Community agencies, such as the employment service, neighbor-

John L. O'Brian

hood youth clubs, welfare units, and charitable organizations, should be represented on panels or in discussion sessions to establish direction to, as well as understanding of, the problem of educating the disadvantaged.

The Educational Processes experiences should be coordinated with the Educational Practicum course. This would be especially appropriate in connection with the study of methods and program development. It is recommended that the students be given opportunity to discuss and demonstrate certain methods or procedures they have found to be effective. Films and other educational media should be used where appropriate.

COURSE OUTLINE

UNIT I   CURRICULUM DEVELOPMENT

Purpose: The unit dealing with curriculum development is intended to establish a framework into which the total program of educational experiences for the disadvantaged may evolve.

TOPICS FOR DISCUSSION

A. Bases for curriculum decisions.
1. The nature of the student to be served.
2. The objectives and purposes of the school.
3. The social and cultural values of the community.
4. The teacher's level of participation in the various phases of curriculum development and implementation.
5. The attitudes, aspirations, and values existing in the community and among the employers of the product of the school.
B. Principles of curriculum development.
C. Curriculum change and innovation.
D. Curricular patterns appropriate for the education of the disadvantaged.
E. Curricular variations based upon the location of vocational education in the school.
1. Separate vocational schools.
2. Vocational schools as a part of the comprehensive high school.
3. Area vocational centers sharing time with the regular high school.
4. Postsecondary schools.

UNIT II PROGRAM DEVELOPMENT

Purpose: This unit is intended to enable the student to develop background and understanding in the nature and process of program development for the disadvantaged.

TOPICS FOR DISCUSSION

A. The nature and process of educational program planning.
B. Community involvement in program planning.
C. Factors influencing the development of a program.
D. Programs of special significance to the education of the disadvantaged.
   1. The Carrollton School, Baltimore, Md.
   2. The Octavius Catto Public School, Philadelphia, Pa.
E. Research in the area of program planning and administration.
F. The cluster concept program.
G. Work-study programs.
H. Cooperative programs.
I. Placement and follow-up.

UNIT III METHODS OF TEACHING

Purpose: This unit is designed to acquaint the teacher with a number of instructional procedures appropriate to a wide variety of student abilities as well as a wide range of educational objectives.

TOPICS FOR DISCUSSION

A. Methodology and educational perspective.
B. Teaching with the use of instructional aids.
C. Teaching using the unit approach.
D. Teaching using the problem approach.
E. Teaching using the individual project approach.
F. Teaching using the group approach.
   1. The group project.
   2. The line production.
G. Teaching and learning through role playing.
H. Teaching using the research and experimentation approach.
I. Teaching with programmed instructional materials.
J. Teaching with instruction sheets.
K. The discovery method of teaching.

222
John L. O'Brian

L. Team teaching concepts and procedures.

M. Seminar and conference procedures in teaching.

UNIT IV   PROGRAM AND CURRICULUM
EVALUATION

Purpose: This unit is intended to increase the teacher's effectiveness in the area of program and curricular evaluation.

TOPICS FOR DISCUSSION

A. Principles and concepts of educational evaluation.

B. Evaluation based upon achievement of objectives or proposed outcomes.

C. Evaluation based upon placement and performance on the job.

D. Evaluation based upon immediate and long-range goals.

E. Evaluation and the literature in the field.

F. Research findings in educational evaluation.

G. Community studies related to the evaluation of education.

SUGGESTED READING LIST

UNIT I.   CURRICULUM DEVELOPMENT

1. Anderson, Vernon E. *Principles and Procedures of Curriculum Development.* New York: Ronald Press, 1956.

2. _____ and William T. Gruhn. *Principles and Practices of Secondary Education.* New York: Ronald Press, 1962. Chapters 5, 7, and 12.

3. Arnstein, George E. "The Technological Context of Vocational Education," in *Vocational Education.* National Society for the Study of Education Yearbook, 64. Part I. 1965.

4. Barlow, Melvin L. "The Challenge to Vocational Education," in *Vocational Education.* National Society for the Study of Education Yearbook, 64. Part I. 1965.

5. Davis, A. *Social-Class Influences Upon Learning.* Cambridge, Mass.: Harvard University Press, 1948.

6. Doll, Ronald C. *Curriculum Improvement: Decision-Making and Process.* Boston: Allyn and Bacon, Inc., 1965. Chapters 3, 5, 6, 8, and 11.

7. Ginzberg, Eli. "Social and Economic Trends," in *Vocational Education.* National Society for the Study of Education Yearbook, 64. Part I. 1965.

*A Master's Degree Program for the Preparation of Teachers
of Disadvantaged Youth*

8. Goldberg, Miriam L. "Factors Affecting Educational Attainment in Depressed Urban Areas," in *Education in Depressed Areas,* ed. A. H. Passow. New York: Teachers College, Columbia University, 1963.

9. Gwynn, J. Minor. *Curriculum Principles and Social Trends.* New York: Macmillan Co., 1962.

10. Haskew, Lawrence D., and Inez W. Tumlin. "Vocational Education in the Curriculum of the Common School," in *Vocational Education.* National Society for the Study of Education Yearbook, 64. Part 1. 1965.

11. Hass, Glen, and Kimball Wiles. *Readings in Curriculum.* Boston: Allyn and Bacon, Inc., 1965. Parts I and II, Section 7.

12. Krug, Edward A. *Curriculum Planning.* New York: Harper & Row, 1950.

13. Oliver, Albert J. *Curriculum Improvement—A Guide to Problems, Principles and Procedures.* New York: Dodd, Mead and Co., 1965. Section 11.

14. Riessman, Frank. *The Culturally Deprived Child.* New York: Harper & Row, 1962.

15. Spodek, Bernard (ed.). *Preparing Teachers of Disadvantaged Young Children.* Summary of Proceedings of a Conference of Directors of NDEA Institutes for Teachers of Disadvantaged Youth, Milwaukee, University of Wisconsin, 1965.

16. Stratemeyer, Florence B., Hamden L. Forkner, and Margaret G. McKim. *Developing a Curriculum for Modern Living.* New York: Columbia University Press, 1948. Chapters 1, 2, 5, 7, and 8.

17. Venable, Tom C. *Patterns in Secondary School Curriculum.* New York: Harper & Row, 1958. Parts I and II.

18. Wiles, Kimball. *The Changing Curriculum of the American High School.* Englewood Cliffs, N. J.: Prentice-Hall, Inc., 1963.

UNIT II. PROGRAM DEVELOPMENT

1. Anderson, Vernon E. *Principles and Procedures of Curriculum Development.* New York: Ronald Press, 1956. Part IV.

2. Bates, Charles D. "North Carolina's State-Wide Program Introducing Students to Industry," *School Shop,* 25 (1966), 59–61.

3. Bloom, Benjamin S., Allison Davis, and Robert Hess. *Compensatory Education for Cultural Deprivation.* New York: Holt, Rinehart & Winston, 1965.

4. Courtney, Wayne J. *Research Proposal for the Identification and Comparison of the Common Training Needs and Requirements for*

John L. O'Brian

Teachers of Vocational Education. Menomonie, Wisc.: Stout State University, 1965.

5. Deutsch, Martin. "Minority Groups and Class Status as Related to Social and Personality Factors in Scholastic Achievement." (Monograph, Society for Applied Anthropology, New York, 1960.)

6. Grambs, Jean D., and William J. Iverson. *Modern Methods in Secondary Education.* New York: Dryden Press, 1952. Chapter 11.

7. Lee, A. M. *Research Proposal for the Identification of Common Courses in Paramedical Education.* Tempe: Arizona State University, 1965.

8. McCarthy, John A. *Vocational Education: America's Greatest Resource.* Chicago: American Technical Society, 1952.

9. Oliver, Albert I. *Curriculum Improvement—A Guide to Problems, Principles, and Procedures.* New York: Dodd, Mead and Co., 1965. Section III.

10. Olson, Jerry C. "The Marriageability of Vocational Education," *School Shop,* 25 (October 1965), 39–42.

11. ———. "Pittsburgh's OVT Program Features Open-Ended Occupational Education," *School Shop,* 25 (April 1966), 80–83.

12. Rakestraw, C. E. *Training High School Youth for Employment.* Chicago: American Technical Society, 1951.

13. Roberts, Roy W. *Vocational and Practical Arts Education.* New York: Harper & Row, 1965.

14. Super, Donald E., and Phoebe L. Overstreet. *The Vocational Maturity of Ninth-Grade Boys.* New York: Columbia University Press, 1960.

15. Turnquist, Carl H. "Galaxy Approach to Education for the World of Work," *School Shop,* 25 (November 1965), 25–27.

16. Venn, Grant. *Man, Education and Work.* Washington, D. C.: The American Council on Education, 1964.

17. Venable, Tom C. *Patterns in Secondary School Curriculum.* New York: Harper & Row, 1958. Chapters 18 and 19.

18. Walsh, John P., and William Selden. "Vocational Education in Secondary School," in *Vocational Education.* National Society for the Study of Education Yearbook, 64. Part I. 1965.

UNIT III. METHODS OF TEACHING

A. TEACHING METHODOLOGY AND EDUCATIONAL PERSPECTIVE

1. Darling, Glenn H. "The Delinquent in the School," *The Clearing House,* 37 (April 1963), 483–486.

2. Educational Policies Commission. *Education and the Disadvantaged American.* Washington, D.C.: The National Education Association, 1962.
3. Friese, John F. *Course Making in Industrial Education.* Peoria, Ill.: Charles A. Bennett Co., 1946. Chapter 14.
4. Hoch, Oscar. "A Proposal for a Workable Approach to Deal with the Underachiever," *The High School Journal,* 45 (November 1961), 78–84.
5. Ingram, Christine P. *Education of the Slow-Learning Child.* New York: Ronald Press, 1953.
6. Israel, Saul. "Don't Forget the 'Slow Learner,' " *The Bulletin of the National Association of Secondary School Principals,* March 1962.
7. Kirk, Samuel A., and G. Orville Johnson. *Educating the Retarded Child.* Boston: Houghton Mifflin Co., 1951. Chapters 9 and 10.
8. Lee, Florence Henry (ed.). *Principles and Practices of Teaching in Secondary Schools.* New York: David McKay Co., 1965.
9. McKean, Robert C. *Principles and Methods in Secondary Education.* Columbus, Ohio: Charles E. Merrill Books, 1962. Chapter 24.
10. Roberts, Roy W. *Vocational and Practical Arts.* New York: Harper & Row, 1965.
11. Walsh, John P., and William Selden. "Vocational Education in Secondary School," in *Vocational Education.* National Society for the Study of Education Yearbook, 64. Part I. 1965.
12. Yoakam, Gerald A., and R. G. Simpson. *Modern Methods and Techniques of Teaching.* New York: Macmillan Co., 1963. Chapters 1 and 2.

B. TEACHING WITH THE USE OF INSTRUCTIONAL AIDS

1. Brown, J. W., R. B. Lewis, and F. F. Harcleroad. *Audio-Visual Instruction.* New York: McGraw-Hill Book Co., 1959.
2. Cross, A. J. F., and I. F. Cypher. *Audio-Visual Education.* New York: Thomas Y. Crowell Co., 1961.
3. DeKieffer, Robert, and L. W. Cochran. *Manual of Audio-Visual Techniques.* Englewood Cliffs, N. J.: Prentice-Hall, Inc., 1955.
4. Golden, Ruth I. "Slow Learners—Instructional Tapes and Insight," *The English Journal,* 51 (September 1962), 418–420.
5. Kinder, James S. *Audio-Visual Materials and Techniques.* New York: American Book Co., 1959.
6. Ozalid Audio Visual Department. *They See What You Mean.* Johnson City, New York: Ozalid Division of General Airline and Film Corporation, 1959.

John L. O'Brian

7. Taylor, L. O., Don R. McMahill, and B. L. Taylor. *The American Secondary School.* New York: Appleton-Century-Crofts, 1960. Chapter 2.
8. Visual Instruction Bureau. "Models: A New Concept in Teaching Aids," *The Texas Outlook,* 43 (July 1959), 14–15.
9. Weaver, Gilbert C., and Elroy W. Bollinger. *Visual Aids—Their Construction and Use.* Princeton, N. J.: D. Van Nostrand Co., 1957.
10. Wittich, Walter A., and C. F. Schuller. *Audio-Visual Materials: Their Nature and Use.* New York: Harper & Row, 1962.

C. TEACHING USING THE UNIT APPROACH

1. Butler, Frank A. *The Improvement of Teaching in Secondary Schools.* Chicago: The University of Chicago Press, 1947. Chapter 10.
2. Giachino, J. W., and Ralph O. Gallington. *Course Construction in Industrial Arts and Vocational Education.* Chicago: American Technical Society, 1961. Chapter 16.
3. Gwynn, J. Minor. *Curriculum Principles and Social Trends.* New York: Macmillan Co., 1960, pp. 157, 178–202.
4. Hammond, James J. "The Unit Method of Teaching at the Junior School Level," *The Industrial Arts Teacher,* 18 (March-April 1959), 16–20.
5. McKean, Robert C. *Principles and Methods in Secondary Education.* Columbus, Ohio: Charles E. Merrill Books, 1962. Chapter 4.
6. Smith, B. Othanel, W. O. Stanley, and J. H. Shores. *Fundamentals of Curriculum Development.* New York: World Book Co., 1950. Chapter 23.
7. Strickland, Ruth G. *How to Build a Unit of Work.* Office of Education Bulletin 15. Washington, D.C.: U.S. Government Printing Office, 1956.
8. Taylor, L. O., D. R. McMahill, and B. L. Taylor. *The American Secondary School.* New York: Appleton-Century-Crofts, 1960, pp. 202–212.
9. Venable, Tom C. *Patterns in Secondary School Curriculum.* New York: Harper & Row, 1958. Chapter 9.

D. TEACHING USING THE PROBLEM APPROACH

1. Briggs, Frances. "Problem-Centered Approaches to Teaching," *The High School Journal,* 46 (March 1963), 196–204.
2. Getzels, J. W. "Creative Thinking, Problem-Solving, and Instruction," in *Theories of Learning.* National Society for the Study of Education Yearbook, 63. 1964.

3. McKean, Robert C. *Principles and Methods in Secondary Education.* Columbus, Ohio: Charles E. Merrill Books, 1962. Chapter 4.

4. Phillips, Kenneth. "The Project Approach vs. The Problem Approach to Industrial Arts Education," *The Industrial Arts Teacher,* 20 (January–February 1961), 10.

5. Yoakam, Gerald A., and R. G. Simpson. *Modern Methods and Techniques of Teaching.* New York: Macmillan Co., 1963. Chapter 6.

E. TEACHING USING THE INDIVIDUAL PROJECT APPROACH

1. Butler, Frank A. *The Improvement of Teaching in Secondary Schools.* Chicago: University of Chicago Press, 1947. Chapter 12.

2. McKean, Robert C. *Principles and Methods in Secondary Education.* Columbus, Ohio: Charles E. Merrill Books, 1962. Chapter 4.

3. Yoakam, Gerald A., and R. G. Simpson. *Modern Methods and Techniques of Teaching.* New York: Macmillan Co., 1963. Chapter 9.

4. Zirbes, Laura, et al. "Fostering Individualization in the Classroom," in *Individualizing Instruction.* Association for Supervision and Curriculum Development Yearbook, 1964.

F. TEACHING USING THE GROUP APPROACH: THE GROUP PROJECT; THE LINE PRODUCTION

1. Baxter, Bernice, and Rosaline Cassidy. *Group Experience, the Democratic Way.* New York: Harper & Row, 1943.

2. Bender, Louis W., and W. C. Sharpe, "A Junior-High School Course for Disadvantaged Students," *The Bulletin of the National Association of Secondary School Principals,* March 1963.

3. Faunce, Roland C., and J. Clute Morrel. *Teaching and Learning in the Junior High School.* San Francisco, Calif.: Wadsworth Publishing Co., 1961. Chapter 7.

4. Grambs, Jean D., W. J. Iverson, and F. K. Patterson. *Modern Methods in Secondary Education.* New York: Holt, Rinehart & Winston, 1959. Chapter 10.

5. Gwynn, J. Minor. *Curriculum Principles and Social Trends.* New York: Macmillan Co., 1960, pp. 122, 312–316, 662–666.

6. Haws, Robert W., and Carl J. Schaefer. *Manufacturing in the School Shop.* Chicago: American Technical Society, 1960.

7. Keane, George. *Teaching Industry Through Production.* Washington, D.C.: National Education Association, 1963.

John L. O'Brian

8. Kettering, Charles F., and Allen Orth. *American Battle for Abundance.* Detroit, Mich.: General Motors Corporation, 1955.

9. Roby, Wallace, and Lloyd Wolf. "The Line Production Job in Industrial Arts Teaching," *The Industrial Arts Teacher,* 16 (November–December 1956), 9–14.

10. Stiles, Lindly J., and Mattie F. Dorsey. *Democratic Teaching in Secondary Schools.* Chicago: J. B. Lippincott Co., 1950. Chapters 12–15.

11. Vance, Stanley. *Industrial Structure and Policy.* Englewood Cliffs, N. J.: Prentice-Hall, Inc., 1961.

12. Young, Talmage B. "The Group Project as a Beginning 1-A Experience," *Industrial Arts and Vocational Education,* October 1960, p. 27.

G. TEACHING AND LEARNING THROUGH ROLE-PLAYING

1. Blackledge, Walter L., and Ethel H. Blackledge. "Role-Playing Prepares Students for Job Interviews," *Business Education World,* 42 (October 1961), 22–23, 30–31.

2. DePhillips, Frank A., W. M. Berliner, and James J. Cribbin. *Management of Training Programs.* Homewood, Ill.: Richard D. Irwin, Inc., 1960, pp. 177–180.

3. Grambs, Jean D., W. J. Iverson, and F. K. Patterson. *Modern Methods in Secondary Education.* New York: Holt, Rinehart & Winston, 1959, pp. 160, 252–264, 561–564.

4. Planty, Earl G., W. S. McCord, and C. A. Efferson. *Training Employees and Managers for Production and Teamwork.* New York: Ronald Press, 1948, pp. 121, 140, 183–185.

5. Riessman, Frank. "Some Suggestions for Teaching the Culturally Deprived," *N.E.A. Journal,* 52 (April 1963), 20–22.

H. TEACHING USING THE RESEARCH AND
EXPERIMENTATION APPROACH

1. Arthur, Earl W. "How to Use a Research-Experimentation Approach," *Industrial Arts and Vocational Education,* November 1960, p. 23.

2. Keeny, Alan P., and Donald Maley. "Montgomery County, Maryland, Research and Experimentation in Industrial Arts," *The Bulletin of the National Association of Secondary School Principals,* 46 (February 1962), 86–90.

3. Maley, Donald. "Research and Experimentation in the Junior High

A Master's Degree Program for the Preparation of Teachers of Disadvantaged Youth

School," *The Industrial Arts Teacher,* 18 (March–April 1959), 12–16.

4. Yoakam, Gerald A., and R. G. Simpson. *Modern Methods and Techniques of Teaching.* New York: Macmillan Co., 1963. Chapter 7.

I. TEACHING WITH INSTRUCTION SHEETS

1. Giachino, J. W., and Ralph O. Gallington. *Course Construction in Industrial Arts and Vocational Education.* Chicago: American Technical Society, 1961. Chapter 17.

2. Hill, Warren E., and Claude H. Ewing. *Materials and Methods for Vocational Training.* New York: McGraw-Hill Book Co., 1942. Chapters 5, 6, and 7.

3. Selvidge, R. W. *Individual Instruction Sheets.* Peoria, Ill.: Charles A. Bennett Co., 1934.

J. TEACHING WITH PROGRAMMED INSTRUCTIONAL MATERIALS

1. Finn, J. D. "Automation and Education: I. General Aspects," *Audio-Visual Communications Review,* 5, No. 1 (1957), 343–360.

2. ———. "Automation and Education: II. Automatizing the Classroom," *Audio-Visual Communications Review,* 5, No. 2 (1957), 451–467.

3. ———. "From State to Automation," *Audio-Visual Instruction,* 4 (1959), 84–85, 100–101.

4. ———. "Teaching Machines," *National Education Association Journal,* 49 (1960), 41–44.

5. Fund for the Advancement of Education. *Four Case Studies of Programmed Instruction.* New York: The Fund for Advancement of Education, 1964.

6. Jensen, A. R. "Teaching Machines and Individual Differences," *Automated Teaching Bulletin,* 1 (1960), 12–17.

7. Luce, G. G. "Can Machines Replace Teacher?" *The Saturday Evening Post,* 233 (September 24, 1960), 36–37, 102, 104–106.

8. Lumsdaine, A. A. "Teaching Machines and Programmed Individual Instruction." Paper presented at American Psychological Association meeting, Chicago, 1960.

9. ———. "Educational Technology, Programmed Learnings, and Instructional Science," in *Theories of Learning.* National Society for the Study of Education Yearbook, 63. 1964.

10. ——— and Robert Glaser (eds.). *Teaching Machines and Programmed Learning—A Source Book.* Washington, D.C.: The National Education Association, 1961.

11. Stolurow, Lawrence M. *Teaching by Machine.* OE–3410 Cooperative Research Monograph No. 6. Washington, D.C.: U.S. Government Printing Office, 1963.

K. THE DISCOVERY METHOD OF TEACHING

1. Alberty, Harold. *Reorganizing the High School Curriculum.* New York: Macmillan Co., 1953. Chapter 5.
2. Bottrell, Harold R. *Introduction to Education: Understanding Teaching Through Developmental Laboratory Experiences.* Harrisburg, Pa.: Stackpole Co., 1955.
3. Bruner, Jerome Seymour. *On Knowing.* Cambridge, Mass.: Harvard University Press, 1962.
4. ————. *The Process of Education.* Cambridge, Mass.: Harvard University Press, 1960.
5. Faunce, Roland C., and J. Clute Morrel. *Teaching and Learning in the Junior High School.* San Francisco, Calif.: Wadsworth Publishing Co., 1961. Chapter 8.
6. Johnston, Herbert. *A Philosophy of Education.* New York: McGraw-Hill Book Co., 1963.
7. Noar, Gertrude. *Teaching and Learning the Democratic Way.* Englewood Cliffs, N. J.: Prentice-Hall, Inc., 1963.
8. Watson, Goodwin (ed.). *No Room at the Bottom—Automation and the Reluctant Learner.* Washington, D.C.: The National Education Association, 1963. Chapter 4.

L. TEAM TEACHING CONCEPT AND PRACTICE

1. Lee, Florence Henry. *Principles and Practices of Teaching in Secondary Schools.* New York: David McKay Co., 1965, pp. 336–340.
2. McKean, Robert C. *Principles and Methods in Secondary Education.* Columbus, Ohio: Charles E. Merrill Books, 1962. Chapter 4.
3. Norton, M. S. "Approaches to Team Teaching," *The Bulletin of the National Association of Secondary School Principals,* 44 (October 1960), 89–92.

UNIT IV. PROGRAM AND CURRICULUM EVALUATION

1. Anderson, Vernon E. *Principles and Procedures of Curriculum Development.* New York: Ronald Press, 1956. Chapter 17.
2. ———— and William T. Gruhn. *Principles and Practices of Secondary Education.* New York: Ronald Press, 1962. Chapter 19.
3. Doll, Ronald C. *Curriculum Improvement: Decision-Making and Process.* Boston: Allyn and Bacon, Inc., 1965. Chapter 12.
4. Grambs, Jean D., and William J. Iverson. *Modern Methods in Sec-*

ondary Education. New York: Dryden Press, 1952. Section IV.

5. Leonard, J. Paul. *Developing the Secondary School Curriculum.* New York: Holt, Rinehart & Winston, 1946. Chapter 15.

6. Oliver, Albert I. *Curriculum Improvement—A Guide to Problems, Principles, and Procedures.* New York: Dodd, Mead and Co., 1965. Section IV.

7. Stratemeyer, Florence E., Hamden L. Forkner and Margaret G. McKim. *Developing a Curriculum for Modern Living.* New York: Columbia University, 1948. Chapter 10.

Educational Practicum for Teaching Disadvantaged Youth

The Educational Practicum is the cap-stone of the sequence of experiences designed to train teachers of disadvantaged youth. It provides a laboratory setting to put into action educational activities involving the teacher trainee's background experiences in such disciplines as social psychology, psychology, sociology, anthropology, and education. It is designed to bring to fruition the experiences and competencies developed in the teacher training sequence for master teachers of disadvantaged youth, that is, putting theory into practice. The practicum will provide a broad range of actual teaching and administrative experiences as well as experiences with the ancillary services that are associated with schools serving disadvantaged youth. Integrated with the practicum is a weekly seminar designed to discuss and resolve common as well as unique problems encountered by the teacher trainees.

Objectives: The Educational Practicum would be organized in a manner designed to achieve the following objectives:

1. To assist the student in understanding the "world of the disadvantaged" in relation to the school setting.

2. To provide the student with an awareness of the multiresponsibilities of the educational system as it relates to the disadvantaged.

3. To provide the student an opportunity to observe a master teacher in the teacher-learner process.

4. To make the student aware of the problems experienced administrators and pupil-personnel faculty face as they involve themselves with disadvantaged youth.

5. To gain teaching experience under the supervision of an ex-

232
John L. O'Brian

perienced teacher or, if in an administrative or ancillary area, to gain experience in the particular area under the supervision of experienced personnel.

6. To provide competencies in curriculum development and revision.

7. To develop an awareness of the need to use a number of different methods of teaching which appear appropriate for students of varying backgrounds and abilities.

8. To obtain experience and competency in using a wide range of instructional media appropriate for the teaching of the disadvantaged.

9. To become aware of and acquire competencies in designing learning experiences required for a range of abilities and social differences.

10. To use and become aware of a number of evaluation and measurement techniques in appraising student's progress, as well as self-evaluation.

11. To understand the need for and experience in using community data and resources in the establishment of direction for educational experiences for the disadvantaged.

12. To become aware of the need for interacting with fellow students and their supervisors pertaining to philosophical, pedagogical, and other areas of common concern which have evolved as a result of the trainee's practicum experiences.

General Comments: The Educational Practicum course will be offered on the time equivalency of a four-credit course. It is recommended that this practicum be supervised by several members of the program staff each dealing with a small number of students. These university supervisors should have experience and familiarity with public school settings.

The Educational Practicum should be coordinated with the Educational Processes course and the Seminar in Learning, Development, and Measurement. The curriculum was designed so that these three programs would run concurrently enabling each to supplement the other. A suggested overall organizational pattern for the practicum is given below:

1. A general orientation including the responsibilities of student teaching should be held. This orientation should be under the direction of the university supervisor in cooperation with the master teachers or school supervisors.
2. Assignment of trainees to the master teacher or supervisor.

A Master's Degree Program for the Preparation of Teachers of Disadvantaged Youth

3. Observation of school areas and activities other than the trainee's area of specialization.
4. Observation of trainee's master teacher or supervisor.
5. Opportunity for the trainee to teach in his own area of competence.
6. Daily conference with the master teacher during the teaching experience phase for the purpose of:
   a. Discussing specific problems that have arisen.
   b. Evaluating the trainee's daily planning.
   c. Self-evaluation by the trainee.
7. Periodic observation of the trainee by the university supervisor.
8. Weekly seminars involving one or more of the master teachers, the university supervisor, and the professors responsible for the Seminar in Learning, Development, and Measurement and the Educational Processes course. The purpose of this seminar would be to discuss common and unique problems and to devise ways of alleviating them.
9. Final evaluation made cooperatively by the master teacher, the university supervisor, and the teacher trainee.

COURSE OUTLINE

UNIT I   THE OBSERVATION PHASE

Purpose: The objectives of this unit are to provide an opportunity for the teacher trainee to observe a master teacher working with the disadvantaged youth, to become acclimated, and to get to know the students.

A. The following are typical observations and goals the teacher trainee should realize from this phase of the practicum:
   1. The personal attributes of the cooperating teacher.
   2. Means of establishing rapport with the student.
   3. Studying the learning process as it relates to the physical aspects of the program.
   4. Studying the learning process as it relates to the master teacher's involvement in:
      a. Motivating the disadvantaged.
      b. Providing for individual differences through subject matter selection, building on previous experience of the pupils, use of teaching aids, use of questioning techniques, use of general classroom management techniques and routine, organization of teaching units, and so on.

John L. O'Brian

5. Studying the learning process as it relates to the disadvantaged youth regarding their:
   a. Attention and participation.
   b. Interest.
   c. Individual differences.
   d. Involvement in individual and group work.
6. Analyzing the observation phase to provide opportunity for the teacher trainee to:
   a. Identify methods and techniques that contribute to the effective teaching of the disadvantaged.
   b. Interpret and analyze the laws of learning as they apply to the disadvantaged.

UNIT II   THE TEACHING EXPERIENCE PHASE

Purpose: The function of this unit is to provide the teacher trainee with the opportunity to apply the techniques, methods, and knowledge gained in the Seminar in Learning, Development, and Measurement, in the Educational Processes course, and in the observation phase of the Educational Practicum.

A. During the teaching experience phase the teacher trainee should become involved in:
   1. Using various methods appropriate for teaching the disadvantaged, such as:
      a. The unit method.
      b. The problem approach.
      c. The individual project approach.
      d. The discovery method.
      e. Team teaching.
   2. Using various techniques and materials appropriate for teaching the disadvantaged, such as:
      a. Role-playing.
      b. Programmed learning.
      c. Work experience activities.
      d. A variety of audio and visual materials.
   3. Building or using evaluation procedures to assess the progress of students.
   4. Daily planning for lessons to be taught (these should be evaluated cooperatively by the teacher trainee and the master teacher).
   5. Using and understanding the value and shortcomings of cu-

mulative and anecdotal records as they relate to providing information for more effective teaching.

6. Face-to-face contact with parents or guardians of the pupils.
7. Developing the necessary procedures to set up a cooperative program for one or more students.

UNIT III FINAL EVALUATION

Purpose: The purpose of this evaluation is to provide a final learning experience for the teacher trainee. Continuous evaluation will have taken place throughout the practicum through conferences with the master teacher and the university supervisor.

A. The final evaluation will be made cooperatively by the master teacher, the university supervisor, and the teacher trainee. The evaluation should include at least the following:

1. Personal qualities.
   a. Emotional stability.
   b. Adaptability.
   c. Cooperation.
   d. Stamina.
   e. Speech.
   f. Appearance.
2. Teacher-pupil relationships.
   a. Classroom atmosphere.
   b. Pupil freedom.
   c. Pupil control.
3. Classroom teaching.
   a. Effective planning and preparation.
   b. Effective presentation and involvement.
   c. Adequate record keeping and follow-up.
   d. Attention to special needs.
   e. Handling of routine matters.
4. Out-of-class responsibilities.
   a. Individual attention to pupils who have problems—school and personal.
   b. Participation in school related activities.
5. Professional relationships.
   a. Attitude toward total school program.
   b. Cooperation with school staff.

c. Involvement with and attitudes toward parents and the community.

6. Seminar participation.

UNIT IV SEMINAR PHASE

Purpose: The purpose of the seminar is to provide an opportunity to discuss common and unique problems arising out of the practicum experience and to devise ways of solving these problems.

A. The seminar will be conducted on a weekly basis throughout the duration of the practicum.

B. The seminar will be conducted on a team basis with master teachers, the university supervisor, and the professors of the Seminar in Learning, Development, and Measurement and the Educational Processes course comprising the team. The university supervisor will coordinate the seminar.

Suggested Agencies: The following agencies are submitted as suggested agencies for the placement of students for the practicum experience. The list is suggestive; no attempt has been made to provide an exhaustive list. The agencies are not listed in any order of preference.

A. The Job Corps—men and women.

B. Multiskilled centers (MDTA).

C. Specific programs at the high school level designed for the disadvantaged.

D. Special demonstration programs.

E. Residential schools similar to those approved under P. L. 88–210, Section 14.

F. Discipline schools where the majority of the youth in attendance are also disadvantaged.

Seminar in Professional Issues

This seminar is a critical and intensive analysis of current issues in education (general and vocational) as they apply to the disadvantaged person. Issues that grow out of the experiences of the curriculum will be integrated and related to education.

Objectives: It is the purpose of this seminar to realize the following:

1. To provide a "bridge experience" between the professional training received and the profession.

2. To provide opportunity to share ideas, to discuss issues, and to offer viewpoints concerning current issues in the field as they relate to the disadvantaged.

3. To evaluate the experiences received in the total curriculum.

General Comments: The Seminar in Professional Issues will be offered on the time equivalency of a three-credit course. The seminar is to be conducted by the students under the guidance of the seminar supervisor (preferably the director of the program). It should be an experience that is not preplanned but where the students themselves determine the content and issues of the seminar. The emphasis should be on student-planned content.

COURSE OUTLINE

UNIT I SUGGESTED TOPICS

Purpose: The topics suggested in this unit are offered as examples of issues that may develop in the seminar. They are offered as a guide and are not intended to be used as subject matter content. It should be emphasized that the seminar content should grow out of the experiences and issues that have evolved from the totality of experiences of the students—both academic and practical. A format such as this will foster topics that are germane to the experiences of the participants. It is anticipated that many topics and issues will arise out of the on-going interaction of the seminar.

EXAMPLES OF ANTICIPATED SEMINAR TOPICS

A. Automation and its impact on semiskilled and unskilled occupations.

B. Grouping practices and integrating the disadvantaged youth into a total school environment.

C. Hiring practices and the minority groups.

D. Educational programs for the disadvantaged.

E. Means of dealing with peer influences.

F. Motivation and the disadvantaged youth.

G. Testing as a selection device.

H. The degree to which society is adequately fulfilling its responsibility to the disadvantaged.

238
John L. O'Brian

I.   The degree to which the disadvantaged person is responsible for his own condition.
J.   The advisability of the poor participating in the administration of poverty programs.
K.   The advisability of training the disadvantaged for semiskilled and unskilled jobs that may be eliminated by automation.
L.   The guaranteed annual wage.
M.   Work and/or leisure.
N.   Police protection in urban communities.
O.   Sex, drugs, and life.
P.   Crime and class.
Q.   Vocational education versus general education.
R.   Societal rewards and their distribution.

Integrating Option

The Integrating Option provides a dual track for the curriculum. In some institutions a Master's Project is a mandated requirement for the degree; in other institutions this requirement may be waived. Therefore, two options are presented for consideration. The Committee favored the Evaluative Paper option as opposed to the Master's Project. This value judgment is based on the comprehensiveness of the curriculum and the opinion that the goals and objectives of the curriculum can be achieved without this culminating exercise. An inspection of Figure 10–1 shows that it is recommended that three credits be given for the successful completion of the Master's Project and that the Evaluative Paper not receive any credit. A total of thirty-three credits will be earned for those following the Master's Project track and a total of thirty credits will be earned by those following the Evaluative Paper track.

Objectives: The integrating Option is aimed at achieving certain outcomes. These are expressed as objectives such as those listed below:

A. *Master's Project*
    1. To provide the candidate with an opportunity to gather data in an operational setting.
    2. To provide the candidate with the opportunity to use the concepts learned in the classroom and in the field experiences to solve a practical problem previously identified.
    3. To provide opportunity to assess the candidate's performance and application of concepts learned under actual conditions as a practitioner and problem-solver.

B. *Evaluative Paper*
  1. To provide the candidate with an opportunity to review his experiences and to evaluate the worthwhileness of these experiences.
  2. To identify the strengths of the curriculum.
  3. To identify the weaknesses of the curriculum.
  4. To identify areas whereby the curriculum can be improved and made more functional.

General Comments: In those instances where the Master's Project is selected the Project should carry three credits; where the Evaluative Paper is selected no credit is recommended. Both routes present a means for the student to integrate his experiences. The emphasis, however, will be different. The Master's Project is an individual investigation, study, critical analysis, evaluation, or pilot project concerned with the education of disadvantaged youth. Each student will be required to develop, carry out, and report the results of his project in a Master's Paper. The Evaluative Paper is an evaluation by the individual of the total experiences received in his Master's program. In all cases the course will be structured for each individual, taking account of his interests.

COURSE OUTLINE

A. *Option 1: Master's Project*
  1. The project will be structured to provide individual consultation with an appointed adviser.
     a. Identification of a problem area to be studied.
     b. Approval of the problem by the candidate's committee.
     c. Execution of the study.
     d. Presentation of problem via a Master's Paper.
B. *Option 2: Evaluative Paper*
  1. The paper will be guided by oral and written criteria.
     a. The student will be required to evaluate the entire curriculum in terms of what he has obtained.
     b. The student will be required to evaluate the entire curriculum in terms of how it failed to meet his needs.
     c. The student will be required to make recommendations for the improvement of the curriculum.
     d. The student will be required to project ways and means

240
John L. O'Brian

the concepts learned could be applied to his home-school situation.

Recommendation

A MOST important element of any curriculum or program of studies is an evaluation of its effectiveness. To a minor degree this has been built into the curriculum under the aegis of the Evaluative Paper. However, there is no assurance that this track of the Integrating Option will be utilized by all institutions electing to use this curriculum. Even where the Evaluative Paper is used, it is recognized that an evaluation of the scope and depth necessary would not result. Therefore, it is recommended that those implementing the curriculum be cognizant of the need to develop adequate evaluation procedures.

11 Human Relations Institute for Teachers of Disadvantaged Children

Harry L. Miller

HUNTER COLLEGE,
THE CITY UNIVERSITY OF NEW YORK

I N THE SUMMER of 1965, Hunter College conducted a six-week institute for 45 elementary school teachers working in urban slum areas, choosing as its primary emphasis the aim of increasing the self-understanding and human relations skills of the institute participants. The Program was funded by the U.S. Office of Education as one of about 75 training institutes that constituted the first group of NDEA grants directed at elementary teaching.

The decision of the Office of Education to make funds available for the training of teachers of the socially disadvantaged child was a particularly welcome one for teacher training institutions in metropolitan areas. New York's central city and large pockets in the immediate metropolitan area surrounding it (in Newark, Yonkers, and other areas) present an extraordinarily difficult challenge to the schools. This is particularly true of those at the elementary level whose total populations may be restricted by neighborhood segregation to children of families living in deep poverty and social alienation.

The dimensions of that challenge are too well known to require any extensive elaboration. In about half of Manhattan's elementary schools, for example, over 85 per cent of the children are nonwhite or Puerto Rican, the overwhelming proportion of them disadvantaged, by any definition. Pupil transiency rates in about half of Manhattan schools are well above 50 per cent. In schools characterized by heavy in-migration, from the south or from Puerto Rico, reading achievement may average as much as three grades below level. Such schools characteristically employ higher proportions of inexperienced and out-of-license teachers than do schools in other areas.

Although the city has moved in a number of directions to meet the problem by providing greater and more varied resources and by designating certain schools as requiring special administrative and staff effort, the central and crucial need that remains is the training of teachers to enable them to cope more creatively with the special problems they face in these schools. No amount of administrative reorganization is likely to be effective if those who teach in the specially organized schools persist in the teaching patterns and attitudes that have been ineffective in the past.

The problem of defining the type of training that is likely to be most effective in meeting these difficulties is a complex one. At the present time, lacking any sure knowledge of the kind of teaching or teacher that is likely to make the difference, it is perhaps best to experiment with a variety of approaches. The planning of this institute was based on the conclusion of many observers of the urban education scene that the problems of the slum school are due at least as much to the alienation of the school staffs as they are to the cultural alienation of the child. If true, then an important objective for teacher training should be to help teachers become more aware of their own feelings, more willing to express them, and better able to accept the expressed feelings of others. Such training might well contribute to the closing of the communication gap between teacher and pupil so evident in those schools, where each group comes into the situation with very different values and experience.[1]

1. *Editor's Note.* The approaches used in this and the previous chapter are comparable. Both chapters (and those that follow) acknowledge that much of the difficulty facing the urban teacher is in the domain of sensitivity to the values and feelings of children outside their range of personal experience. Thus, training must be undertaken to broaden this experience and supplement the process of self-discovery.

Harry L. Miller

Program Design: Objectives and Activities

A PROGRAM was designed for the institute based on the premise outlined above. This program sought to realize a number of clearly separate objectives by scheduling relatively discrete blocks of time for special activities devoted to particular aims. The program is shown graphically in Figure 11–1.

The first of these activity blocks, and the most directly relevant to the major emphasis of the institute as a whole, was composed of a series of sensitivity training sessions given in the form of T-Groups. This is a learning device developed over the past fifteen years by the National Training Laboratory. Such training proceeds as an unstructured series of discussions in which a skilled trainer helps participants understand and deal with their own developing interactions and the feelings that accompany them. Bradford et al. (1964, p. 16) give the following specification of the hoped-for outcomes of such training showing clearly the relevance of the learning format for the purposes of the institute:

> One hoped for outcome for the participant is increased awareness and sensitivity to emotional reactions and expressions in himself and others. Without such awareness . . . he functions in partial blindness to the complex of human factors which every situation embodies. . . . Another desired objective is greater ability to perceive and to learn from the consequences of his actions through attention to feelings, his own and others'. Emphasis is placed on the development of sensitivity to cues furnished by the behavior of others and ability to utilize feedback in understanding his own behavior. . . . The staff also attempts to stimulate the clarification and development of personal values and goals consonant with a democratic and scientific approach to problems of social and personal decision, and action. Some of the more important learnings seem to result when individuals publicly confront previously unperceived discrepancies in their values, and when they receive non-judgmental support in attempts to resolve these discrepancies.

Because groups of 8–12 are optimal for such training, the number of institute participants was set at 45, to permit the formation of four groups, each with its own trainer. A period of approximately a week and a half was set aside for the T-Group sessions.

The second major block of activities was a teaching practicum, in which participants worked under supervision in a nearby elementary

INSTITUTE SCHEDULE						
Time	First Week	Second Week	Third Week	Fourth Week	Fifth Week	Sixth Week
Mornings	Workshop Input Sessions	*Block One — Teaching Practicum* Monday — Planning for the week Tuesday — Planning and preparation for the field trip Wednesday — Field trip Thursday — Classroom activity based on field trip (language skills emphasized) Friday — Analysis and evaluation of the week's work				*Block Five General Sessions* 1. Planning for future teaching approaches 2. General reporting on experiences
Afternoons	*Block Two* *Sensitivity Training* *(T-Group Sessions)*	*Block Three* *Lecture — Discussion Sessions* 1. Reading 2. Lectures 3. Discussion	*Block Four* *Understanding the Community* 1. Reading 2. Lectures 3. Discussions 4. Developing social psychological backgrounds			

Figure 11-1. The institute schedule for the six-week period.

school with a group of children recruited for the summer. The complex nature of this operation is indicated by the following description of its various elements.

Input sessions were held during the morning portion of the first week. These were designed to precede the Teaching Practicum. The sessions were devoted to examining available special curriculum materials, conferring with visiting specialists engaged in running experimental school programs, attending staff lectures on curriculum, and evaluating teaching methods deemed appropriate for the disadvantaged child.

The Teaching Practicum was held during the morning session of the next four weeks. A number of activities constituted the Practicum. One of the major ones was that of working with children from disadvantaged areas where new materials and approaches were tried. A general pattern, adopted and followed each of the four weeks, was to devote Monday morning to planning the week; Tuesday morning to planning and preparing the children for a field trip that would take place on Wednesday; Wednesday morning to the field trip; Thursday morn-

Harry L. Miller

ing to classroom work utilizing the field trip experiences and emphasizing language skills; Friday morning to evaluation of the week's work. Each institute member was required to keep a diary describing his experiences with the children and to keep notes on progress and the results of experimentation with materials developed and methods used.

The aims for the practicum were to make participants aware of the range of new materials and teaching techniques developed for work with disadvantaged children, to encourage them to be creative in developing their own materials and techniques, and to practice the insights gained in the T-Groups as they developed relationships with the children.

A third block of time (approximately a week and a half) was devoted to a series of lecture-discussion sessions aimed at improving participants' understanding of the research and theory available on the social, cultural, and psychological roots of the problems of the disadvantaged child's schooling. These sessions were based on a series of assigned readings, not only in a volume of collected pieces but in a specially organized library of books, fugitive materials, and journal articles. Discussions focused on such topics as the following:

1. The subcultural value systems in the American social class system, and their relation to achievement motivation.
2. The opportunity structure; poverty and its effects.
3. The nature of cognitive deprivation in lower-class living.
4. Social mobility, social class, and intelligence.
5. The personality correlates of disadvantaged status.
6. The relation between segregation and achievement.
7. Experimental work on teaching and learning styles, on the success of model programs, and on new curricula.

Most of these sessions were conducted by a member of the staff, but on three occasions they featured visiting specialists who reported on a specific body of experience or research.

A fourth block of work concentrated on understanding the community that surrounds the slum school, and particularly the urban ghetto in which so many of them are located in cities like New York. Several sessions were held at the college, with visiting community experts discussing problems of housing and health, delinquency, job training, and so on. Others were held in Harlem and Bedford Stuyvesant, where the group visited a variety of social centers and talked with local social workers.

Block five, which was a series of general sessions, concentrated on planning for future teaching approaches and reporting on experiences.

Timing

Because many of these blocks of activity had, of necessity, to overlap, a number of adjustments in the ideal schedule had to be made. The following allocation of time over the six-week period represents a considerable number of compromises:

The T-Group Sessions were held in the afternoons of the first week and a half. Four T-Group specialists, each with a responsibility for a group of 8–12 people, conducted these sessions. Two of the four stayed on after this intensive period and worked informally with groups or individuals. The T-Groups, as originally composed, also met several times during the final three weeks of the institute.

The Teaching Practicum occupied the mornings of the second, third, fourth, and fifth weeks. Mornings of the final week of the institute were spent in general reporting on and evaluation of the practicum experience and in describing instructional units developed by the participants.

Research and Theory sessions began after the end of the T-Group sessions, that is, in the middle of the second week. They were held two afternoons each week until the end of the Institute.

Understanding the Community sessions occupied every afternoon of the fourth week. The week began and ended with a session at the college; field trips were made during the middle of the week.

Selection of Participants

RECRUITING of institute participants was limited to the New York metropolitan area. A large proportion of those finally selected were from the city itself. A few of the participants came from New Jersey and Long Island. Each applicant was required to have at least one year of teaching experience, and of those selected, almost half had between six and ten years of teaching. Almost a quarter of those selected had more than ten years of experience. The modal age was between 35 and 39 years.

The 700 applications reviewed were screened for a variety of abilities and experiences. Each was first given a composite rating representing weighted scores based on teaching experience, academic record, principal's recommendation, the interest expressed by the principal in making use of the teacher's institute experience, and the statement by the applicant of how *he* intended to make use of the experience.

The original intention had been to invite teams of at least two teachers from the same school on the assumption that team members could support one another in changing practices in the school. When the ratings of applicants from the same school were considered, however, it became clear that the Institute could not wholly be composed of teams without sacrificing quality, if one supposed that the composite scores of individuals did indeed reflect quality. If one person from a particular school had a high score, the other applicants from the same school tended to score below the cut-off point that had been established. There were some schools, however, from which pairs of high scorers could be selected; these schools were checked with a person intimately familiar with the New York system, to obtain an assessment of the likelihood that the school principal would welcome innovation. The eventual selection included eight two-person teams, plus a five-member team from the school in which the practicum was to be conducted. The remaining members of the Institute were singles.

Evaluation

ALL available evidence, both subjective and objective, suggests that the human relations training that was at the heart of the institute succeeded in at least its immediate purpose, though there was no opportunity of assessing objectively whether it made a difference in classroom behavior.

Two objective measures, before and after the institute, assessed the impact of the T-Group experience. One was an instrument composed primarily of a series of incidents involving minority group members; in each case, the respondent was to select a statement that he thought would most accurately describe the feelings of the person involved. The comparison of before and after scores showed a trend in the desired direction. The mean score on the pretest was so high, however, that the change was not significant. New York City teachers are so sensitive to matters of race relations that the pretest results are probably not valid. Several members of the group privately confessed, during the Institute, that they had not recorded their real feelings.

The second instrument, developed by Boris Gertz, one of the training staff, attempted to measure the primary objectives of the T-Group experience rather than secondary outcomes. This perhaps accounts for its greater success in this instance. The scores represent changes in two variables: willingness to be open about one's own feelings with pupils, colleagues, and superiors; and willingness to give other persons in these categories feedback about one's own feelings about them. The raw scores are summarized below in Tables 11–1 and 11–2 as the pre- and post-test means for the four groups. Table 11–1 shows the willingness

TABLE 11–1. Pre- and Post-test Scores on the Openness Factor for the Four T-Groups in the Institute

	STUDENTS		COLLEAGUES		SUPERVISORS		OVERALL	
	Pre-test	Post-test	Pre-test	Post-test	Pre-test	Post-test	Pre-test	Post-test
Gp. A	27	36	25	31	30	27	24	31
Gp. B	26	26	27	26	19	19	24	24
Gp. C	28	32	27	29	19	23	24	28
Gp. D	28	30	27	32	21	27	26	30

TABLE 11–2. Pre- and Post-test Scores on the Feedback Factor for the Four T-Groups in the Institute

	STUDENTS		COLLEAGUES		SUPERVISORS		OVERALL	
	Pre-test	Post-test	Pre-test	Post-test	Pre-test	Post-test	Pre-test	Post-test
Gp. A	29	36	34	39	33	39	32	37
Gp. B	30	31	33	32	33	33	32	32
Gp. C	29	37	34	39	32	34	32	37
Gp. D	31	33	34	38	31	34	33	35

of the Institute participants to be open about their feelings with pupils, colleagues, and superiors. Table 11–2 shows the willingness of the Institute participants to give other persons in these categories feedback about their own feelings about them. The response changes shown in Tables 11–1 and 11–2 were then tested for significance in a statistical study undertaken with a combined group, including the four Hunter T-Groups and three similar groups at Lesley College. Since there was no difference between the college mean scores, the results of the test, given in Table 11–3, can be assumed to apply to the Hunter scores generally. Although it is clear from the raw data that some of the

Harry L. Miller

TABLE 11–3. Analysis of Variance Results of Pre- and Post-test Differences Attributable to T-Group Experience, for All Groups

	F-RATIOS	
	Openness	Feedback
With Students	16.422**	18.495**
With Colleagues	14.535*	32.868***
With Supervisors	20.634***	15.987*
Overall	26.344***	30.869***

***p < .0000
 **p < .0001
  *p < .0005

Note: These data are used with the kind permission of Dr. Boris Gertz of Lesley College and Dr. Jay Hall of the South West Center for Law and Behavioral Science at the University of Texas.

groups were affected to a considerably greater extent than others by the T-Groups, the training produced highly significant differences in both openness and feedback tendencies in the group as a whole.

A variety of subjective evidence supports the conclusions drawn from the use of Gertz's instrument. Many participants remarked that they had found the experience powerful and awakening; and there was occasional evidence in the diaries that teachers were seeing children and other teachers in consciously new ways. On their own initiative the group organized a reunion during the following spring; over half of the Institute members attended. It was clear from the ensuing discussion that the T-Group was the most vital and lasting element of the Institute experience. Many stated that they could attest to its effect on their relations with their pupils.

The T-Group training staff felt that the sessions did not produce as great results as hoped for. Not that one can expect great growth on the part of all who go through a T-Group experience. Herbert Thelen has speculated that about a third of the members of such groups really change a good deal, another third get at least considerable cognitive insight, and the remainder are not greatly affected. But very high group cohesiveness that usually results from the "cultural island" effect of a residential training experience, and that tends to increase the impact of the T-Group method, did not materialize. In this case, where participants were not living together, and where physical facilities were neither quiet nor comfortable, group cohesiveness remained low. The training staff members were emphatic in their recommendations that if T-Group methods were to be a part of such institutes in the future, at least that

Human Relations Institute for Teachers of Disadvantaged Children

part of the program should be held in an off-campus, residential setting. Most of the participants, when queried, agreed with the staff.

The effectiveness of the Teaching Practicum (the second major element of the Institute) must be based on subjective evidence. Participants were asked to write their reactions to the experience and to make suggestions for improvement. A summary of the comments received in which more than two persons in the group made the same comment is shown in Table 11–4.

TABLE 11–4. Reactions to and Suggestions for Improving the Institute

Number of Persons	Comment
10	Need more clearcut objectives.
10	Need more time with the children.
7	Need more relevant kinds of children.
4	Need more time for planning.
4	Field trip orientation is binding.
4	Need more direction from the staff.
3	Need more experimentation and derived conclusions.
3	Need more opportunity to do what *I* want to do.

Out of the extensive comments from which those in Table 11–4 are summarized, one can draw a number of conclusions. There was a great deal of frustration over the amount of time available to do what needed to be done, frustration which the staff shared. The two staff members supervising the Practicum, for example, seldom found time for the individual conferences that they felt were necessary. A number of children in the laboratory school were far from disadvantaged; this was a result of severe recruiting difficulties. The summer of 1965 was the first year of a massive summer program initiated by Head Start, and there was brisk competition for the children who would have provided a relevant challenge for the Institute teachers.

Another concern expressed both by the participants and the staff raise more fundamental questions about the design of the Teaching Practicum, and about such an activity in general as part of a concentrated summer training experience. If one assumes, as the staff did, that any significant teacher growth depends on actual practice, under supervision, it is possible to describe minimum requirements for such an activity and evaluate this specific design against them; for example:

Harry L. Miller

1. Participants must be exposed first to a body of theory and precept for a sufficiently long period to enable them to digest it. Input of this kind in the Institute was not large enough in quantity because of time pressures, nor was there time for digestion before the actual work in the classroom began. Some of it came *after* work began, and when participants were already feeling the strain of meeting with children every day.

2. Participants need enough time to plan experimental procedures that each one would like to try out, procedures that grow out of the input data and are relevant to them. This could be done in small groups or as teams of three or four. It is clear from some of the difficulties encountered that such planning groups need considerable help in translating abstraction or example into ideas for classroom experimentation; if the planning is done in small groups, one would need a fair number of staff resources to aid him.

3. Ideally then, a group of forty-five teachers should have access to a number of classes of children over a period of several weeks. Provisions should be made to meet each morning for experimental lessons conducted by one teacher and observed by another and, at least occasionally, by a trained supervisor. The afternoons might be devoted to analysis of what happened in the morning with the attendance, at least part of the time, of the supervisors. This would require many children and a fair-sized supervisory staff for that period of time.

If one takes this model seriously, a number of alternative ways of dealing with it are suggested. One alternative is to discard the Practicum as a realistic element of training in a concentrated summer institute. One could certainly argue in support of this view, that teachers ought to have some relief from the pressures of the classroom, from which they come, without a break, into an institute. It may well be that a long period of reflection and an immersion in the adult world would be ultimately more useful for elementary school teachers than to be plunged back almost immediately into the situation from which they come.

Yet, most of what we know about training suggests that we cannot depend on transfer of learning to the real situation without some practice under conditions of reinforcement. The alternative, then, is to devise some practical activities that include at least some of the most important elements of the model. In this Institute, for example, the goals of the laboratory school could have been made far clearer; the complaints about ambiguity of goals have considerable foundation, and it may have been a mistake to rely, in this complex problem area, on the classic workshop techniques. With some minor additions to the staff for brief periods of time, more guidance might have been given to planning and some concentrated supervision provided on a sampling basis.

Apart from the measurement of changes induced by the human relations training and the subjective reactions to the laboratory school experience, there is available one set of data on general shifts of attitude as a result of the Institute. On the last afternoon, participants were asked to look through a questionnaire that they had filled out during the first week and indicate whether they would now (1) add anything to what they had written previously, (2) delete anything, or (3) change the emphasis they had originally given to any statement. The original responses had shown, in many instances, a considerable degree of sophistication, so there is again some difficulty in assessing change from a previously fairly high point.

It is instructive that in the changes made there is an overwhelming trend toward an emphasis on a need for sensitivity and understanding. For example, in answer to the question of what teachers of disadvantaged children need in order to improve, common responses were: (1) more sensitivity; (2) understanding of the culture; (3) know oneself better; (4) accept the child as he *is*; and (5) understand how the child learns.

Second, the bulk of responses lie in the area of what the school, and particularly what the teacher, can do about the achievement problem. This reflects a healthy change in the direction of a belief that the problems lie as much with the school as with the child and his culture. Common changes in original responses added such statements as: (1) the teacher should have faith in the potential of the child— handicaps should be a challenge; (2) schools should provide more relevant and meaningful materials and curriculum; (3) parents should have respect for teachers.

There was a considerable shift in the direction of differentiating among the children as a group, and a rejection of stereotyping and middle-class patronizing. A parallel trend was found toward seeing differences as just that, without applying value judgments to them, and toward accepting children as they are. One participant for example, deleted his original comment that, "they are not appreciative of what the school tries to do for them," adding a marginal note, "that's patronizing."

Finally, there are in these changes an almost equal emphasis on the importance of cultural differences and on the need of the school to adapt to those differences by experimenting with curriculum and materials.

Although these data hardly constitute hard evidence of fundamental change, they do provide some hopeful indications of real growth in acceptance of responsibility, determination, and a sense of direction for future work.

_____ Some Recommendations for Institutes
with a Human Relations Focus

VIEWED as a whole, the outcomes of this Institute would encourage an emphasis on human relations training in future summer programs for teachers of the disadvantaged, with the following changes made in the pattern described:

1. Radically change the recruiting procedure by restricting participants to four or five schools, with sympathetic and interested principals, from which teams of eight to ten teachers could be recruited, and include some supervisors.

2. This recruiting procedure would necessitate change in the design of human relations training, in addition to other changes that seem appropriate. The T-Groups would now be "family groups" and would address themselves to personal growth in self-understanding where this would be relevant to school problems. The training period exclusively should occupy the first two weeks or ten days of the Institute and take place in a residential setting. Two weeks are preferable; this would permit some work on the conditions for creativity.

3. The second two weeks should focus on two activities: input of theory, research, and precept; and intensive planning sessions in small groups for the coming classroom sessions. Visiting experts should be used for periods of two or three days not only to make presentations, but to sit in with planning groups to help them develop ideas for experimental procedures and demonstration lessons.

4. A third two-week period should be spent teaching in a practicum. The morning should be used for classroom instruction and the afternoon for review and evaluation. Ideally, a group of regular summer

Human Relations Institute for Teachers of Disadvantaged Children

elementary schools that are relatively close to one another should be made available for this period. If the Institute participants were grouped in teams of four, then only ten or eleven regular classes would be required. These could be arranged using only two or three schools. The supervisory staff should not have too great a difficulty covering that number of classes regularly.

5. A three- or four-day additional period for general evaluation and reporting would be useful. This would bring the total time for the Institute to about six and a half weeks, slightly longer than the present one.

_____Reference

BRADFORD, LELAND, JACK R. GIBB and KENNETH D. BENNE (eds.). *T-Group Theory and Laboratory Method.* New York: John Wiley & Sons, 1964.

256
Harry L. Miller

12 The Project Beacon Training Program

Julian Roberts and
Doxey A. Wilkerson

FERKAUF GRADUATE SCHOOL OF EDUCATION
YESHIVA UNIVERSITY

FERKAUF GRADUATE SCHOOL'S Project Beacon is a long-range program addressed to many aspects of the education of socially disadvantaged children. It involves a variety of research and evaluation projects, extended training programs and short-time institutes, preservice programs and in-service programs, information retrieval and dissemination, annual invitational conferences, demonstration programs in selected schools on different levels, and other projects. It is a comprehensive program now in its third year of development. Some of its projects are well under way; others are just beginning; and others are still "gleams in the eye." The purpose of the whole is to help advance theory and practice in the education of socially disadvantaged children, and thereby to make some contributions to the improvement of education for all children.

The personnel-training aspects of Yeshiva's Project Beacon are broader than the preparation of teachers. Programs are under way to prepare school psychologists, educational psychologists, guidance specialists, administrators, and supervisors, as well as teachers—all for work in depressed-area schools and other agencies. The focus of this paper is on the preservice program to prepare teachers for urban slum schools called the Project Beacon Training Program. Interpretation is made of (1) some of the underlying premises of this program, (2) approaches and problems with the theoretical studies required of students, (3) approaches and problems with the internship experiences provided for students, and (4) approaches and problems involved in evaluating the program.

Premises and Goals

THE very recent and now burgeoning movement to improve the education of socially disadvantaged children has articulated a wide range of sometimes conflicting perceptions and guiding principles; and it may be advisable briefly to outline without elaboration or argument, some of the premises that define the Project Beacon Training Program point of view.

First, lower-class and minority-group children in urban slums, among whom the socially disadvantaged predominate, are characterized by a wide range of individual differences—in self-concept, motivation, general conduct and academic performance; to perceive them as a homogeneous group is to think in terms of a harmful stereotype.

Second, the academic retardation and deviant interpersonal behavior commonly observed among socially disadvantaged children are functions of social conditioning, not of biological inheritance. Moreover, in addition to the negative cultural influences generally associated with poverty and discrimination in the home and community, negative influences in the school itself contribute substantially to impede normative academic performance among socially disadvantaged children.

Third, the academic and related handicap common among socially disadvantaged children can be minimized, if not fully overcome, through appropriate curricular experiences.

Fourth, in order to develop such appropriate curricular experiences with disadvantaged children, teachers need to be equipped with special theoretical insights, attitudes and classroom skills relevant to the special learning problems involved.

258

Julian Roberts and Doxey A. Wilkerson

Fifth, the special professional equipment required for effective work with disadvantaged children can be developed by teachers and prospective teachers through an integrated program of relevant theoretical studies and guided field experience.

Sixth, on the preservice level, liberal arts college graduates who have good academic records and who evidence genuine interest in working in depressed-area schools are generally good prospects for participation in a teacher education program oriented toward improved school experiences for disadvantaged children.

Most of these propositions are yet to be firmly validated by empirical evidence, and some of them are the subjects of current debate among professional educators. However, the Project Beacon Training Program is not intended to provide the answers to the many complex questions involved in the education of disadvantaged children, but rather as an effort at discovery and trial. It is intended as "an experimental teacher-education program which seeks, through problem-solving and tested laboratory experience, to discover and develop effective approaches to promoting the emotional and cognitive growth of socially disadvantaged children." The premises outlined above define the major guidelines of this approach to this task of discovery and development.

The objectives of the program reflect the general point of view here defined. They are:

1. Understanding of the biological, social, and psychological forces that shape human development and learning in general, and of the special influences affecting the development and learning of disadvantaged children and youth.

2. Understanding of community organization and process in general, and as reflected in depressed-area urban communities.

3. Understanding of modern principles of curriculum development and teaching methods, and of adaptations required for the effective guidance of learning by socially disadvantaged children and youth.

4. Skill in classroom instruction and management in depressed-area schools.

5. Empathy with socially disadvantaged people and ability to interact with them effectively for the attainment of worthy school and community goals.

6. Readiness and ability to use techniques of educational research in approaching problems in the education of disadvantaged youth.

7. Abiding commitment to professional service in depressed-area urban schools.

An analysis of the theoretical studies and internship experiences through which an attempt is made to implement these principles and realize these objectives follows.

_____Theoretical Studies at Yeshiva University

THE Project Beacon Training Program began in 1963–64 with ten liberal arts college graduates, each of whom was awarded a scholarship of $2400—$400 by the University and $2000 by Mobilization for Youth, the comprehensive demonstration project for the control of deliquency in Manhattan's Lower East Side. There were also ten students in the program during 1964–65, and thirteen during 1965–66. The scholarships, with some variations in amounts, were also awarded during the second and third years. Beginning with 1966–67, twenty students were to be admitted to the program each year, fifteen of them with Prospective Teacher Fellowship Awards under Title V-C of the Higher Education Act of 1965, and others with preservice fellowship awards from the New York State Education Department. Participants have thus far been restricted to prospective elementary school teachers, although it is planned to develop the program subsequently on the secondary level as well.

Students in the program are required to earn 36 semester hours of credit in courses, seminars, and internship over a period of one four-week summer term and two semesters. Completion of the program qualifies students for the degree of Master of Science in Education and satisfies New York State certification requirements for the elementary grades.

Students in the initial 1963–64 program were required to prepare a thesis, but this requirement proved to be incompatible with the heavy course-and-internship load students had to carry and was subsequently abandoned. The research experience that the thesis requirement was designed to give is currently provided, in part, by a series of investigative reports required in the year-long Internship Seminar.

The theoretical studies required of students during 1965–66 consisted of ten three-hour courses in the psychological and historical foundations of education, in teaching methods, and in seminars associated with internship. Their titles, along with those of the two three-hour internship courses, are listed below by related groups:

Julian Roberts and Doxey A. Wilkerson

Child Development and Learning
Educational Psychology
Social Psychology of Education

History of Educational Thought

Teaching Language Arts, Elementary N-6
Teaching Social Studies, Elementary N-6
Teaching Mathematics, Elementary N-6
Science for Elementary Schools N-6

Internship (Fall)
Internship Seminar (Fall)
Student Teaching in Grades N-6 (Spring)
Internship Seminar (Spring)

Continuing evaluation of the program (by procedures subsequently described) has revealed serious inadequacies in this program of theoretical studies.

In the first place, as an inspection of the above list of titles suggests, the program is thin in theoretical content. Methods of teaching, internship, and related internship seminars constitute two-thirds of the 36 semester hours required in the program as a whole. It appears, that a much larger proportion of students' time should be devoted to behavioral science studies relating to the psychological and sociological influences shaping the development of disadvantaged children.

Second, most of these courses, although relevant, are not focused specifically on the special problems involved in the education of disadvantaged children. This limitation inheres in the fact that all of them (except Internship Seminar, which is discussed subsequently) enroll mainly students who are not participants in the Project Beacon Training Program.

Third, all of these courses (except Internship Seminar) are conducted by teachers who are isolated from the concurrent internship experiences of Beacon students, and hence they are not integrated with those experiences. Indeed, feedback from students suggests that the contents of most of these courses are largely nonfunctional—some say irrelevant—in the field. With one or two exceptions over the three-year period, this appears to be especially true of the several methods courses.

Fourth, the organization of theoretical studies around "regular" courses in which Beacon students constitute a minority of those enrolled tends seriously to limit opportunities for experiment and discovery related to the special problems to which the Project Beacon Training Program is addressed.

Most of the inadequacies stem from the organization of theoretical studies around specific course requirements for certification by the New York State Education Department. Some of them reflect weaknesses in internal procedures. In any case, major correctives were clearly indicated; and a reorganization was agreed upon, beginning in 1966–67, which was intended to improve the theoretical studies of the Project Beacon Training Program. There follows a detailed description of what this reorganization involved.[1]

It was planned (1) to structure all theoretical studies of Beacon students in three broad seminars conducted exclusively for them— in the general fields of psychology, sociology, and curriculum and instruction; (2) to have teachers of the latter two seminars supervise students' concurrent internship experiences during the fall and spring semesters, respectively; and (3) to supplement the theoretical work of the regular seminars with a series of special seminars and all-day workshops, in which students interact with outstanding scholars and practitioners in the field of compensatory education.

Seminars

There follows a tentative outline of the content of the several seminars (here logically organized), together with a description of the procedure by which they were conducted.

SEMINAR ON PSYCHOLOGY OF HUMAN DEVELOPMENT AND LEARNING

1. *Biological and Social Bases of Behavior:* Heredity and Environment; Constitution and Environment; Culture and Behavior.
2. *Learning as a Determinant of Behavior:* Theories of Learning; Patterns of Parenthood; Theories of Personality; Theories of Psychotherapy; Understanding and Thinking; Skills; Evaluating Teaching and Learning.

1. The revised program described in the following few pages was introduced in the 1966–67 academic year, with special approval by the New York State Education Department.

Julian Roberts and Doxey A. Wilkerson

3. *The Teacher-Pupil Transaction:* Human Relations in the School; Group Life in the Classroom; Mental Health of the Teacher; Classroom Social Structure as a Mental Health Problem.
4. *Individual Differences:* Motivation; Readiness; Levels of Aspiration; Incentives; Adapting Schooling to Individual Differences.
5. *Special Problems in Urban Education:* Disadvantaged Youth; Children with Special Learning Problems (for example, brain injured, perceptual difficulties, emotionally disturbed, and so on); Counseling and Guidance Problems with Pupils and Their Parents.

SEMINAR ON SOCIAL ORGANIZATION AND PROCESS

1. *Culture:* Meaning and Content of Culture; Process of Socialization in Family, Community, and School.
2. *Social Organization:* Norms; Statuses; Groups; Associations and Institutions; Social Stratification and Mobility; Social Disorganization.
3. *Poverty:* Typography of "The Poor"; Economics of Poverty; Culture of Poverty; Poverty and the School.
4. *Racial and Ethnic Groups:* History and Demography in New York City; Patterns of Discrimination; Problems and Processes of Integration; Intergroup Relations and the School.
5. *Social and Cultural Change:* Behavioral Change and Opportunity Structure; Conflicting Values and Goals; Decision-Making and Power; Public Opinion; Strategy for Institutional Change; Role of the School.

SEMINAR ON CURRICULUM AND INSTRUCTION

1. *Bases of Curriculum Decision-Making:* Changing Purposes of Public Education; Social Trends and Needs; Developmental Needs of Children and Youth; Conflicting Values and Goals; Developments in Educational Theory and Research; Perceived Inadequacies of Current Programs, Especially Those Serving Disadvantaged Youth.
2. *Process of Curriculum Development:* Determining Objectives; Selecting Learning Activities and Instructional Materials; Organizing Learning Experiences (Curriculum Design); Evaluating Outcomes.
3. *Modern Methods and Materials of Instruction:* Reading; Language Arts; Social Studies; Mathematics; Science; English; Foreign Language; Physical Education; Music and Art.
4. *Adapting Instruction to Special Learning Problems of Disadvantaged Pupils:* Perception, Concept-Formation and Cognitive Development;

Language Development; Self-Concept; Alienation; Academic Motivation; Social Values and General Conduct; Talented and Well-Behaved Youth Among the Disadvantaged.

5. *Planning and Conducting Instruction:* Learning Activities Appropriate for Different Types of Objectives (that is, knowledges, attitudes, skills); Planning Large Units and Daily Lessons; Grouping; Individualizing Instruction; Evaluating Outcomes.

6. *Classroom Management:* Uses of Structure and Routine; Interrelations of "Curriculum" and "Discipline"; Interrelations of Home and School; Constructive Aprpoaches to Norm-Varying Behavior; Intergroup Relations in the Classroom.

7. *Teachers and School Administration:* The Teacher and Decision-Making; Administering the Daily Schedule; Records and Reports; Certification and Personnel Policies of the New York City Board of Education.

PROCEDURES IN CONDUCTING SEMINARS

In each of these three seminars, the process of instruction will be characterized by the following approaches and emphases:

1. Instruction will be organized around specific problems relating to the education of disadvantaged children and youth. On the basis of internship experiences and preliminary study of the literature, trainees will participate with instructors in identifying and defining the specific problems to be studied and also in planning the approach to such study. Instructors are responsible for guaranteeing that the problems are so selected and developed as to embrace the several areas of content indicated by the preceding outline.

2. Individual and group assignments in relation to the problems selected for study will be differentiated on the basis of trainees' varying interests and professional goals.

3. For the most part, all trainees will work together as one group in each seminar. From time to time, participants with common interests in early-elementary or upper-elementary teaching will work together as subgroups and will report the results of their work to the seminar as a whole for discussion.

4. Emphasis will be placed throughout upon thorough knowledge and critical evaluation of the literature, efforts at problem solving and

Julian Roberts and Doxey A. Wilkerson

discovery, and integration of theoretical study with concurrent internship experiences.

5. One or more minor research projects involving original investigation and analysis will be required of each trainee in each seminar.

6. Instructors of the three seminars will meet regularly for instructional planning and for assessing the development of individual trainees.

7. Members of the faculty of the Ferkauf Graduate School of Education will participate, for brief or extended periods of time, in guiding seminar study and discussion relating to their respective areas of specialization. They will serve during such periods as co-teachers with the regular instructors.

Special Seminars and All-Day Workshops

On six occasions during the eleven-month program, outstanding scholars and creative thinkers will be invited to the University to address participants in the Project Beacon Training Program. Attendance at these Special Seminars will be open to faculty members and graduate students, but participation in the discussion will be restricted to students in the program and instructors of the regular seminars. These Special Seminars will bring participants into contact with persons who have challenging and provocative ideas in the area of urban education.

Four All-Day Workshops will be conducted during the course of the program, each providing opportunity for in-depth discussion of significant innovative ideas and practices in the urban education of disadvantaged youth. These workshops will also be organized around eminent scholars and practitioners in the field.

This reorganization and redirection of the theoretical studies of the Project Beacon Training Program will not automatically correct the weaknesses noted in the current program; effective implementation, of course, will prove decisive with this or any other administrative structure. However, the planned changes should very greatly strengthen the program of theoretical studies.

Internship in the Field

IF THERE is anything distinctive about the Project Beacon Training Program, aside from the ideological bias previously defined, it is to be found in the full academic year of internship experiences required of all students, particularly that part which involves them in interaction with the people and institutions of a slum neighborhood. Underlying this internship program, of course, are certain assumptions, the validity of which is attested only by informal evidence; and it may be helpful to define them at the outset.

First, it is assumed that effectiveness in classroom teaching and management in a slum school is enhanced by first-hand acquaintance with the home and community environment in which disadvantaged children are socialized. Information and insights gained from the literature of poverty are likely to be deepened and made more functional by a variety of direct experiences with the people, social institutions, and organizations in a depressed neighborhood.

Second, it is assumed that pre-existing democratic values and wholesome attitudes toward lower-class populations tend, with such direct experience, to develop into genuine empathy. There is an important difference between positive attitudes *toward* socially disadvantaged people and that fuller understanding which, on the basis of knowing individuals and families, enables one to project his own personality into theirs, to *share in* their perceptions and feelings and motives.

Third, it is assumed that extended and varied student teaching in a slum school, even where the quality of the educational program is less than superior, can serve to extend and integrate professional theory and knowledge, to crystallize values and attitudes, and to begin the development of instructional and management skills essential for effective performance in depressed-area schools.

Fourth, it is assumed that some internship experience with depressed-area schools that are functioning on a high level of quality—at least through observation—is essential in order to help define realizable standards of professional competence and to place one's own student teaching experiences in perspective.

It is perhaps unnecessary to add that it is *not* assumed that the values here outlined will emerge automatically from internship experience in lower-class neighborhoods and schools. On the contrary, their realization depends in large measure upon appropriate guidance by University personnel in the course of day-to-day supervision in the field and in concurrent study and discussion in the Internship Seminar.

There follows a brief description of and evaluative comments on the internship experiences provided during 1965–66 for students in the Project Beacon Training Program.

Julian Roberts and Doxey A. Wilkerson

Internship in the Neighborhoods: Fall Semester

Internship experiences in a slum neighborhood are concentrated in the fall semester and are conducted mainly through agencies of Mobilization for Youth (MFY), a comprehensive demonstration program directed toward the control of delinquency on Manhattan's Lower East Side. The area involved is the historic initial area of residence for immigrants from Europe, especially Jews. Currently, however, its population is approximately 33 per cent Puerto Rican and 10 per cent Negro, the remainder consisting of varied ethnic groups—Jews, Chinese, Italians, and others. It is an area of slum tenements and low-income housing projects, widespread poverty, and the whole range of social pathology usually associated with these conditions.

Throughout the fall semester Beacon students are assigned to work in the following MFY activities and programs in this area, partly in the schools, but mainly in nonschool situations.

1. *Lecture-discussions conducted by MFY personnel*—on the programs of Mobilization for Youth, the Puerto Rican Community, the Negro Community, the Prevailing Pattern of Poverty (based upon MFY interviews), Community Organization, Strategy for Institutional Change, and the MFY Program of Research and Evaluation.

2. *Neighborhood Service Centers*—interviewing families in their homes; helping process clients at the centers; accompanying social workers in case-work, involving contacts with police, courts, housing, and welfare authorities.

3. *Homework Helper Program*—after-school tutoring of elementary pupils on a one-to-one basis; walking pupils home after the tutoring sessions.

4. *Higher Education Program*—tutoring disadvantaged freshman college students on a one-to-one basis, students admitted to junior college on a trial basis despite deficiencies in their high school records.

5. *Mobilization Reading Program*—assisting Mobilization Reading Teachers assigned to local elementary schools for diagnosis and remedy of special reading problems among pupils.[2]

Other fall-term internship experiences include: (1) observation in one elementary-school classroom for the first six weeks of the term,

---

2. For students who are majoring in guidance, work with counselors at a high school in the area is substituted for work with Mobilization Reading Teachers.

beginning the first day of school; (2) an informal session with leaders of the Negro Action Group (NAG), which is active in pressing for school improvement in the area; and (3) a field trip to visit the experimental nursery schools conducted in depressed-area schools by the Institute of Developmental Studies.

Students devote between 15 and 19 hours a week on these internship assignments. Past experience suggests that this load is too heavy, considering the fact that students also carry 12 credit-hours of course and seminar work at the University, and it will be reduced.

The schedule of student participation varies among the several MFY programs, work with two or three of them proceeding simultaneously. The amounts of time also vary—from three to six hours a week and from four to ten weeks—for the several programs. Past experience suggests that this pattern of internship assignments, although providing a varied and profitable experience, tends to be somewhat superficial; students do not remain with most programs long enough to get deeply involved. With the next group of interns, a varied series of orientation experiences over a period of about six weeks will be provided; and then each student will be assigned to one program for more sustained and intensive involvement.

Although the Director of the Project Beacon Training Program maintains contact with all interns in the field and with the agencies in which they work, his supervisory intervention is minimal; for the most part his relations are with the directors of the MFY programs involved, not with the personnel immediately in charge of the interns. Day-to-day supervision is given by the MFY officials with whom the students work directly. All of them are conscientious about their responsibility for the development of the trainees, but it is perhaps inevitable that they differ in the validity of their supervisory perceptions and approaches. The necessary corrective appears to be more direct consultation than now obtains between the Director and the individual field-work supervisors immediately in charge of the interns.

Internship in the Schools: Spring Semester

As has been noted, interns are provided limited experiences in public school programs in the fall semester—mainly through observations during the first six weeks of the term and through work with Mobilization Reading Teachers. In the spring semester, they are assigned to full-

Julian Roberts and Doxey A. Wilkerson

time student teaching (or guidance work) in schools in the MFY area.

Although the time that Beacon interns devote to student teaching—all day, five days a week for 17 weeks—exceeds by far that which prevails among other pre-service programs, the general pattern of the student teaching experience is fairly conventional—except, perhaps, that it is restricted to depressed-area schools. It involves a period of observation and limited participation in the classroom, followed by the occasional teaching of single lessons and more frequent small group instruction, and in time by all-day responsibility for the class. The pace at which an intern proceeds through these stages depends upon his own rate of development and the perceptions and preferences of the cooperating teacher.

Limited opportunity has been provided for student teachers to observe classes other than those to which they were assigned, including the classes of other interns. Feedback from such observations suggested that the experience was very helpful, and more such inter-class observations are planned for the coming spring semester. Included will be several demonstration lessons taught by Beacon interns with all of their colleagues looking on, followed by discussions of the lessons in Internship Seminar. This innovation should enhance interns' perceptions of the classroom process and thereby further their professional growth.

During the first year of the Project Beacon Training Program, the students all took and passed examinations for substitue teaching licenses during the fall semester and were placed in schools as substitute teachers (with pay) for their spring-term internship. This arrangement seemed unsatisfactory. It saddled interns at the outset with greater responsibility than most of them were equipped to assume; it deprived them of the help that a perceptive cooperating teacher can give; and it removed the internship experience farther from University influence than is normally the case. This practice was abandoned after that one semester of experience.

It is expected that cooperating teachers will confer regularly with student teachers and give careful guidance to their work, in recognition of which service the teachers are offered tuition-free courses at the University. For the most part, cooperating teachers assume their responsibilities with seriousness and dedication, often spending much more time with student teachers than can be compensated by a free course; but, of course, there are unfortunate exceptions. Moreover, only rarely does a cooperating teacher have time during the school day for unhurried conferences with student teachers; and the after-school time available is limited for even the most conscientious personnel. A potential solution involves paying cooperating teachers an attractive stipend for regular after-school conferences with Beacon interns.

A big unsolved problem of the program is that of selecting cooperating teachers who will contribute maximally to the development of interns. The professional and personal qualities of the cooperating teachers decisively condition the value of the student teaching experience, and it is expected that these qualities will vary among the personnel involved. Most of the cooperating teachers with whom interns have worked were able and helpful professionals, but a few of them, for various reasons, tended to impede rather than to further the students' development. In the past, the selection of cooperating teachers has been made by the MFY Director of Laboratory Schools in consultation with principals and the Director of the Beacon Program; but there has been very limited choice because of the great competition among many institutions for student teaching positions in the area. The solution of the problem probably lies in identifying a corps of desirable cooperating teachers and developing special institutional arrangements with them —such as adjunct faculty status and extra pay—to the end of insuring their availability to our program.

On at least one occasion during the spring semester, interns go together on an all-day field trip to visit schools where outstanding work is being done with socially disadvantaged children. Last spring the students visited classes in Greenburgh School District No. 8, at Hartsdale, New York. The experience was so valuable that it is to be repeated this spring.

Internship Seminar: Fall and Spring Semesters

As the program is currently organized, interns meet once a week throughout the year in a seminar conducted by the Director. This Internship Seminar undertakes to serve two interrelated purposes, with differing emphases during the fall and spring semesters.

One general purpose is to further develop students' theoretical understanding of selected problems and issues involved in the education of socially disadvantaged children. During the fall semester, emphasis is placed on the impact of social disadvantage upon learning and on school-community relations in slum areas. During the spring semester,

Julian Roberts and Doxey A. Wilkerson

emphasis is placed on special problems in guiding learning and in classroom management in depressed-area schools, and also on aspects of curriculum development. Procedures during both semesters consist mainly of the preparation, presentation, and discussion of investigative reports by individual students and committees. There are also four or five guest lecturers during the academic year.

The other general purpose is to help students interpret their concurrent internship experiences in the light of relevant theory. Emphases vary with the content of those experiences. The main procedure is informal discussion.

Attention has been called to the plan to organize the entire Project Beacon Training Program on the basis of three broad seminars—Psychology of Human Development and Learning, Social Organization and Process, and Curriculum and Instruction—and to have the instructors of the latter two seminars supervise internship experiences during the fall and spring semesters. When this is done, the special Internship Seminar will be discontinued, and its functions will be transferred to the regular seminars.

Approaches to Evaluation

ALTHOUGH the problems of systemic evaluation in teacher education are very complex and difficult, continuous efforts to cope with them are important. Meaningful guidelines for the further development of programs can best be formulated in the light of reliable evidence concerning the effectiveness, or even the relevance, of the classroom and field experiences with which students are currently provided.

Evaluative judgments concerning specific aspects of the Project Beacon Training Program are interspersed throughout this analysis, along with brief comments on steps being taken to correct perceived inadequacies. Attention is here restricted to current and projected approaches to evaluation of the program as a whole.

The general purpose of the program is to equip prospective teachers and other professional personnel for effective service in depressed-area urban schools. Four relevant evaluative criteria, therefore, are (1) the extent to which graduates of the program obtain positions in such schools; (2) the quality of their performance as professionals in the schools where they are employed; (3) the assessment of students' performance by their classroom teachers and internship supervisors, especially the latter; and (4) probably the most significant of them all, the appraisal by Beacon trainees of their experiences in the program, as perceived during the period of training and during the first year of professional employment.

These, then, are the four criteria by which the program is now being evaluated. It will be noted that all but one of them, job-placement, call for appraisal on the basis of subjective judgments. This fact reflects a deliberate decision; approaches using objective data that are both meaningful for the program and possible to obtain have not yet been developed.

The following are the procedures by which data relevant to these several criteria are now obtained:

1. *Job-placement*—questionnaires to graduates, supplemented by direct contacts.

2. *Quality of graduates' performance on the job*—questionnaires to supervisors in the schools where graduates are employed.

3a. *Assessments of trainees' performance by classroom teachers*— compilation of grades reported to the Registrar; also (beginning this year) rating scales executed by teachers, plus supplementary comments.

3b. *Assessments of trainees' performance by internship supervisors* —rating scales executed by persons directly in charge of the several internship programs, plus supplementary comments; administered at the end of internship in each program.

4a. *Appraisals by interns of their classroom and internship experiences during the program*—questionnaires at the end of the fall and spring semesters.

4b. *Appraisals by interns of their experiences in the program after graduation*—questionnaires to graduates, supplemented by occasional and informal direct contacts.

A substantial report based on these several groups of data for 1964–65 trainees was recently submitted by a special Faculty Evaluation Committee for the Project Beacon Training Program. Several general findings and proposals of the report are noted below:

1. With one or two exceptions, teachers adjudged the achievement of Beacon students in their courses and seminars as satisfactory or better.

2. Without exception, the performance of students in their several fall-semester internship assignments in Mobilization for Youth programs was adjudged by supervisors as "Good," "Very Good," or "Excellent"; although specific weaknesses of certain students were identified.

Julian Roberts and Doxey A. Wilkerson

3. Without exception, the student teaching performance of interns during the spring semester was adjudged by supervisors as "Very Good" or "Excellent," although supplementary comments indicated certain strengths and weaknesses peculiar to individual interns.

4. During their participation in the program, students expressed positive appraisals of most of their courses and seminars. However, their appraisals of their several methods courses—except for The Teaching of Reading—was generally negative. The content of these courses was said to be largely irrelevant to or nonfunctional in their student teaching situations.

5. During their participation in the program, students expressed generally positive appraisals of their internship experiences in MFY programs and in the public schools, especially the latter. However, they identified a number of weaknesses in both areas of internship.

6. There follows a summary of the current occupations of ten participants in the program during 1964–65:

Two are teaching in depressed-area public schools on Manhattan's Lower East Side, one in the school where she did student teaching.

One is teaching in a depressed-area public school in New Haven, Connecticut.

One is the assistant to the Director of MFY's Higher Education Program, in which she did much of her internship.

One is teaching in a cathedral school in New York City. (She is disappointed at not being placed in a slum school this year, owing to her delay in taking the licensing examination.)

One is employed as a counselor by Mobilization for Youth.

Two are enrolled in doctoral studies at Yeshiva University.

One is a housewife and plans to return to the University for doctoral studies.

One is on the West Coast, not teaching, occupation unknown.

7. Most of the questionnaires calling for assessments by supervisors of the professional performance of 1964–65 graduates in their current positions were returned. They report at least satisfactory performance for beginning teachers.

The general picture that emerges from the recent evaluation report is that of a program which, despite the weaknesses that have been noted, is substantially serving the purpose for which it was designed.

Past experience with the evaluative criteria and procedures here reported indicates that they are valid and practical. Aside from some refinement of the investigative instruments, these approaches will continue to be used.

An additional procedure planned for subsequent evaluations is to bring graduates of the program to the campus periodically during the first year of employment; to have them record on tape "critical incidents" that reveal strengths and weaknesses in their professional preparation; and to participate with faculty members in retrospective appraisal of their experiences in the training program.

Another innovation planned for subsequent evaluations is to have faculty members observe graduates of the program in their classrooms, recording selected behaviors and judgments on a carefully devised observation schedule.

Still another evaluative innovation being considered is that of administering a social values test (such as that developed by Dr. Henry Meyers at the University of Michigan) to trainees when they enter the program and at the end of their internship in the schools. This would permit testing of the hypothesis that one's general social outlook is significantly related to his effectiveness as a teacher of socially disadvantaged children.

Summary

AN ATTEMPT has been made here to interpret the purpose of the Project Beacon Training Program and its underlying premises; to describe the program in considerable detail; to outline an approach to evaluating the program; and in the course of the whole, to reveal some of the inadequacies perceived and plans for correcting them. Past experience thus far suggests that the innovations reported herein may have relevance to all teacher education programs directed to the preparation of teachers for public elementary, secondary, and vocational schools in disadvantaged areas.

Julian Roberts and Doxey A. Wilkerson

13 A Master's Degree in Urban Education and Total Mobilization of Resources for Change

Maurie Hillson and
Francis P. Purcell
RUTGERS UNIVERSITY

Introduction

A MAJOR PROBLEM confronting those who attempt to create better education for youth in the inner city is the lack of adequately educated and trained teachers. Research indicates that youth of the inner city are educable. Companion research indicates that the assignments to inner city schools result in the placement of less able teachers rather than more able teachers. There are a host of reasons for this. Lack of understanding concerning the life circumstances of low-income people, stereotypic ideas concerning their desire and motivation, fear of harm because of the location of the inner city schools, and the scarcity of programs, even simple courses or seminars for teachers, all combine to establish what is a critical paucity of skilled teachers for this large portion of our school population.

There is, however, a fomentation within educational and governmental circles about this problem. There is a need for programs that are specifically oriented toward creating teachers for the urban areas. Programs must be created to educate and train teachers for positions in these schools so that stabilization and educational redirection can be achieved and educational accomplishments can be realized by inner city youth.

A graduate program for experienced teachers with specific objectives to create a master teacher for inner city or for urban children is very desirable. The need for a graduate school of education in a major metropolitanized state to commit itself to such an activity is not only essential, but mandatory and urgent.

The commitment to such a program cannot be piecemeal. The addition of a course, or seminar here or there, which carries a title that reflects the current vogue is only educational tinkering. The assignment of a student to a slum school for student teaching without the necessary background and carefully nurtured experience in both knowledge and work with low-income youth is frequently useless. It does, in fact, result in negative feelings toward the schools, the youth, and the desire to teach in such schools.

What is necessary is a cohesively well-thought-out program that aims at the creation of a "community teacher." The essential elements of such a program need to be fitted into a matrix so that, at the completion of the experience, the teacher will be one who is competent, creative, and committed. Within this matrix, the coordination of graduate work, practical clinical experience, and depth in total community understanding must neatly intertwine and fruitfully underpin the attainment of the objectives of the whole program: an experienced, thoroughly educated master teacher for inner city communities.

The collection of research is replete with materials that attest to the idea that the earlier the pattern is set for wholesome education the better the chance for continued growth. The need for teaching youngsters well in their early years is crucial. Assigning a priority based on the ability of a graduate school of education to make a meaningful impact leads to the conclusion that an intensive quality program in preschool and elementary education is the first order of commitment. By recruiting into the program carefully selected "fellows" from an inner city for a summer program plus a full academic year, the graduate school can create a group of teachers who can return to their schools and become agents of educational change. After the fellow returns to the school, by his association with a continuing university-fostered edu-

Maurie Hillson and Francis P. Purcell

cational program, he can serve through the expansion of his ideas, in recruiting other fellows for the program, and as a master teacher for the clinical experiences of the up-coming fellows. Emanating out of the graduate school of education will be a constant flow of fellows. In addition, the organization of a council concerned with the education of youth in the inner city should be created. This council can foster the informational flow attendant on the methods, materials, content, and strategies that are being proved useful in the education of youth in the inner city.

The following pages describe the framework of a Design for Urban Education, which has been initiated by Rutgers and the Newark Board of Education. An Experienced Teacher Fellowship Program should become an integral part of this project. The Design for Urban Education is fully funded by Elementary and Secondary Education Act funds. The inclusion of an Experienced Teacher Fellowship Program, funded under the Higher Education Act, would provide a unique example of the integration of two federal acts to support education.

Rationale and Objectives

The School and University Relationship: An Educational Innovation

Probably the acid test of any institution and the continued vitality of that institution will be seen in the way it reacts to adversity. If the institution can find justification for failure and if it easily accepts defeat, then it will play no part in the progress of mankind. If that same institution sees a challenge in its adversity and it converts threatened defeat into victory, it will continue to serve society. The urban schools face adversity. They face the acid test. The schools of education and universities that prepare teachers face adversity. For the past few years, with rare exception, educators have only seen the challenge within circumscribed limits. They have tinkered with or readjusted areas of concern, but they never dealt with the main issues. Attempts to take a critical look at programs have not always met with success. Sacrosanct symbols and traditions that have long been useless in this automative age are still being imposed on our dynamic culture. Colleges that prepare teachers, state departments of education, specific school systems, teachers, administrators, and the patrons of the schools have not dealt

A Master's Degree in Urban Education and Total Mobilization of Resources for Change

with the totality of the issue that faces them. Within urban areas frequently more time is spent on creating heat rather than light. The problem is one of vast proportions. Many items of concern face the urban schools. The following list is by no means exhaustive in nature:

1. How do we keep teachers abreast of the expansion of knowledge?

2. How do we keep teachers abreast of the cognitive functions of people as revealed by the intensive research in the area?

3. How do we teach teachers about the variations that exist in the learning theories and to pluck from these variations the applications that will work for them?

4. How do we apprise the school and the teachers in the school of the anthropological and sociological determinants in our culture so they do not continue to deal with their youngsters in a simplistic psychological fashion?

5. How do we retool teachers to understand and work with these items so that they better educate their charges?

6. How do we inform teachers of the newer ways of the organization for learning which seem to be showing superior gains over the traditional ways?

7. How do we bring into being the innovated programs of nongrading, team teaching, teacher redeployment, collaborative and coordinate planning, and multiage, multilevel grouping plans?

New Directions Are Indicated

Some say the answer is in-service education. In-service education, however, is only one way and it is not enough. What is needed is a matrix, an environment, a milieu, in which the exchange of ideas, techniques, and information, as well as the newer investigations of all of those factors cited above and more, can take place. This will be fostered and assured by a new kind of organization. This new framework can serve to move us directionally toward higher levels of intellection as well as toward much higher levels of humanistic forbearance. The concepts that covering material is teaching, that what is learned today is applicable always, and that research is only theoretical and nonapplicable to the classroom, need to be eliminated. Teachers need to know the theory of as well as the practice of education at the classroom level. Teachers need to know that what is learned today may be

Maurie Hillson and Francis P. Purcell

glaringly obsolete tomorrow. There now exist large areas of research on how and what children can learn and the frameworks of organization that support the better teaching-learning situation. It seems obvious that with all of the problems facing the schools it is necessary to come up with an educational program that can serve our nation better by creating a discernably better product; a child possessed of a better education; one with a greater intellectual attainment; one who also inherently adopts the value structure that squares with and furthers the democratic concept.

A School-University Symbiosis: Action and Research

A school and university relationship for educational development can serve as the matrix for creating an educational symbiosis between schools and universities. Symbiosis represents a mutually advantageous relationship between two organisms. The university and the school can have such a relationship and through it the archaic strictures that work against continued growth and development might be removed. The activities of such a relationship can be action and research oriented, can be adjunctive in terms of classroom participation, can be supportive of educational programs, can be additive in terms of the services that are being given within the community. It can be a relationship that never creates any usurpation of each participant's prerogatives but rather one of coalescence for the greater good of everyone served. The experience that can be gained by university students in the practical situation of the school and the university relationship can be so real and positive, that when school systems hire them after their intern or practicum year, they are a cut above the present available corps of teachers. They are ready to participate in the on-going growth and programs of youngsters that cry for continuous expert help. Teachers come with greater insight into learning. They cost less because they are ready to "really" teach. This school and university relationship can attempt to do many things. But basically it will attempt to create a complete utilization of resources for educational development both of the university and the schools. It will attempt to eliminate the gap that one so frequently finds existing between research and theory and practice. It can establish machinery for quicker action on newer and better programs. It can eliminate that chasm that exists between theoretical expression and clinical reality in the whole area of teacher education.

A Rapprochement

It is over the last fifteen years that American public schools have entered into an era of development marked by rapprochement between scholars and school men. There is, at long last, a rapidly growing awareness by all concerned that the intellectual vitality of the schools depends upon their proximity to the sources of productive scholarship. It is known now that cooperative endeavors can produce not only substantial curriculum changes but also new perspectives in many areas; for example, the education of teachers, or the problems of communication which often exist between schools and universities. In the past, and currently, the education of teachers has been too much a compound of verbiage and minutia. This can be attributed to a number of causes. Salient among them is the fact that training teachers is too far removed from the reality of practice. The school and university relationship can re-establish the practical situation in such a way that reality can no longer be lost. The lack of a free flow of communication results in a waste of time between developments on the national scene and the introduction and trial of these developments in local classroom settings. To bring a school and university together symbiotically also brings with it the immediate establishment of those programs and the use of those materials that through research have proved worthy in the education of our young. An arrangement between a university and a school system may be somewhat analogous to a medical school and teaching hospital relationship. The medical school must have a teaching hospital in order to have a logical arrangement in which to explore possible solutions to the problems that face its profession.

The school and university relationship can represent a professional partnership. It can be mutually advantageous to all involved from an educational point of view. Details of the arrangement are evolutionary. Directions of energies are to be based on cooperative insights into priority areas. The success of such an arrangement can be evaluated in terms of the product it creates and the continuing up-grading of the organizations that make up the committed partnership.

Areas of Educational Development and Organization

Within the setting of the community school there needs to be a new set of organizational procedures. These are both vertical and horizontal

Maurie Hillson and Francis P. Purcell

in nature. They differ from those customary organizational patterns extant in the schools. It is obvious that for the programs of the community school, one cannot operate on a set of assumptions that are used to underpin the programs that now abound in the land. The programs of the school are dedicated to sending into the mainstream of life youngsters who have the total awareness of the need to acquire knowledge and intellectual and vocational skills, and who once having acquired them, recognize their responsibility to use them intelligently for the good of all so that they can make a contribution to the highest concept of human dignity.

There will be, therefore, a program that will emphasize several areas of development. First, and basic to the total educational program, will be the development of the concept of individualization in education. Second, will be the establishment of programs that are essentially nongraded so that individualization can, in fact, occur. Third, the program will create team approaches, or collaborative or coordinate approaches, to the education of youngsters so that both individualization and nongraded education will certainly take place. Fourth, the attempt will be made to bring about differentiated categories or structures that will be more in keeping with the differentiation of youngsters' needs.

To this end, then, within the school the educational organization for vertical progression through the years will be as follows: A preschool program which will be followed by a nongraded primary program through the youngsters' fourth year in school, upon which will be built a middle school made up of the fifth, sixth, seventh, and eighth years of the youngsters' academic life, which will be followed by an upper school program of the ninth, tenth, eleventh, and twelfth years. In addition to this, there will be a capstone experience of the thirteenth and fourteenth year or the choice of an initial experience of the first two years of college prior to transfer to a basic four-year institution. The seventeenth year, or the fifth year, should be a Master's level program in cooperation with a university and an Experienced Teacher Fellowship Program. This would ensure and maintain a clinically oriented professional package at the Master's Degree level.

Innovative Teaching

Within this vertical progression will be created a viable systems approach to innovated teaching. The horizontal grouping procedures will basically consist of teacher redeployment, collaborative instruction, and team teaching. Added to this will be student team learning programs; home-work helper programs; multiage, multilevel learning partner programs; audiovisual approaches to organization; programmed learning and teaching machine projects; individualized learning contracts; guidance approaches; activity approaches; and an organics approach to teaching, which focuses on the learner and makes him central in the learning situation.

These programs will be model programs. Teachers will be trained to become masters in the art of this kind of teaching and in the science of this kind of learning. The fifth-year university students will have vast opportunities to work in intimate clinical relationships. A part of the program will be the pre-education activities aimed at the screening, training, and retooling of in-service teachers for these new innovations and changes in educational activities.

These and additional areas make up a total activity, which becomes a true innovated and exemplary idea worthy of strong support. The program of community and school relations is one such activity.

The School as an Agent of Change

Historically, the school has been viewed as a potential instrument to promote the general welfare of the communities. Generations of school officials have sought various means to establish closer ties to the community. One such effort is through the development of a community school. The concept of the community school has not been fully, or for that matter, partially tried. Yet, as urban problems mushroom and the well-documented inability of schools to cope with the learning problems of the disadvantaged are coupled with the inability of existing community agencies to deal with urban problems, compelling arguments can be advanced for the establishment of a community school. Although schools in the past have developed programs that used the community as a resource for curriculum enrichment, vocational schools have taken advantage of work experiences in the community, and some schools have placed emphasis on becoming a center of community activity by providing physical facilities. Few, if any, have mounted concentrated efforts in community service. Yet, if schools are to fulfill their basic function of education and training, those well-documented conditions in the community which prevent learning in the school must be altered. Essentially, if urban schools are to be a major vehicle of cul-

Maurie Hillson and Francis P. Purcell

tural assimilation for immigrant groups or for those socially bypassed, a kind of mutuality and reciprocity must be established which promotes community change and change in the school.

Areas of Mutual Concern

Educators and social scientists are deeply concerned as many urban schools have become increasingly ineffective as educational establishments for low-income youth while simultaneously developing bureaucratized insensitivities to the needs of the community. The term bureaucratic seems apt inasmuch as it refers to social processes that are relatively impersonal and seemingly beyond the control of professional administrators within the structure. So much is this the case that private foundations and even the federal government have funded organizations expressly designed as agents of change with the urban school as the target (Mobilization for Youth, Inc., and Haryou Act, and so on).

For all its weaknesses and past errors, the school is still a potentially viable social instrument to produce change and progress. A *community school* must see its education responsibilities as extending beyond the classroom boundaries. Thus, programs will be established to carry out on-going community development functions. These will be in the areas of educational techniques to engage local people in the identification of social problems (housing, unemployment, delinquency) and the means to their solution (program development, coordination of services, mobilization of resources). These and others will be used, tested, and developed.

An Agreement

The desire is to educate a community teacher both through in-service training and at the graduate preparation level. The idea is to educate a teacher who would not only be competent in educational technology, but who would understand and be able to contribute to the solutions of the problems of the inner city, to poverty and its attendant evils.

Clearly, the problem of the inner city school rests in part upon the inability of graduate schools of education to produce teachers qualified and skilled in teaching under the conditions of the inner city. Research

A Master's Degree in Urban Education and Total Mobilization of Resources for Change

journals are replete with evidence that such schools attract the least ex-perienced teacher and retain the least able.

In order to fulfill this mission, clinical professorships will be established. Graduate students need opportunities to experience directly and observe the problems faced by the inner city school system. The program will then move forward, preparing both the structure for urban education and the professional personnel to staff the educational structure created.

The community school will become the center for developing any programs funded by the recent federal legislation because of its ready access to information, research, and first-hand experiences within the inner city. The school is one of the most stable institutional organizations within the inner city. It becomes a logical focus to design and mount programs that would assist in the physical and social development of the entire community. Therefore, this plan envisions the school as assuming and taking on, in cooperation with urban planning centers, a community development function. The community development function would proceed along the lines of social planning in contrast to purely physical planning. The social workers involved in such an operation would not be of the clinical variety, but would be those who are able to work with community and neighborhood groups toward the identification and solution of community-determined problems. They would be skillful in the identification and mobilization of resources that can be located by virtue of various program developmental activities. Immediately, such programs with which graduate schools of education have had experience could be proposed and developed; for example, Upward Bound, Rutgers Education Action Program (REAP), Operation Head Start, and eventually neighborhood job corps and so on.

The university will fulfill its obligation in the area of educational research by carefully recording and inventorying successful and unsuccessful educational efforts as they relate to elementary, secondary, and graduate education. The educational variables will be carefully controlled so that reliable and valid information can be made generally available. Deliberate effort will be made to avoid strictly behavioral science research, although the insights and strategy of behavioral scientists will be put to use to determine valid and reliable educational strategy and content.[1]

1. *Editor's Note.* Universities located near poverty centers are urged to develop programs to train teachers for the disadvantaged. The three programs reported previously imply this; in this chapter the request is explicit.

Maurie Hillson and Francis P. Purcell

_____Program Content and Its Organization

THE proposed Master's Program entails a summer session plus a full academic year. The successful completion of the program will bring with it the awarding of a Master's Degree in Urban Education.

In broad outline the elements of the program are as follows: The fellows will take course work designed to provide both a theoretical and practical orientation to the problems arising in inner city areas relevant to education. This will require an intensive analysis of the character of the social and cultural milieu of cities and the factors that affect urban education. The problems of social class values as determinants of the direction of the process of education will be given considerable attention.

A very vital school and community component will be a part of the fellow's program. In order to become a community teacher one must have a clear and deep understanding of the dimensions of community organization and development. Clinical participation in the community will be arranged and coordinated with the programs that are being mounted under the several acts of Congress concerning the welfare of low-income people.

The problems of many urban youth seem to be directly related to their inability to read. A major part of this program will deal with the methods and materials of diagnosing the disabilities of children and the teaching of reading. A special emphasis on the preparation of materials for and adaptation of instruction to the specific problems inherent in urban elementary schools will be made. The development of diagnostic abilities will be addressed. Developmental reading strategies that have worked well and that can work well will be explored and evaluated. Clinical activities that allow for in-depth activities concerning these areas will be established, demonstrated, and used in practicum situations.

The curriculum pattern of a graduate school of education would have to be altered in this proposed program. The times and the needs of our society call for bold departures. The customary ways of approaching the academic experience offer little relevance for experienced teacher fellows who will seek experience and knowledge that will be immediately translatable into action when they return to the communities from whence they came.

To that end this program will use an "overarching fellow tandem" approach; that is, a team of two fellows will constitute a tandem. These two fellows will become involved participant observers in a whole variety of activities that make up the myriad dimensions of a community.

Not only will they as individual fellows participate in course work aimed at building their necessary backgrounds, but in addition they will involve themselves in clinical experiences in the schools, in the home, and in the community. A faculty team approach to these experiences will be employed. If the number of fellows is 16, then 8 tandems will operate. These tandems will relate to one another in larger programs and seminars so that the collectivities of insights and learnings can be synthesized into meaningful wholes. This will hopefully lead to integrative insights concerning the community, social change, the schools, and the teaching of children in the inner city.

Each teacher-fellow in this program is to attempt to establish competence in teaching in the inner city. This necessarily requires ability in the diagnosis and teaching of reading. But there are the other very important capabilities concerning the methods of teaching the substantive areas of the elementary school curriculum that are necessary. The hope of many educators is that as educational innovation catches up, teachers will be able to specialize so that they can make a more forceful impact in the area they teach. Team teaching, nongraded education, various types of grouping procedures and patterns aimed at both the consolidation of divergent learning abilities and levels exist in the land. However, any quick survey of current practices will yield the fact that it is in the middle- and upper-income suburban communities that one sees most of these organizational innovations. This is unfortunate. The dimensions of these patterns seem more realistically appropriate for overcoming many of the problems evidenced in inner city schools. Nevertheless, reality insists that these fellows will, for the most part, return to school systems that operate "self-contained" classrooms or variations thereof. It behooves us to create opportunities for their garnering of greater depth in substantive areas. However, the combination of factors and strategies built upon these factors will allow for different approaches to teaching the inner city child. For example, a course in the language arts for elementary children when oriented toward the inner city child will make maximum use of live case studies, focal-needs teaching, and other innovations.

A series of seminars, clinical experiences, and courses will be set up to capitalize on the innovations cited above. These will be operated by participation in the public school classrooms and in home visitations by tandems of fellows. The outline of the experiences as well as an introduction delineating the integrated aspects of this program follows. These courses represent a progression. They begin at a point aimed at bringing

Maurie Hillson and Francis P. Purcell

about a conceptualization of the generalized problem attendant on the culture of poverty and the problems of disadvantaged youth. They progress toward specific educational insights and strategies, methods, and approaches that seek to definitively ameliorate this kind of an existence.

The first set of courses will attempt to state the problems in broad terms. Along with these, and interwoven in an integrated fashion, will be suggested work in the methods of teaching, the specifics of problems found in the public schools, and other insights that will lead to the alleviation or elimination of some of the problems. Therefore, both educational method and intellectual insight become one in the teacher's background as he moves toward the area of competency necessary to address the problems of education in the inner city schools. For example, the Community Relations Course is offered at the same time as Language Learning: Diagnosis, Correction, and Materials. The reason for this is, that in order to understand the basic nature of the language problems faced by youth in disadvantaged areas, one must have a total insight into the various aspects of their total life style. The community relations attendant on the life style of these youngsters, their use of neighborhood patois, and their obvious abilities and capabilities must be understood. Their use of different language patterns makes it necessary for the teacher to have both a background understanding of this, as well as an understanding of how to teach alternative aspects of language use that are more in keeping with the standards expected by the schools.

The entire educational program would seek to foster the kinds of relationships where the insightful background of the teacher literally forces the seeking of new techniques that make it certain that youngsters are taught alternate situations.

The other courses within the conspectus will proceed along this same line. The growth of intellect on the part of the teacher, as well as the growth of his ability to make an intellectual assessment of the situation, will underpin the need for seeking newer and different ways of dealing with a population who are impoverished or who are representative of the culture of poverty. The general courses that have to do with the sociology of the family and the home visitation will insist upon a kind of reduction of social distance. These will bring a nearness that will increase both insight and sympathy and should result in better or more fruitful educational strategies attendant on the needs of the youngsters who populate the school. This, of course, will bring about the

287
A Master's Degree in Urban Education and Total Mobilization
of Resources for Change

commensurate growth in their basic intellectual abilities as well as performances. This is what we are seeking with this kind of activity.

What follows then is, in barest outline, a series of titles and courses set forth in summary form. These summaries serve as broad statements of the content as well as the orientation that will mark the total program, which is as fully conceived and well integrated as one can hope for in addressing the problem of creating better prepared teachers.

I. Urban Schools and the Elementary School Curriculum

    A. Problems in Elementary Education
    B. Problems and Techniques in Teaching:
        Mathematics in the Elementary School
        Science in the Elementary School
        Social Studies in the Elementary School
        Language Arts in the Elementary School
    C. Language Learning: Diagnosis, Curriculum, and Materials
    D. Early Childhood Education and the Problem of Disadvantagement
    E. The Enriching Arts in Elementary Education
    F. Field Participation in Selected Schools by Tandems of Fellows:
        Presentations, Critical Observations, Evaluations, Seminar Case Presentations, Suggested Redirections of Educational Activities

II. Urban Schools and the Urban Society

    A. Disadvantaged Child and the Culture of Poverty
    B. Developmental Psychology: Early and Middle Years of Childhood
    C. Community Relations
    D. Community Studies and Education
    E. Sociological Foundations of Education
    F. Society and Education
    G. Social Class Influence on Education
    H. The School as a Social System
    I. Home and School Visitation Program

Maurie Hillson and Francis P. Purcell

A General Conspectus of the Summer Session and the School Year

SUMMER SESSION   CREDITS

Language Learning: Diagnosis, Curriculum, and Materials	3
Community Relations	3
Home Visitations (no credit)	
TOTAL	**6**

Academic Year (no semester break as such)
(This is a "break-away" schedule. Courses and seminars will begin, continue, break away from formal meetings to move to field experiences and field experience seminar, then reconstitute for final summations and synthesizing courses and seminars.)

AREAS OF CONCENTRATION   CREDITS
URBAN SCHOOLS AND THE ELEMENTARY
SCHOOL CURRICULUM

Problems in Elementary Education (3)   **3**
  (Elect 9 credits from the following:)
Problems and Techniques in Teaching Mathematics (3)
Problems and Techniques in Teaching Science (3)
Problems and Techniques in Teaching Social Studies (3)
Problems and Techniques in Teaching Language Arts (3)   **9**
Early Childhood Education and the Problem of
  Disadvantage (2)
The Enriching Arts in Elementary Education (3)
Home Visitations (no credit)

                             TOTAL   12

URBAN SCHOOLS AND THE URBAN SOCIETY   CREDITS
  (Elect 12 credits from the following:)

  The Disadvantaged Child and The Culture
    of Poverty   (3)
  Developmental Psychology: Early and Middle
    Years of Childhood   (3)
  Community Studies and Education   (3)
  Sociological Foundations of Education   (3)   Total   12
  Society and Education   (3)
  Social Class Influence on Education   (3)
  The School as a Social System   (3)
  Home and School Visitations (no credit)

                            TOTAL   12
                      GRAND TOTAL   30

A Master's Degree in Urban Education and Total Mobilization of Resources for Change

TANDEMS of teachers will participate in the practicum situations in various prototype communities that make up an inner city. The fellows will have several well-organized clinical experiences. They will observe carefully scheduled demonstration classes by master teachers in urban education. They will participate both in the school and the community in aspects of the home visitation experience. The program is so set up that activities termed clinical or practical are directly related to the basic theoretical assumptions discussed in class courses and seminars. The "break-away" scheduling, which starts with substantive course class work, breaks away for participation and observation, reconvenes for final synthesis and summation, and will also have a highly integrative activity of year-long on-going seminars. Selected elementary schools in which teachers are doing exemplary work in urban programs will be used. These teachers will serve as University Adjuncts in Urban Education and be much like clinical professors. They will participate with the fellows in seminars and serve to integrate the experiences that the fellows are having. They will also serve as liaison to the community in the home visitation program and in general be part of the University Urban Education Team that is mounting the program of educating teachers for the inner city.

The Areas of Concentration

Problems in Elementary Education

This course presupposes a background of training and experience in the field of elementary education. It acquaints students with contemporary research in the field and surveys the problems of the elementary school and its pupils as they assume their roles in modern society.

It will probe deeply into the problems of education in the inner city school. Using the findings of social science, it will assess the problems facing the school and will survey the materials and programs being established to address these problems. Facets of parental alientation from the school, multiproblemed children from slum neighborhoods, strategies for creating meaningful contact with culturally different

Maurie Hillson and Francis P. Purcell

learners, and aspects of intervention for the redirection of education will be studied.

Problems and Techniques in Teaching Mathematics in the Elementary School

This is an advanced course for fully certified elementary teachers to provide richer understanding of the impact on the elementary school of new developments in mathematics and new refinements in the teaching of mathematics. Content, method, material, and general curricular implications will be considered. Special attention will be given to research and results of experimentation.

The course will orient itself toward the refinements of approach and content attendant to the needs of the child in the inner city classrooms.

Problems and Techniques in Teaching Science in the Elementary School

This is an advanced course for fully certified elementary teachers to provide richer understanding of the impact on the elementary school of new developments in science and new refinements in the teaching of science. Content, method, material, and general curricular implications will be considered. Special attention will be given to research and results of experimentation.

The recent findings concerning programs in operation in inner city neighborhoods will be studied in depth and curricular ideas based on areas of meaningful contact will be developed.

Problems and Techniques in Teaching Social Studies in the Elementary School

This is an advanced course for fully certified elementary teachers to provide richer understanding of the impact on the elementary school of new developments in social studies and new refinements in the teaching of social studies. Content, method, material, and general curricular implications will be considered. Special attention will be given to research and results of experimentation.

A Master's Degree in Urban Education and Total Mobilization of Resources for Change

Materials and strategies relevant to inner city life will be considered. The use of inquiry and process approaches will be carefully explored to assess the viability of these ideas and their inclusion in the elementary school curriculum of the inner city.

Problems and Techniques in Teaching Language Arts in the Elementary School

This is an advanced course for fully certified elementary teachers to provide richer understanding of the impact on the elementary school of new developments in language arts and new refinements in the teaching of language arts. Content, method, material, and general curricular implications will be considered. Special attention will be given to research and results of experimentation.

This course will address in depth the whole area of communication, linguistics, and language learning attendant on the life style of inner city children. It will draw from the research the relevant findings concerning the teaching of standard English as a second language, the use of neighborhood patois as bases for language building, and the many other findings related to teaching children of the inner city.

Language Learning: Diagnosis, Curriculum, and Materials [2]

This course is an introduction and study of the various aspects of the diagnosis of language disabilities with additional study of the types of curricula activities, the scope, and the sequence needed to correct or eliminate the diagnosed problems. The orientation of the course is on the language problems of the inner city child. The assessment of needs and constructive programs to overcome deficiencies so as to ensure opportunity for greater school success will be of focal concern. Methods of diagnosis as well as methods of corrective teaching procedures will be studied and analyzed. Grouping procedures for teaching children with various problems will be surveyed and strategies for attacking various problems will be analyzed.

2. Required in the summer session.

Maurie Hillson and Francis P. Purcell

Early Childhood Education and the Problem of Disadvantage

This is a course that will provide for a study into the impact that research has made in early childhood education. The newer programs of early childhood education will be carefully reviewed. The various methods of approach to early childhood education will be studied and evaluated in light of the present findings. The aspects of programs of early childhood education attendant on cognitive and social development and training will be studied and analyzed. Problems in curriculum building for early childhood programs will be addressed. Teaching strategies and methods of approach will also be considered to round out a treatment in-depth of early childhood education and the problems of disadvantage.

The Enriching Arts in Elementary Education

Music, Arts and Crafts, Drama, Dance, and Art, and the techniques and methods of creating worthwhile approaches to these so that they are relevant to the child in the inner city, will be addressed in this course. The course will provide for the teacher a greater understanding of the new developments in teaching materials in these areas as well as the techniques for creating motivation and desire for participation in various cultural activities. Methods of creating opportunity for greater and more varied stimulation as a precursor to participation in the enriching arts will be studied and analyzed.

Developmental Psychology: Early and Middle Years of Childhood

This course deals with the continuities and discontinuities in development, and the relationships among the physical, intellectual, social, and emotional growth aspects. It integrates concepts derived from learning, clinical studies, and cultural and sociological studies with general behavior theory. Although this course considers child development in its broadest terms, the emphasis is on those concepts that have particular relevance for an understanding of the characteristics of disadvantaged children or particular usefulness in the classroom situation.

Community Relations

The concept of the school as coordinating agency among other child and youth service agencies provides the motivation of this course. It considers interpretation of the school program as a basis for community support; the position of education personnel with respect to social leadership; lay participation in program planning and evaluation; and the influence of such groups as patrons, religious and civic groups, patriotic organizations, charities, the press, and labor and management groups. It refers to current practice and research in the field. It develops principles underlying an effective program.

This course will present the point of view that the school, being one of the more stable social institutions within the inner city, is in a unique position to carry out community development efforts as a total community school. The course will explore the manner in which local persons can be involved in the life and planning of a school. The course will directly try to reverse the trend that has permitted the school to become separate, aloof, and insulated from the needs, desires, hopes, and aspirations of the people they are supposed to serve. The course will emphasize the concept of the school's accountability and responsiveness to local persons of all walks of life.

Community Studies and Education

An examination of differences in values, social structure, and customary behavior of the subcultures that exist within contemporary American communities and between community types (metropolis, suburb, town, rural village) will be undertaken. The influences of these differences on individual motivation and behavior and on community-school relations will be studied.

This course will focus primarily upon the phenomena and the change of American communities from rural to urban to metropolitanized areas. The economic, social, and political constraints to which the metropolitan region are subjected will be examined in detail so that the student will come to understand the variety of problems and issues that modern man must confront as the society becomes increasingly metropolitanized. The process by which the central city has become isolated from the remainder of the metropolitan region and the implications this has for education will be focused upon. The student will be expected to use social system theory in analyzing community structures.

Maurie Hillson and Francis P. Purcell

Sociological Foundations of Education

This course provides an introduction to some of the leading principles of sociology and anthropology and an exploration of their function in education. Some of the major topics are: the concepts of status and role in the school; role conflicts; the social system and culture of the school; social class differences in education; and functional analyses of educational problems.

The course will examine in detail, in depth and breadth, the concept of a culture of poverty. The problems of disadvantagement among large numbers of minority-group people will be viewed from the various concepts identified above. Of particular concern is the concept of social assimilation and acculturation and the function of the school in relation to this process. The school will be identified as a key social institution that expedites and facilitates the social assimilation of minority-group people and the major means by which people attain upward social mobility. The course will seek to divert the student from an overemphasis on the concepts of motivational psychology and assist the student in viewing the social structures that play a deterministic role in social behavior. Normative and deviant behavior will be examined in light of the findings of the structural and functional social scientist in order to locate within the social structure those factors that can be looked upon as deterministic.

Society and Education

This course provides an examination of the consequences for the school system of our emerging corporate urban society with its new occupational, social, and valuational systems. Not only will the consequences for the school system be examined in terms of increased metropolitanization, but the consequences to society for the establishment of a viable education system will also be studied. Alternative means to this end as well as the whole function of public education as it is experienced in urban areas will be examined. The apparent failures of the current educational system to educate large numbers of our youths will be explored. The manner in which the school is functional for large segments of the population and dysfunctional for other, equally large segments of the population will be analyzed. The school will be examined in terms of the growing body of literature concerning this phenomenon. Cultural studies will be used so that a comparative basis for American education in society can be understood.

Social Class Influence on Education

The different theories of social stratification current today in sociology and anthropology and underlying educational policies and practices will be examined, with emphasis on the works of Warner, Davis, and their critics. Among the major topics are social class structure, indicators of class position, differences in socialization and mobility, testing, biases, and critiques of social class influences in education.

The probability that social stratification, as it currently stands, provides for less and less opportunity for upward social mobility will be explored. The emergence of a new working class will be examined and the consequences this has for the greater American society will be studied. Differentials in educational success as it relates to social class will be focused upon. The problem of class conflict as the low-income youth meets the middle-class teacher will be identified in terms of the way teachers can reduce social distance.

The School as a Social System

A study in detail of the influences of the social organization of people in the school on teaching, administration, and learning. A scheme is presented for analyzing and understanding school and classroom as social systems. Among the major topics are: student cliques and achievement; informal organization of the faculty; relation of formal and informal organization; values and the school social system; school culture; and resistance to change.

The school will be viewed as a social system that is relatively open or relatively closed. The concept of total institutions in American society will be examined. The course will attempt to view the extent to which a school can be operated as a democratic organization or one which is largely totalitarian in nature. The degree to which students and faculty can become involved with parents in the formulation of educational policy will be explored.

Maurie Hillson and Francis P. Purcell

The Culture of Poverty and
the Disadvantaged Child

This will be a course that focuses primarily on the problem of education and the disadvantaged child. The concept of disadvantagement will be carefully analyzed and the problem of referring to one culture as inferior or disadvantaged in comparison with another will be critically reviewed. The course will attempt to point out the viability and complexities of all subcultures within the larger culture. Such concepts as social role, culture, value stretch, role sets, and so on will be conceptual tools for viewing the phenomenon of the economically disadvantaged in an affluent society.

The irrelevancies of such standardized measuring instruments as the intelligence tests and the various achievement tests as means to trap poor youths into making blue-collar and lower-class decisions, will receive close attention. The language of poverty used by low-income youths will also receive careful scrutiny and the value and richness of the language and vernacular of low-income individuals will be closely examined. The problems of automation and lack of opportunity for cultural assimilation will also occupy a prominent place in this course.

Problems of Urban Education

This will be a final seminar that will bring to bear the ideas and theories developed in other places in this sequence of courses on the whole problem of urban education. The place of the school in community rehabilitation projects, community renewal projects, and public housing will be examined. The concept of economic base studies and the implications for schools will provide the teacher with a more sophisticated outlook on the relationship of the school to the urban metropolitanized area. The phenomena of population agglomeration and subsequent decentralization of organizational form and the implication this has for the school will be studied. The social process by which we produce superior suburban schools and inferior urban schools will be the focus of the content in this course.

The various innovations that have been experimented with during the past few years to equalize quality education in the United States will be examined. Such concepts as the nongraded school will be included.

Experienced Teacher-Fellow Home-Visit Course [3]

ASSUMPTIONS

1. Inasmuch as the school systems have undertaken several of the basic socialization functions of the family, some degree of enmity, that is, social conflict, is in any case an inevitable outcome.
2. Should this tendency (social conflict) occur in the context of social class disparity, which is frequently the case of the educated, socially mobile teacher and the socially static untutored lower-class parent, the situation develops along the lines of in-group and out-group phenomena.
3. If to these foregoing conditions is added the factor of race, language, and ethnic differences (that is, Negro, White, Spanish, English), outright social alienation is a distinct possibility.
4. The phenomenon of social alienation and in-group versus out-group perceptions may be but one of the conditions associated with the failure of the school to meet the educative needs of many pupils, but it looms as one of the prior conditions. Should this condition go unresolved not only does it undermine other solutions to educative problems of the lower-class child, it tends to further the intractability of the problem itself.

PROPOSITION

It is therefore proposed that as an integral part of the special course orienting teachers to the life style of lower-class individuals, a section be devoted to instructing teachers on the social science techniques in family study. The proposition is that mutually distrustful in-group versus out-group perceptions will be significantly reduced as each (the family and teachers) gains knowledge of the other as a person, status differences not withstanding; furthermore, status, class, and ethnic differences need not remain as insurmountable barriers that divest children of their capacity for full utilization of the school system.

PLAN

A programmed means to this end is contemplated by providing the teacher with an understanding of certain interpersonal skills and knowl-

3. This course is fully delineated, since it is a fundamental aspect of the whole program.

Maurie Hillson and Francis P. Purcell

edge in family study as has been developed in social science. The transmission of these skills, not intended to train fellows as social scientists but to enhance their skills as teachers, will take place through a series of academic seminars. The content of these seminars will be drawn from the social sciences and will be designed to lessen the integrative task of the teacher and facilitate her relationship with parents and pupils.

Should the dissonance of in-group versus out-group social perceptions be reduced, teachers will be in an informed position to intelligently suggest curriculum and program changes within the school consistent with the learning patterns of the lower-class child and to implement innovations that emanate from other levels and sources.

According to this plan, the fellows will attempt to make an assessment of the educative needs of a given child by observing the primary focus of the child's life style, his family orientation.

The plan calls for the fellow to develop an *empathic relationship* with a child of the family she will eventually contact *in the home.* The signal to visit the home will come from the child in the form of specific acts indicating acceptance of the teacher as a helpful adult authority figure, that is, as the one who gradually initiated tension-reducing tactics and facilitates reciprocation. The home visit will then appear to be one in a series of tension-reducing activities emanating from the teacher as a natural outgrowth from the child's graduated and reciprocated tension-reducing tactics. The intent is to establish a "field of forces" with positive valences (home $+ -$ school $+$) for teacher and child.

Adequate preparation and time must be allowed to ready the fellow and family for the first of the contemplated visits; that is, a *positive* signal should be indicated before the visit is scheduled.

It is noted that the teacher will be exposed to substantial theoretical content during the teaching of this course. It can be assumed that the seminars led by social science faculty will adequately present content covering the "why" dimensions, and the sessions described here aim to teach "what" and "how." In addition, the small group characteristics of these sessions give rise to the possibility of primary group development that could sustain positive motivations and identifications with the community, allay anxieties, and reduce resistances.

It is anticipated that much reworking of the theoretical material will occur within the small group sessions with the faculty which will provide an opportunity to fuse this content into the stream of social science knowledge being presented.

Index

Index

303

Ausubel, Pearl, 8, 18, 213, 218
Authority, 16–17, 32

BALDWIN, James, 180, 193
Baltimore, Md., 123–24
Banks, W. R., 191
Barlow, M., 102, 107, 144, 151, 223
Barnett, L. J., 200
Barzun, Jacques, 201
Bascom, W., 24, 33
Bates, C. D., 224
Baxter, Bernice, 228
Becker, H. S., 200, 201
Bell, R. R., 199
Bender, Louis W., 228
Bendix, R., 198
Benne, Kenneth, 245, 256
Berger, P., 45, 46, 198
Berliner, W. M., 229
Bernstein, Basil, 6, 18, 211, 216
Bettelheim, Bruno, 191
Bibb, Leon, 181
Bierstedt, R., 201
Biological deprivation, 3–4
Blackledge, Ethel H., 229
Blackledge, W. L., 229
Blackman, L. S., 86, 91
Black power, 52n.
Blau, P. M., 201
Bloom, Benjamin S., 5, 8, 18, 80, 90, 211, 214, 216, 224
Boas, Franz, 191
Boger, J. H., 6, 9, 18, 212, 216
Bollinger, E. W., 227
Botkin, B., 192
Bottrel, H. R., 231
Bradford, Leland, 245, 256
Braly, K. W., 190
Brazziel, W. F., 10, 18, 212, 216
Breckenridge, Marian E., 4, 18, 210, 215
Bredemeier, Harry C., 198
Brehm, J. W., 16, 18, 214, 218
Bremmer, R., 198
Briggs, Frances, 227
Brim, A. G., Jr., 198

Brim, Orville, 43, 46
Brink, W., 191
Bronfenbrenner, Urie, 7, 18, 212, 217
Brookover, W. B., 201
Brooks, L., 89, 90
Brown, B., 188
Brown, C., 180
Brown, F., 188
Brown, J. S., 16, 18, 214, 218
Brown, J. W., 226
Bruner, Jerome S., 231
Bryan, H. M., 77
Buchheimer, Arnold, 49, 60, 76
Buchheimer, Naomi, 76
Bugelski, B., 214
Burchill, G. W., 67, 68, 73, 76
Burns, W. H., 191
Buros, Oscar K., 215
Butler, F. A., 227, 228

CALDWELL, E., 180
California State Board of Education, 77
Caplow, T., 201
Carriker, William R., 79
Carrollton School, 125–31
  approach, 125
  course descriptions, 128–31
  faculty, 127
  problem, 125
  program, 126, 127
  student body 126
Cassidy, Rosaline, 228
Caudill, H., 25, 33, 180
Centers, Richard, 198
Chernak, Sidney N., 123
Church, Joseph, 214
Churn, B., 189
Clark, Kenneth B., 24, 33, 180, 187, 188, 189, 191, 199
Clark, M., 24, 33
Cleft, V. A., 187
Cliff, V., 46
Cloward, S. M., 201
Coch, L., 15, 18, 214, 218